ACTIVATING THE SUPERNATURAL IN YOU!

SHAKING HEAVEN AND EARTH

DENNIS REANIER

Published by XP Publishing,
P. O. Box 1017 Maricopa, Arizona, 85139
www.XPPublishing.com

ISBN: 978-1-936101-67-2

Dedication

I dedicate my life and this book to my wife and best friend, Tammi. You are a carrier of His presence; I would be nothing without you in my life! Thank you for challenging me to never settle for less than God's best; your partnership means more to me than you will ever know. You are an incredible mother and model to our four daughters. You are the best wife that God could have ever given me! You will always be the queen of my life. I love you!

I also dedicate this book…

To my four princesses Jordan, Raegan, Naomi, and Josie. I am so proud of each one of you, and could not imagine a life without you! You bring so much joy and fulfillment to my life. My greatest reward is being your dad!

To my mom, Susan Brewer, who accepted Jesus Christ two weeks before she passed away from lung cancer on May 29, 1999!

To my cousin, Rich Powell, for being a good friend who supported and believed in me!

To my father-in-law and mother-in-law, Brad and Lynn Cooper, for accepting me as your own son!

To my spiritual father, Ray Larson, for leading me to Christ and imparting so much into my life spiritually!

To my other spiritual father, Paul Parker, for imparting the Father's heart into my life.

To Wesley Campbell and Sean Smith, for making spiritual deposits that have forever enriched my life!

To Brian and Nicole McConville, along with the leadership team and people at Word of Life Christian Center. Without your sacrifice this book would never have been written! It is a privilege to be able to serve you in such freedom as your friend and pastor!

ENDORSEMENTS

Shaking Heaven & Earth is a catalyst for the convergence of the current reformation to launch the ordinary believer into a life of the extraordinary as they are activated in the supernatural. Dennis' book is full of revelation about your identity and inheritance that will take you off the "limitation" network and put you on the "all things possible" network in order to possess your birthright! *Shaking Heaven & Earth* is a must read for every believer, leader, and pastor.

RANDY CLARK
GLOBAL AWAKENING MINISTRIES
INTERNATIONAL CONFERENCE SPEAKER
AUTHOR OF *THERE IS MORE*

Shaking Heaven & Earth is a revelatory experience containing the practical tools to launch the average Christian into a spiritual reformation. Every believer who puts into practice the principles of this book will be activated in a life of miracles to change recorded history.

WESLEY CAMPBELL
FOUNDER OF REVIVAL NOW MINISTRIES,
PRAYING THE BIBLE INTERNATIONAL, AND BE A HERO
AUTHOR OF *WELCOMING A VISITATION OF THE HOLY SPIRIT*

This book challenges believers to live in a relationship with God resulting in revelation, rather than settling for the empty promises of religion. *Shaking Heaven & Earth* will help propel your faith into action in order to see the promises of heaven manifesting through "you" today on earth!

STACEY CAMPBELL
FOUNDER OF REVIVAL NOW MINISTRIES,
PRAYING THE BIBLE INTERNATIONAL, AND BE A HERO
AUTHOR OF *ECSTATIC PROPHECY*

Shaking Heaven & Earth is a divine manual that is a right-on-time holy summons to impact this world and inhabit our birthright. While reading this manuscript, I found myself wanting to underline, take notes and, yes, pray! When I wrote *Prophetic Evangelism*, I had a sense that it was a revelation that had a "NOW" stamp on it by the Holy Spirit. I can honestly tell you that I feel the same way about this book!

SEAN SMITH
SEANSMITHMINISTRIES.ORG
AUTHOR OF *PROPHETIC EVANGELISM*

Dennis Reanier has accurately captured the key principles to live a victorious spiritual life. As I have watched this man of God pursue the presence of God over the last 22 years I have come to know his passion for revealing the kingdom of God. His personal pursuit of God is a journey that has brought knowledge and revelation that will help transform your life. All who give an ear and a heart to the principles herein will gain vital truths for victorious living, with the life of God's power being revealed in and through "YOU."

DR. RAY LARSON
7DEGREES.ORG
FOUNDER OF 7 DEGREES
AUTHOR OF *MARKETPLACE MINISTRY*

Have you ever thought there must be a way to live the Christian life apart from formulas and ten steps to…whatever? Have you ever felt like you have invited Father God into your plans rather than hearing His and moving accordingly? My excellent friend and son in the Lord, Dennis Reanier, like Mary of Bethany, has chosen the better part. He has challenged us to live a faith life based on saying what we hear the Father saying and doing what we see Him doing according to Jesus' example in John, chapter five.

No great hero of the faith had a great plan and carried it out. They all heard from on high, decided to act on what they heard and received supernatural ability to carry out the assignment. I highly recommend this book to you. More importantly, I recommend his life to you. Dennis has made it real, not easy. He has opened up his life in Jesus with all the beauty and ashes, and invited us to join him in this great adventure. I received the invitation with great anticipation and encourage you to do the same.

PAUL PARKER
GENERNATIONS.ORG
FOUNDER OF GENERATIONS COMMUNITY CHURCH

Shaking Heaven & Earth totally shook my world! Dennis has opened up for me a brand new revelation of what MY promise land looks like AND how to take it. I am confident that it will do the same for everyone who reads it. Get ready! Principals that you have known with your mind will become life in your spirit and will thrust you forward in your journey into the heavenly kingdom realms.

ELIZABETH A. NIXON, ESQ.
WHITE QUILL MEDIA
AUTHOR OF *DECREES INSPIRED BY THE PSALMS*
WWW.WHITEQUILLMEDIA.COM

TABLE OF CONTENTS

FOREWORD

BY WESLEY AND STACEY CAMPBELL

SHAKING HEAVEN & EARTH is a must read for every believer who desires to experience the abundant Christian life! Though all things are possible, not every believer experiences their full potential. *Shaking Heaven & Earth* will help you to experience the Christian life you have always dreamed of. What Dennis has laid out are the practical tools necessary to launch the average Christian into a spiritual reformation. With each page you read, real faith will rise in your heart. We believe that every believer who puts into practice the principles of this book will become world changers who are activated into a life of miracles.

Few manuscripts contain the insight or revelation that can bring passionate and radical change to the everyday Christian life. That is why we are excited to recommend *Shaking Heaven & Earth*. It will accomplish what you want to happen in your heart – the hope and inspiration that you can actually experience the promises of the Bible for yourself!

We have known and respected Dennis Reanier for over five years. In that time we have watched his ministry grow; we've developed a deep friendship as we have worked as business and ministry partners. To date, this book is his finest contribution to the body of Christ. For this reason we are able to say that the message contained in the pages of this book is consistent with the life of the author.

In *Shaking Heaven & Earth* you will understand your true identity in Christ, the character of God, and the authority, dominion, and resources that He has given to us. You will realize how we are set free from the captivity of a religious mindset: one that attempts to enslave many in logic and reason based on information but is void of intimacy with a loving God. This book will equip you to live in genuine relationship with the Holy Spirit, resulting in revelation that results in an inheritance mindset rather than settling for the empty promises of religion. *Shaking Heaven & Earth* is sure to propel your faith into action in order to manifest heaven through "you" today on earth!

Finally, we believe that *Shaking Heaven*...will impart wisdom and revelation that can thrust you into the spectacular plan of God for your life. If enough believers get ahold of the message in this book, it will transform the body of Christ into a powerful force, greater than anything we have seen in recorded history. Please don't just read quickly through the pages of *Shaking Heaven & Earth*. As the ancients read, studied, prayed, and spoke the revelation, so you must study, question, dissect, and discuss every single chapter in this book until it's a part of who you are. If you do, you will easily find what many Christians have searched their whole lives for: passion, power, prosperity, and, most importantly, a deep intimate fulfilling relationship with our Lord and Savior Jesus Christ. You won't only be blessed as you read *Shaking Heaven*...you'll be transformed!

WESLEY AND STACEY CAMPBELL

FOREWORD

BY SEAN SMITH

I TRULY BELIEVE THAT GOD is looking to release what's on His Mind in order for a people to embody His Voice. When revelation meets proclamation, there is a dynamic created that shakes atoms and atmospheres. In this age, darkness is hot on attempting to steal the church's proclamations and practices. This is evident in the modern experimentation with spirits and spirituality. Putting it all together, this is a crucial time to possess the fullness of God's promises and contend to pierce this present darkness with God's weaponry.

Shaking Heaven & Earth is a divine manual that is a right-on-time holy summons to impact this world and inhabit our birth rite. While reading this manuscript, I found myself wanting to underline, take notes and, yes, pray! This work combines a great depth with great dynamism. I was thoroughly challenged by the heart of this prophetic treatise, while feeling the passion of the Spirit that prevails. Dennis Reanier pens like a veteran writer who has a holy assignment from the Father. Dennis has pulled from years of ministry to the body of Christ. He intertwines interesting personal stories along with prophetic insights that

13

engage the reader. There is a simplicity that causes his deep revelations to come across as so practical. Many times I have read books that seem to rehash a theme that feels like you have read it before. But this work is fresh, original and carries an authentic ring which hits you immediately and carries you till its conclusion.

There are certain "discoveries" in my spiritual journey that will forever mark my walk. I can vividly remember reading certain books and messages that opened new wells and doors in my Christian experience. I'm convinced that there are potential discoveries of significance that are unknowingly walked over daily. While we were looking for something else, some treasures remain hidden. Many believers can know Jesus but live in different dimensions of Jesus.

Shaking Heaven & Earth is about moving out of the fringes of the faith into the fullness of our inheritance. This manual takes you from the history of the Israelites to the prophetic words of the apostles. When I wrote *Prophetic Evangelism,* I had a sense that it was a revelation that had a "NOW" stamp on it by the Holy Spirit. I can honestly tell you that I feel the same way about this manuscript.

I highly recommend this fiery prophetic revelation that my good friend, Dennis Reanier, has written. I have seen his life up close and have personally witnessed his integrity and spiritual passion. In a day where many are taking shortcuts, I can truly vouch for Dennis and affirm that he has allowed God to take him on the path of God's complete processing. I can guarantee that this book will not just be a "one-pass" perusal, but you will be compelled to pour your spirit over *Shaking Heaven & Earth* again and again. Get ready to be blasted into a new level of activation, while being challenged to come into a higher dimension of influence in your world.

SEAN SMITH
SEANSMITHMINISTRIES.ORG
AUTHOR OF *PROPHETIC EVANGELISM*

CHAPTER 1

A Voice Calling in the Wilderness

WHILE I WAS IN PRAYER ONE DAY, I heard the Lord say in my spirit, "I am a voice calling in the wilderness." I understood this to mean that God was meeting His people in the wilderness so that He could develop an intimate relationship with them that would result in the possession of their promised land. The wilderness is the way of the flesh, bondage, negativity, doubt, deception, fear and failure...the place God often meets His people...right where they are living! The promised land is the way of the Spirit...freedom, faith, relationship, revelation, and the abundant life...a place where God's people begin to experience and live in the things they believe about their faith in Him.

The Lord was leading those who had been wounded through the trials of life's circumstances inflicted by the enemy to meet with Him. Many of His people felt so defeated that they had begun to give up on their relationship with God! The daily grind of the day-to-day tribulations were slowly wearing down these saints, keeping them from seeking after Him with all their heart, soul, strength, and mind. The purpose of God meeting His people in the wilderness was to turn the trials meant for their harm into their good! The Lord did not want to punish or make life difficult for the saints, but He wanted to draw them into a closer relationship with Him in order to increase their desire to wait on Holy Spirit. Then they could learn to overcome through a relationship based on the revelation of Christ's accomplishments rather than by their own strengths and abilities.

There is "a voice of one who cries: Prepare in the wilderness the way of the Lord [*clear away the obstacles*]; make straight and smooth in the desert a highway for our God!"[1]

MY PANORAMIC VISION

This declaration was followed by a panoramic vision, as if I were looking from an airplane window. A bright and glowing light illuminated the picture that I saw. Everything in the vision had the appearance of being white and yet was transparent. I could see in the spirit through every object that would have been made of solid matter in the natural, thus impossible to see through in the flesh. I then saw an opening in the heavens between the clouds. Out of the opening appeared two very large arms with hands that wore thin white gloves. One hand was grasping a bow while the other hand was pulling an arrow back against the tension of the string in order to release it high into the heavens.

When I looked to see where the arrow was going, I was surprised to see hundreds, maybe even thousands, of arrows that had already been launched into the heavens. Once an arrow was launched it would multiply into many arrows of differing

[1] Isaiah 40:3 AMP

sizes. Some had peaked in the air so that they were beginning to plummet toward the earth. All the while, there were still different groupings of arrows preparing to hit at different times. Some were not far from hitting the surface of the earth, while others were much higher up, and some were still preparing to peak in the air before they plummeted back to the earth. All the while, arrows were continually being launched one after the other.

At first it appeared as if these arrows would land randomly throughout the world. As I looked closer, the majority were landing within the borders of the United States, although there were pockets of arrows hitting other people groups and nations. Some of the arrows that were previously launched had already hit the earth. I then felt Holy Spirit whisper, "What you are seeing in this vision cannot be seen by many of those who call themselves My people. I am not allowing them to discern the spiritual realm while they are living out their daily lives in the natural realm, as they have become paralyzed by interpreting the things I am saying to them in the Spirit through the appearance of natural circumstances that require solutions that can only be understood in the reality of the spiritual realm. It is causing My people frustration, because they think that what that they are seeing is Me (God)."

For those who cannot see in the Spirit, it is like the clandestine arrows that were used at night for surprise attacks back in the French/English war. Often they would shoot arrows at the opposing force that had been lit aflame into the night air for all to see. When they wanted to catch their enemy off guard, they would launch these arrows into the dark without any flame so that the enemy they were aiming to hit could not see or even know what was coming until the arrow had already pierced their body. I asked the Lord, "What does the vision I am seeing mean?"

THE MEANING OF THE VISION

He explained to me that He was going to use the enemy's own weapons against him by using these attacks to prepare His church to be a pure and spotless bride. I understood that by "pure and spotless" the Lord was referring more to the state of our hearts than our actions. He was looking for people with hearts that were perfect toward Him. He was not looking for people who never make mistakes. He was looking for people whose hearts were fully devoted to Him. These were people who had committed their hearts one hundred percent to Him alone. I heard Holy Spirit say:

"Without purity there will be no power to overcome! I have already begun to prepare My church by developing them in relationship with My Spirit, resulting in purity of heart. Then they can walk in the necessary revelation and power of My accomplishments to experience the abundant life and usher in the emerging agenda of the end time harvest."

THE LORD CONTINUED:

"Those who cannot see the arrows are those who confess to being born again by the Spirit, but they only live and make decisions by what they see with their natural eyes. Since these are spiritual arrows, they never even see them coming. It is important to understand that I have not called My people to live by what they see or understand in the natural. 'For we walk by faith (*we regulate our lives and conduct ourselves by our conviction or belief respecting man's relationship to God and divine things, with trust and holy fervor; thus we walk*), not by sight or appearance.'[2]

"I have called My people as a spiritual people. My desire is to relate to them as Holy Spirit. I want them to ascend in the Spirit to gain revelation through relationship, and then to descend to earth imparting revelation into their natural circumstances and lives. It is impossible for My people to do this without having established their identity through intimacy with Me."

In Matthew 16:17-19 (AMP), Jesus says:

Blessed (*happy, fortunate, and to be envied*) are you, Simon Bar-Jonah. For flesh and blood (*men*) have not revealed this to you, but My Father who is in heaven. And I tell you, you are Peter (*Greek, Petros – a large piece of rock*), and on this rock (*Greek, petra – a huge rock like Gilbraltar*) I will build My church, and the gates of Hades (*the powers of the infernal region*) shall not overpower it (*or be strong to its detriment or hold against it*). I will give you the keys of the kingdom of heaven; and whatever you bind (*declare to be improper and unlawful*) on earth must be what is already bound in heaven; and whatever you loose (*declare lawful*) on earth must be what is already loosed in heaven.

In this passage Jesus says, Simon Bar-Jonah did not understand who He was through mere human understanding, but by revelation given to him by His Father. As a result of Simon Bar-Jonah receiving revelation, Jesus finds it necessary to give him a new identity with the name *Peter*, meaning *rock*. The name *Peter* was to be a monumental reminder to all the church for all

---

[2] 2 Corinthians 5:7 AMP

ages about the importance of receiving their identity through revelation from heaven rather than just getting information from the natural realm. His new name was to represent the rock of revelation in which His new identity was to be built. It was on this rock of revelation that Jesus said, "I will build My church, and the gates of Hades shall not prevail against it."[3] If that is true, then the antithesis is also true, that without revelation the gates of hell could prevail against the church!

REVELATION, FAITH AND POWER

If we are the church, then our ability to prevail is determined by our ability to obtain revelation through our relationship with God. The Lord showed me that to bind and/or loose something on earth, we will have to ascend into heavenly places to obtain revelation in order to know we have authority to bind or loose on earth. We are able to bind and loose on earth by speaking and agreeing with those things that have already been established in heavenly places. God was showing me that there is no reason to try to bind and loose something on earth to change the atmosphere of heaven. It's the spiritual reality that has the authority to change our natural reality.

> IF WE ARE THE CHURCH, THEN OUR ABILITY TO PREVAIL IS DETERMINED BY OUR ABILITY TO OBTAIN REVELATION THROUGH OUR RELATIONSHIP WITH GOD.

The Lord continued to reveal to me that those who cannot see are constantly being hit by these arrows, thinking that life is always giving them a hard time. They get knocked down,

[3] Matthew 16:18 NKJV

feeling discouraged, confused, disillusioned and ready to give up. When they finally pick themselves up again, they begin to work and strive in the same manner they did before they got knocked down. Since they cannot see these arrows, it is only a matter of time before they get hit again by one of them and go through this process all over again. After experiencing this cycle repeatedly, they finally decide to give up, defeated, weary and discouraged, never able to possess the promises of God.

AT THIS POINT, I HEARD THE LORD SAY:

"Many of My people are in this place because they have not been equipped to walk by faith. Many of them have come to believe that if they confess the information of the Scriptures over their circumstances, I will perform for them. 'Faith comes by hearing, and hearing by the word of God.'[4] Faith comes by receiving the very words of Jesus from the heavenly realm concerning our circumstances through the Holy Spirit. Unless they get a revelation of the Scriptures for their lives and circumstances through a relationship with Holy Spirit, it will not keep the gates of hell from prevailing against them! It will continue to produce confusion, discouragement, deception, and disillusionment about the legitimacy of Scripture, robbing them of the opportunity to live the abundant life!"

THE LORD CONTINUED:

"This is not my work. It is the work of the accuser. It is the enemy who has disguised himself as an angel of light. So 'take up the shield of faith, with which you can extinguish all the flaming arrows of the evil one.'[5] Remember the white gloves being worn

[4] Romans 10:17 NKJV
[5] Ephesians 6:16 NIV

on the hands that gripped the bow and the arrow? They were being worn to keep from having any identifiable or traceable evidence in the natural of where the arrows had originated from in the spirit. Even though the arrows were producing many manifestations in the natural arena, many of my people had no discernment as to whether the spiritual origin was based in truth or deception. They could not see into the spiritual realm. Since it is coming from the heavens, they automatically assume that it is Me (God)."

The names written on the arrows were accusation, selfishness, criticism, pride, independence, deception, frustration, confusion, disillusionment, past hurts, fear of failure, fear of man, false judgment, poverty, sickness, disease, defeat and division that would result in manifesting difficulties through circumstances that were bringing hardships into many believers' lives. All the while, Holy Spirit had preordained a plan to turn these experiences that the enemy intended to use for the destruction of His people to good! He was releasing revelation through relationship to warn His people of harm in order to lead them into His promises, so the saints would learn to trust in the accomplishments of Jesus Christ rather than trusting in their own strengths and abilities to possess His promises.

REVELATION AND PROTECTION UNDER HIS SHADOW

Notice that there are pockets where the arrows are falling that have much larger arrows than other surrounding areas. The territories in which you see larger arrows falling are geographical areas where the names of the spirit on those arrows are gaining more control and power resulting in more darkness.

Some of the results were manifesting in rising crime, higher divorce rates, child abuse, drug and alcohol abuse, economic collapses, sickness, disease, war and even terrorist attacks. I asked the Lord, "How could this happen?"

Where there is a decrease in the unity of my people agreeing with the reality of heaven through relationship with Holy Spirit, there is an increase in the power of darkness that will manifest in the natural realm.

The Lord reminded me from Ephesians, chapter six, that this is a spiritual battle in which much of His church has been trying to fight in the natural. It says,

Put on God's whole armor (*the armor of a heavy-armed soldier which God supplies*), that you may be able successfully to stand up against (*all*) the strategies and the deceits of the devil. For we are not wrestling with flesh and blood, (*contending only with physical opponents*), but against the despotisms, against the powers, against (*the master spirits who are*) the world rulers of this present darkness, against the spirit forces of wickedness in the heavenly (*supernatural*) sphere. Therefore put on God's complete armor, that you may be able to resist and stand your ground on the evil day (*of danger*), and having done all (*the crisis demands*), to stand (*firmly in your place*). Stand therefore (*hold your ground*), having tightened the belt of truth around your loins and having put on the breastplate of integrity and of moral rectitude and right standing with God, and having shod your feet in preparation (*to face the enemy with the firm-footed stability, the promptness, and the readiness produced by the good news*) of the Gospel of peace. Lift up over all the (*covering*) shield of saving faith, upon which you can quench all the flaming missiles of the wicked (*one*). And take the helmet of salvation and the sword that the Spirit wields, which is the Word of God. Pray at all times (*on every occasion, in every season*) in the Spirit, with all (*manner of*) prayer and entreaty. To that end keep alert and watch with strong purpose and perseverance, interceding in behalf of all the saints (*God's consecrated people*).[6]

Then I saw arrows falling from the sky and trying to pierce other people, but the arrows could not touch them, bouncing off just before piercing them. I asked the Lord, "Why are these arrows not penetrating these people?" From all natural appearances there did not appear to be anything different about those who were being penetrated by the arrows and those who were able to repel the arrows. Holy Spirit said:

"These are those who have been waiting on Me in fellowship to receive their new identity through union with me. These are those who are in a genuine relationship with me resulting in overcoming revelation to experience the abundant life. The arrows cannot touch those who are intimate with Me because they walk in My power!"

Then the Lord brought the Scripture to my mind in Acts 5:15 AMP, where it says:

---

[6]Ephesians 6:11-18 AMP

So that they (*even*) kept carrying out the sick into the streets and placing them on couches and sleeping pads, (*in the hope*) that as Peter passed by, at least his shadow might fall on some of them.

In this passage, Peter is healing people by accident! He isn't trying to be anyone or anything. He is just walking around being himself while his shadow is falling on people who begin to get healed. Peter didn't have a grid for this kind of supernatural phenomena. Jesus never healed anybody with His shadow. There was no previous model for Peter to copy. It is the only time we know of a saint's shadow manifesting in healing.

The word shadow here is the Greek word *episkiazo*. It means to cast shade upon, to envelop in a haze of brilliancy, or to invest with preternatural influence.[7] It is the same word that is used when the Spirit of God overshadowed Mary when she conceived in her womb Jesus Christ, the Son of God.

The angel said to her, The Holy Spirit will come upon you, and the power of the Most High will overshadow you (*like a shining cloud*); and so the holy (*pure, sinless*) Thing (*Offspring*) which shall be born of you will be called the Son of God.[8]

This was not just an ordinary shadow! It is the very surrounding presence of God that provides protection as well as power. Literally, those who have been quickened with the life of Holy Spirit have a shield that surrounds with a cover and empowers them so the enemy and his arrows cannot penetrate their lives, allowing them not only to overcome and possess, but

---

[7] Strong's Exhaustive Concordance, Reference 1982
[8] Luke 1:35 AMP

to experience their promised land. "You, O Lord, are a shield for me, my glory, and the lifter of my head."[9]

FOR RELATIONSHIP WITH HIM, WAIT ON HIM IN PRAYER!

Then Holy Spirit brought me to Acts 2:2-4 AMP, recounting an encounter the disciples were having where "suddenly there came a sound from heaven like the rushing of a violent tempest blast, and it filled the whole house in which they were sitting. And there appeared to them tongues resembling fire, which were separated and distributed and which settled on each one of them. And they were all filled (*diffused throughout their souls*) with the Holy Spirit."

Notice, the word *filled* here means "diffused throughout their souls." Why didn't the author use a word to say "diffused throughout their spirit" instead of the word "soul"? Did the author make a mistake? No, because your spirit is already perfect. According to Ephesians it is the exact same spirit and substance that was in Jesus Christ.

Being filled isn't about getting more of God in your spirit. You already have all of God! It's about getting more revelation of all that is already in your spirit diffused throughout your soul (mind, will, and emotions). So when we say we want more of God, what we are saying is that we want more revelation in our mind, will, and emotions. This is what Paul is talking about when referring to spiritual gifts as "*distinguishing certain Christians, due to the power of divine grace operating in their souls.*"[10]

The above experience was as a result of Jesus' instructions:

---

[9] Psalm 3:3 AMP
[10] 1 Corinthians 12:4 AMP

While being in their company and eating with them, He commanded them not to leave Jerusalem but to wait for what the Father had promised, of which (*He said*) you have heard Me speak. For John baptized with water, but not many days from now you shall be baptized with (placed in, introduced into) the Holy Spirit.[11]

The word *wait* here is the Greek word *perimeno*. It means "to stay around," and "to wait for."[12] It implies waiting in fellowship through relationship with Holy Spirit. Notice that this verse says we are placed in and introduced into the Holy Spirit. Not only is He in us, but we are in Him. We have Him coming and going!

Holy Spirit was revealing to me that the power the disciples received through baptism with the Holy Spirit came as a result of waiting on Him in prayer. It was Holy Spirit in them activating their soul (mind, will, and emotions) with revelation through relationship in order to manifest the power of God in and through them. Then He said, *"Baptism of the Holy Spirit was never meant to be a one-time experience like many of My people have understood."*

The Greek word for *baptized* in the above verse is *baptizo*. It means "to make overwhelmed."[13] It implies repeating the same process until an object is fully saturated and overflowing. It is often illustrated by the picture of a pickle being saturated in dill brine by dipping it over and over again.

Next Holy Spirit took me to Acts 4:31 AMP, where it says:

And when they had prayed, the place in which they were assembled was shaken; and they were all filled with the

---

[11] Acts 1:4-5 AMP
[12] Strong's Exhaustive Concordance, Reference 4037
[13] Strong's Exhaustive Concordance, Reference 907

Holy Spirit, and they continued to speak the Word of God with freedom and boldness and courage.

Then I heard Holy Spirit say something that I had never understood before! "The disciples were all filled with the Holy Spirit, after they had already been filled with the Holy Spirit." The Holy Spirit had just showed me how the disciples were all filled with the Holy Spirit in Acts 2:4 and now He was showing me how they were filled again with the Holy Spirit in Acts 4:31.

Holy Spirit was showing me that those who have been overshadowed by the presence of God are not being touched by the arrows of the accuser. They had made it a lifestyle to continually be filled (diffused throughout their souls) again and again with the Holy Spirit through fellowship in relationship with Him. The result is revelation to see into the spiritual realm and receive protection in the natural realm, all while manifesting His supernatural power with freedom, boldness, and courage to experience the abundant life.

HOLY SPIRIT SAID:

"I am beginning to prepare the way by clearing away the obstacles. I am going to shake the places where My people fellowship in relationship with Me! Everything that can be shaken on earth that is not of Me will be shaken through relationship, resulting in revelation with power to manifest heaven on earth! I will "shake not only the earth, but also heaven"[14] through the Spirit already living in My children. They will testify to the world that I am alive by overcoming every obstacle and possessing their inheritance!"

---

[14] Hebrews 12:26 NKJV

CHAPTER 2

LIVING ON THE

RIGHT SIDE OF THE CROSS

THE VISION I RECEIVED IN THE PREVIOUS CHAPTER came to me during a season of prayer that followed a conference I attended a few years ago in Estes Park, Colorado. Our speaker at the conference was Wesley Campbell, who was ministering to us from his new book, *Praying the Bible*. The conference was very good, but in driving home that week I did not feel as though anything profound had taken place in my personal relationship with God.

It was not until I arrived home from a long road trip that I realized something had been imparted into my life by Holy Spirit. I had a supernatural desire to spend time in the presence of God, through prayer, like I had never experienced in the previous eighteen years of my Christian life. In the past I had prayed more out of discipline, wanting to see God bless my efforts while ministering and preaching. This time something was different because I did not seem to need any motivation to pray.

I could not get enough time in the presence of God! I had a burning desire to spend every moment that I could alone with Holy Spirit. I began praying over twenty-five hours per week. I would begin my times with Holy Spirit by praying the Scriptures. The more I prayed the Scriptures, the more I felt the Spirit of God consuming me with His presence. This led to times of spontaneous prayer, worship, praying in the spirit, and just waiting in the presence of Holy Spirit. His presence was so fulfilling that hours of time would fly by, yet it felt like minutes.

I can still remember seeing my wife, Tammi, peek around the corner of our basement stairs to see if she could interrupt my prayer session with God so we could spend time together. During this time she told others that she did not know what had happened to her husband. My life had been turned upside down! Every waking free moment that I had was being spent in prayer.

Holy Spirit spoke to me once to leave my time of prayer to go and spend time with my wife and children. I began to pray the Bible with our daughters every evening before they went to bed. During this time our oldest daughter, Jordan, was baptized with the Holy Spirit at the age of five. She began to have encounters being activated to hear God's voice in very specific and personal ways!

THE PERSISTENCE AND PURPOSE OF PRAYER

For the first couple of weeks of this experience I did not hear God speak one word! It was not until after I had sought the Lord for a couple of weeks that I began to ask Him why I had not heard Him say anything to me. Holy Spirit responded to me by saying, "I am more interested in your desire to be in My

presence than your desire to hear and do something for Me."
I understood this to mean that God did not intend to speak to
me until I was more concerned about being in relationship with
Him than I was concerned about accomplishing results for Him.

After praying for several more weeks, I began to make the
number of hours that I was going to pray a goal. One particular
week I was one hour short of my intended goal, when I heard
Holy Spirit say He was not interested in being a goal that I had
accomplished. He was interested in my desire to spend time
together in His presence. So He instructed me to end my time of
prayer that week one hour short of my set goal.

Several nights I laid awake all night on my bed anticipating
Jesus and His angels to appear in my room. My body would
shake all night, consumed with the presence of the Lord. I
could feel hot, electric waves rippling through my entire body.
It was during and after this season of my life that I began to
experience new revelations, miracles, and visions (the first being
the opening chapter of this book) from Holy Spirit in ways that
I never had before!

My eyes were opened to a whole new world, a spiritual
world that was able to change the practical realities of my life, a
spiritual world that was able to bring the things I believed about
the Bible in harmony with the things that I was experiencing
from His Word! It was a world that was allowing me to live
in the fulfillment of the promises of God. Until my eyes were
opened to this new world I had unknowingly settled for less than
the promises of God in my life. This book is for those who may
be feeling disillusioned in their current level of faith, realizing
there is a difference between what you believe and what you are
actually experiencing in your everyday life!

EAST OF THE JORDAN

There is an interesting passage of Scripture in the book of Joshua that illustrates how we, as believers, can settle for living short of our promises in God. Joshua addresses *"the Reubenites, the Gadites, and the half-tribe of Manasseh."*[15] He tells the tribes to:

Remember what Moses the servant of the Lord commanded you, saying, the Lord your God is giving you (*of these two and a half tribes a place of*) rest and will give you this land (*east of the Jordan*). Your wives, your little ones, and your cattle shall dwell in the land which Moses gave you on this side of the Jordan, but all your mighty men of valor shall pass on before your brethren (*of the other tribes*) armed, and help them (*possess their land*) until the Lord gives your brethren rest, as He has given you, and they also possess the land the Lord your God is giving them. Then you shall return to the land of your possession and possess it, the land Moses the Lord's servant gave you on the sunrise side of the Jordan.[16]

Moses has just died, and Joshua has been chosen by God to take his place in leading the people of Israel into their promised land. To understand this passage of Scripture, it is important to look at the history of Moses and the Hebrew people. God called Moses to deliver His people from slavery and bondage in Egypt, and to lead them to salvation in the land of Canaan. He was able to lead the people of God successfully to the edge of the Jordan River. There he sent out twelve spies to explore the land that God had promised His children. The Bible says that they spied

---

[15] Joshua 1:12 AMP
[16] Joshua 1:13-15 AMP

out the land for forty days. All of the spies came back agreeing with the report of the Lord. They told Moses that "the land to which you sent us; surely it flows with milk and honey."[17]

If only this had been the end of the report for the twelve spies. Instead, they continue to give a negative report in direct opposition to the Word of the Lord. They began to speak a report filled with doubt and unbelief based on the appearance of their natural circumstances. They told Moses that the land was exactly as God had promised. "But the people who dwell there are strong, and the cities are fortified and very large; moreover, there we saw the sons of Anak (*of great stature and courage*)."[18] Ten of the twelve spies then began to list off all the reasons why they would not be able to possess the promise of God. They incited fear in the people of Israel saying, "we saw the Nephilim (*or giants*), the sons of Anak, who come from the giants; and we were in our own sight as grasshoppers, and so we were in their sight."[19]

Out of the twelve spies that Moses sent to explore the promised land, only Joshua and Caleb continued to believe God at His Word over the circumstances they saw with their natural eyes. In the midst of the negative report to Moses and the people of Israel, "Caleb quieted the people before Moses, and said, Let us go up at once and possess it; we are well able to conquer it."[20] He quieted the ten spies who were speaking fear and doubt, and he began agreeing and declaring faith with God's Word:

Joshua son of Nun and Caleb son of Jephunneh, who were among the scouts who had searched the land, rent their

[17] Numbers 13:27 AMP
[18] Numbers 13:28 AMP
[19] Numbers 13:33 AMP
[20] Numbers 13:30 AMP

clothes, and they said to all the company of Israelites, The land through which we passed as scouts is an exceedingly good land. If the Lord delights in us, then He will bring us into this land and give it to us, a land flowing with milk and honey. Only do not rebel against the Lord, neither fear the people of the land, for they are bread for us. Their defense and the shadow (*of protection*) is removed from over them, but the Lord is with us. Fear them not.[21]

Ten of the spies who searched out the promised land developed a grasshopper mentality as they convinced the people of Israel to believe in their circumstances rather than believe God at His Word. Israel chose to believe a report filled with fear based on the appearance of the natural over the report of God's Word. It caused them to see themselves as small and defeated rather than strong and victorious. They chose to doubt God's supernatural Word and believe the report of the natural. As a result, Moses and the people of Israel were sent back into the wilderness to wander for forty years (a trip that can be walked in 11 days!).

God waited for an entire non-believing generation to pass away before leading His people back to take their promised land. Only Joshua and Caleb, because of their faith in God's Word, were allowed to live long enough to possess the promised land. God even said, Caleb "has a different spirit and has followed Me fully, I will bring Him into the land into which he went, and his descendants shall possess it."[22] Forty years later, Moses attempted to lead God's people into the promised land once again. The Israelites had been in this aimless state of wandering when they were finally presented with an opportunity to go live in the

---

[21] Numbers 14:6-9 AMP
[22] Numbers 14:24 AMP

promises of God. Instead of rejoicing over the opportunity, they would rather keep living the same way that they had already been living. They wanted to settle for less than the promises of God!

STAYING PUT HINDERS GOD'S BLESSINGS

The Israelites were camped on the east side of the Jordan River just before crossing into the promised land. While they were there, the leaders of the tribes of Reuben, Gad, and half the tribe of Manasseh came to Moses and requested to receive the land east of the Jordan for their promised inheritance. They pled with Moses, "If we have found favor in your sight, let this land be given to your servants for a possession. Do not take us over the Jordan."[23]

In response to this strange request, Moses returned a question for a question, asking:

Shall your brethren go to war while you sit here? Why do you discourage the hearts of the Israelites from going over into the land which the Lord has given them? Thus your fathers did when I sent them from Kadesh-barnea to see the land! For when they went up to the Valley of Eshcol and saw the land, they discouraged the hearts of the Israelites from going into the land the Lord had given them.[24]

Moses was angry because the Israelites were about to cross the Jordan and possess the promised land that God swore to their forefathers. And these two and one half tribes approached Moses to tell him that they do not want to go with the rest of God's people to possess their inheritance.

---

[23] Numbers 32:5 AMP
[24] Numbers 32:6-9 AMP

They wanted to stay right where they were!

The first time Israel approached the promised land, they had acted in fear and unbelief. Now, a whole new generation of God's people arrived at the edge of the promised land and wanted to settle for less than the promises of God. So, Moses rebuked them, saying:

> You are risen up in your fathers' stead, a brood of sinful men, to increase still more the fierce anger of the Lord against Israel. For if you turn from following Him, He will again abandon them in the wilderness, and you will destroy all these people.[25]

As a result, the leaders of these two and one half tribes made a proposal to appease God by making a commitment to fight with Moses and the people of Israel, saying:

> We will be armed and ready to go before the Israelites until we have brought them to their place. Our little ones shall dwell in the fortified settlements because of the people in the land. We will not return to our homes until the Israelites have inherited every man his inheritance. For we will not inherit with them on the (*west*) side of Jordan and beyond, because our inheritance is fallen to us on this side of the Jordan eastward.[26]

Moses agreed to their proposal, saying:

> If you will do as you say, going armed before the Lord to war, and every armed man of you will pass over the Jordan before the Lord until He has driven out His enemies before Him and the land is subdued before the

[25] Numbers 32:14-15 AMP
[26] Numbers 32:17-19 AMP

Lord, then afterward you shall return and be guiltless (*in this matter*) before the Lord and before Israel, and this land shall be your possession before the Lord.[27]

Originally Moses was supposed to bring the people of Israel into their promised inheritance, but the Lord would not let him live long enough to set one foot in the promised land. We find out the reason why in an earlier conversation, where the Lord told Moses:

Because you did not believe in (*rely on, cling to*) Me to sanctify Me in the eyes of the Israelites, you therefore shall not bring this congregation into the land which I have given them.[28]

Only Joshua and Caleb had stood up before the people of Israel, while tearing their clothes to speak in opposition to the report of the ten unbelieving spies and to declare their belief in the Word of the Lord! So Moses was not allowed to enter the promised land – only to see it. God showed Moses the promised land before he died, saying:

This is the land which I swore to Abraham, Isaac, and Jacob, saying, I will give it to your descendants. I have let you see it with your eyes, but you shall not go over there.[29]

When Moses died, it was Joshua who received the mantle of leadership to bring God's people into the promised land. Joshua began by preparing Israel to make provisions within three days to cross over the Jordan to finally possess the land that God

---

[27] Numbers 32:20-22 AMP
[28] Numbers 20:12 AMP
[29] Deuteronomy 34:4 AMP

had already given them. It is here that we return to find Joshua reaffirming the agreement made between the leaders of the tribe of Reuben, Gad, and the one half tribe of Manasseh with Moses, to allow these tribes to receive the land east of the Jordan as their inheritance in exchange for their willingness to fight along with the rest of the Israelites to possess the promised land. Essentially they had come to Moses by their own initiative, saying that they wanted to relinquish their rights to the promised land for personal convenience so they could live on the east side of the Jordan. The promised land is on the west side of the Jordan, but they wanted to live on the east side of the Jordan!

They were willing to go across the Jordan and risk their lives fighting in order to help the other nine and one half tribes conquer the promised land of Canaan, but after they possessed the promised land they would not take their share of the inheritance. They would go back and live on the east side of the Jordan.

They chose not to live in the fullness of what God had already given to them. They chose to settle for less than the promises of God! The land east of the Jordan may look like the promised land, but it is not the promised land – it is a place where we can see all of the promises of God, but never actually experience the fulfillment of those promises for ourselves!

THE ABUNDANT LIFE

The promised land is a prophetic picture of what it means for a believer to live the abundant life in the New Testament. The abundant life is about experiencing what you believe about God and the promises of His Word for yourself. It is where you are actually experiencing your faith working in your everyday life. In John 10:10 AMP, Jesus says:

The thief comes only in order to steal and kill and destroy. I came that they may have and enjoy life, and have it in abundance (*to the full, till it overflows*).

Notice that Jesus does not say He came that they may believe to enjoy life, and believe to have it in abundance. Jesus says, *"I came that they may have..."* He came that we would experience life and the joy of life in abundance, to the fullest, and even until it overflows. Jesus wants us to have life and to enjoy our lives so much that it will overflow out of our lives and into the lives of people around us. He does not just want us to believe that we can have life and enjoy our lives. Jesus wants us to experience it for ourselves. It may be difficult for some religious people to understand that Jesus wants us to enjoy our lives, but that is what the Bible says is God's plan for our lives!

Several years ago I went on a short mission trip to Jamaica. During one outreach, we were prayer walking through one of the towns. We were passing by one of the homes when we were engaged in conversation by the parents of a young boy of about eight. They explained to us that their little boy was unable to walk. Holy Spirit led us to lay hands on him and pray for his healing. Instantly, to our amazement, this boy was healed as we helped him struggle to his feet and watched him begin to walk! On that day in Jamaica we got to experience the abundant life!

RELATIONAL DEPENDENCY AND SURRENDERING CONTROL

If we had been afraid to trust God that day in Jamaica we would have never experienced the miraculous. It was in the midst of having to risk failure in our own abilities we learned to be dependent upon God to accomplish the impossible based on His abilities. The things we believed about healing were manifested right before our eyes! The abundant life can only be experienced through a relationship of dependency and trust in God.

In Genesis 32, Jacob had an encounter where he wrestled with God all night. Obviously, Jacob was not a slacker that was easily discouraged! Could you imagine wrestling with God all night? It seems like it was God's plan for Jacob to think that he could possibly win by allowing him to wrestle with Him for such a long time. God could have defeated Jacob at any time!

In the midst of this wrestling match, the Bible says,

When (God) saw that He did not prevail against him, He touched the socket of his hip; and the socket of Jacob's hip was out of joint as He wrestled with him.[30]

Jacob was a young, arrogant man who thought that he could accomplish just about anything on his own, including God's plan for his life. After all, he was successful in stealing his brother's birthright and manipulating his father into speaking his brother's blessing over his own life. The only problem was that no matter how hard he worked and strived to be successful, things never seemed to get any easier.

Now Jacob was trying to manipulate God into blessing him by saying, "I will not let You go unless You bless me!"[31] So then God asked him:

"What is your name?" He said, "Jacob." And He said, "Your name shall no longer be called Jacob, but Israel;

---

[30] Genesis 32:25 NKJV
[31] Genesis 32:26 NKJV

for you have struggled with God and with men, and have prevailed."[32]

Then Jacob asked, saying, "Tell me Your name, I pray. And He said, "Why is it that you ask about My name?" And He blessed him there.[33]

Why did God want to know Jacob's name? The name of a person represented a person's identity. In the Old Testament, knowing someone's name was to essentially have control over that person's life. When Jacob finally surrendered his name to God, he was surrendering His identity and the control of his life to God!

God would not give Jacob His name. Jacob began to receive a revelation about finding his identity through relationship, dependency, and having strength in God during weakness. It was when Jacob finally surrendered control that he received his blessing from God.

"Jacob called the name of the place Peniel: 'For I have seen God face to face, and my life is preserved.'"[34] In other words, it was a place of revelation. Jacob received a revelation of God. He received a revelation of his identity in God! He also received a revelation of his inheritance through spiritual resources when God blessed him with His promises, and preserved his life.

It was an event that Jacob or the children of Israel would not soon forget:

As he crossed over Penuel the sun rose on him, and he limped on his hip. Therefore to this day the children of

[32] Genesis 32:27-28 NKJV
[33] Genesis 32:29 NKJV
[34] Genesis 32:30 NKJV

Israel do not eat the muscle that shrank, which is on the hip socket, because He touched the socket of Jacob's hip in the muscle that shrank.[35]

The word *shrank* here is the Hebrew word *nasheh*. It means "in a sense of failure, rheumatic, or crippled."[36] It is in a sense of failure that we develop a genuine relationship with Jesus. It is that place where we realize that we are crippled in our own abilities. It is where we learn to be dependent upon God's strength, abilities and accomplishments.

As a result, Jacob went on to accomplish more in God as a crippled man with a dislocated hip than he was ever able to accomplish in the full strength of his own abilities. In surrendering the control of our lives, we can finally be trusted with the authority and power of His promises. As His heart and agenda become our heart and agenda, Jesus says:

I do not call you servants (*slaves*) any longer, for the servant does not know what the master is doing (*working out*). But I have called you my friends, because I have made known to you everything that I have heard from my Father. (*I have revealed to you everything that I have learned from Him*).[37]

Just like Jacob, many of us find ourselves wrestling for control of our lives in relationship with God. Often we want to be relationally independent, thinking that we can accomplish just about anything on our own, including God's plan for our life. We tend to leave our state of relational dependency on God

---

[35] Genesis 32:31-32 NKJV
[36] Strong's Exhaustive Concordance, Reference 5384
[37] John 15:15 AMP

to take back the control that we once surrendered to Jesus. It is like we tell God, "Thanks for the help when I really needed it, but I can handle the rest from here!" The only problem is that no matter how hard we work and strive to live the abundant life, it never seems to become a reality.

As a result, we often settle for what looks good now, rather than waiting in dependence on Him for the fulfillment that is only found in His promises. We make major decisions in regards to the direction of our lives based on our current circumstances, perspectives, and feelings. Often it seems that we settle for less than the abundant life, just so we can live where it is comfortable, convenient, and familiar. There are things in this world that appear to be good for our lives, but they are not the promises of God!

Many Christians just want their lives to get a little better. They settle for less than God's promise for an improved way of life. They are willing to trade the promises of God, if they can find relief from their current set of circumstances. They just want to experience a little more peace at home, a little less pain in their body. They are willing to forfeit the promise of God if things could get just a little better!

CHILDREN OF GOD IN RELATIONSHIP WITH HIM

JOHN 1:12 AMP SAYS:

As many as did receive and welcome Him, He gave the authority (*power, privilege, right*) to become the children of God, that is to those who believe in (*adhere to, trust in, and rely on*) His name.

When we receive and welcome Christ into our heart and life, we are children of God. As sons and daughters of the living God we have been given authority to receive the abundant life. We have been given His authority to destroy every obstacle that opposes the promises of God in our life. We do not have to settle for things to be a little better in our life. We have a right to the privileges of God. He has given us the power to possess our promises by trusting in Him!

The New Testament word for *believe* in this passage of Scripture has nothing to do with the existence of someone or something. It is the Greek word *pisteuo*. It means "to have faith (in, upon, or with respect to, a person or thing)."[38] It implies entrusting one's spiritual well being to Christ by adhering to, trusting in, or relying on Him.

Our ability to believe in God requires a relationship with Him. A relationship with someone is a necessary component in order to adhere to something someone has communicated to us. It is vital to have a relationship with someone whom we know to be trustworthy before we can trust them, before we feel like we can rely on them with faith! For example, how will we trust God for our provision if we do not have revelation that He is provision?

A relationship implies a personal exchange of communication and spending time with another. It is an exchange of hearts. Sometimes we will talk to a person that we are in a relationship with and they listen to us. Other times a person that we are in a relationship with will talk to us and we will listen to them.

Imagine if I had married my wife and then quit having a relationship with her, no longer spending time together, talking with her or listening to her! We would not have a very healthy marriage

---

[38] Strong's Exhaustive Concordance, Reference 4100

relationship. My wife would not be happy with the status of our relationship. She would feel like we did not have a relationship. I would not really know her thoughts or feelings. We would not really know each other well enough to trust one another!

The same thing is true in our relationship with God. I have to personally know Him to be trustworthy in order to trust in His name. The true substance of our relationship with God is found in our daily ability to believe in His name. As a result, we are given authority, including the power, privilege, and right to become the children of God. We become heirs in the promises of God. "In Him we also were made (God's) heritage (portion) and we obtained an inheritance."[39] We have already obtained an inheritance that can only be found in Christ! This heritage is the key to releasing the favor necessary in order to experience the abundant life!

A ROYAL PRIESTHOOD

There is much confusion in the body of Christ today about what it means to walk in faith, authority, and the inheritance of God. Many Christians just do not know who they are in Christ!

You are a chosen race, a royal priesthood, a dedicated nation (God's) own purchased, special people, that you may set forth the wonderful deeds and display the virtues and perfections of Him who called you out of darkness into His marvelous light. Once you were not a people (at all), but now you are God's people; once you were unpitied, but now you are pitied and have received mercy.[40]

[39] Ephesians 1:11 AMP
[40] 1 Peter 2:9-10 AMP

47

We are God's very own chosen people, set aside and called for the purpose of manifesting the light and works of God that live within us all while displaying His likeness. Many Christians spend more time contemplating the plans of the enemy than developing faith in God. It is essentially giving the enemy authority in our lives that he does not have the right to exercise. The One who has all authority lives in us and has already defeated the enemy. He has given us His authority to manifest His works and display His likeness. As Christians, we need to spend more time keeping our eyes on the author and finisher of our faith rather than on what the enemy is doing! Spending our entire life in spiritual warfare is to settle for less than the abundant life!

A story about Martin Luther helps to illustrate this point. One night he was fast asleep when he heard some noise in his room. In the dark, he lit a match in order to see what all the commotion was about. His response may be somewhat of a surprise. He said, "Oh, it is just you, Satan!" He then proceeded to blow out the match and lay down to go back to sleep!

LIVING IN DECEPTION

Did you know that you are the only one who can give the enemy authority in your life? He has been successful in keeping God's people from understanding their true identity in Christ so they will hand over their authority to him. He was able to deceive Adam and Eve into believing that they were not like God, even though they were created in His image, so they would eat from the tree of the knowledge of good and evil in order to try and become something that they already were in Him.

Satan also tried to deceive Jesus, although unsuccessfully. In the wilderness, the enemy tried to get Jesus to question His identity by saying, "If you are the Son of God?" Jesus *was* the Son of God! Satan was trying to deceive Jesus about His identity so that He would believe that He still needed to receive all that was already His!

This is the same thing the enemy tries to do with us. He is still trying to do the same thing as when he deceived Adam and Eve about their identity, as well as when he tried to deceive Jesus about His identity. It's not a new idea. The enemy is not creative or original, just consistently persistent about trying to get us to surrender our authority by surrendering our identity. Essentially, we do this when we acknowledge that we have already been given everything we need for victory through His accomplishments, but then make excuses of why it will not work for us!

> Be doers of the Word (*obey the message*), and not merely listeners to it, betraying yourselves (*into deception by reasoning contrary to the Truth*).[41]

For most of us there is a difference between what we believe and what we are actually experiencing in our lives. The above verse is not a call to be doers of the Word through our own strength and ability. It is a call to obey the message based on His revelation that has been diffused through your soul. The things that we are doing ought to be a result of our being.

God is not a hypocrite. God doesn't just heal people. He is healing. A hypocrite is just an actor. An actor is someone who is acting like something they aren't.

---

[41] James 1:22 AMP

In the same way, created in the image of God, we are not called to be hypocrites. We are not to act like something that we are not. We are to act or do out of who we are. Our doing is not to come as a result of merely listening to information but hearing revelation about our true identity so that we do not betray ourselves.

Often, as Christians, we do not pray over our children when they are sick, fearful that we will fail again! God has called believers to a place where we would experience the things that we say we believe based on revelation. "Faith by itself, if it does not have works, is dead."[42] We must activate the things that we believe by faith based in revelation in order to experience the abundant life and reveal that Christ is alive in us.

I once heard Kris Vallotton say that the problem with being deceived is that you don't know you are deceived. We betray ourselves into deception through our own sense and reasoning that is contrary to the Truth! We are deceived when we believe that we can live by faith in a relationship with Christ based on information received through our physical senses by merely listening. It is the fruit of our relationship with Christ that results in revelation through our spiritual senses to know and understand His heart and agenda in order receive and manifest His promises for our lives. It is the evidence of a genuine relationship with God!

JESUS SAID:

I am the Vine; you are the branches. Whoever lives in Me and I in him bears much (*abundant*) fruit. However, apart from Me (*cut off from vital union with Me*) you can do

---

[42] James 2:17 NKJV

nothing. If a person does not dwell in Me, he is thrown out like a (*broken-off*) branch, and withers; such branches are gathered up and thrown into the fire, and they are burned. If you live in Me (*abide vitally united to Me*) and My words remain in you and continue to live in your hearts, ask whatever you will, and it shall be done for you. When you bear (*produce*) much fruit, My Father is honored and glorified, and you show and prove yourselves to be true followers of Mine.[43]

LIVING ON THE RIGHT SIDE OF THE CROSS

I have heard it said that as the Israelites were passing over the Jordan River they could have looked down from an aerial view, with the priests holding the ark of the covenant of the Lord in the middle of the river bed, and seen that their formation took on the shape of the cross. As we study the Scriptures regarding the journey of Joshua and the Israelites, we can see a prophetic parallel between the crossing of the Jordan and the cross of Jesus Christ. Joshua had delivered the people of Israel out of bondage, brought them through the wilderness, across the Jordan River, and into the promised land. In the same way, Christ died on the cross to deliver us from our sin, reconciling us into right relationship with God and setting us free so that we could live the abundant life!

The Israelites wandered in the wilderness on the wrong side of the Jordan, living in the flesh and in bondage and defeat, because they chose to trust the appearance of their circumstances more than they trusted God at His Word. It is the same way for us as believers today when we choose to live the Christian life by

---

[43] John 15:5-8 AMP

trusting in our own strengths and abilities rather than trusting in Christ and His accomplishments on the cross. Joshua was able to finally lead the Israelites to possess their promised land when they learned to trust God at His Word over the appearance of their circumstances. Similarly, as believers we can experience the abundant life when we learn to trust in a relationship based on the revelation of Christ's accomplishments more than on their own wisdom, strength, and abilities.

> WE HAVE ALREADY BEEN GIVEN EVERYTHING WE NEED TO LIVE IN THE PROMISES OF GOD THROUGH CHRIST'S ACCOMPLISHMENTS.

One side of the cross represents living as if Christ never actually paid the total cost for our sin. It is the side of the cross where we are still trying to earn the things that Christ already paid for on the cross, where we try to overcome the impossible on our own. If we choose to live on the wrong side of the cross we will never experience the abundant life.

On the other side of the cross, Jesus has already defeated every enemy. He has already fought every fight we would ever need to fight. We have already been given everything we need to live in the promises of God through Christ's accomplishments. If we choose to live on the right side of the cross, we will experience His promises in our life!

As Joshua gets ready to lead the people of Israel into the promised land after forty years of wandering in the wilderness, he faces one of the greatest challenges of his natural life. He is leading God's people across the Jordan River. It is the only thing standing between the Israelites' end to wandering in the wilderness and the possession of their promised land. The Jordan River represents this impossible obstacle in Joshua's life that has to be overcome in order to possess the promises of God. It is "impossible" because there is nothing that he can do in his own strength and ability to lead God's people across the Jordan. If Joshua leads the people of Israel across the Jordan in his own strength and ability, then the people of God will never live to see the promised land.

JOSHUA IS IN A PLACE OF TOTAL DEPENDENCE UPON GOD

At this point Joshua is standing by the side of the Jordan, looking at the impossible thing he is facing. He is waiting for God to do something, when he hears the Lord say, "This day I will begin to magnify you in the sight of all Israel, so they may know that as I was with Moses, so I will be with you."[44] Joshua finally receives a word from the Lord! All he has to do is trust the spiritual realm based on God at His word, instead of trusting in the appearance of the impossible obstacle standing before him in the natural realm.

In the natural realm nothing has changed, and the Jordan appears to be just as impossible as ever to cross. If Joshua is successful, then the people will determine that the favor of God is with him and they will follow him just like they followed Moses. If he is unsuccessful, then the people will determine that the favor of God is not on Joshua and they will not follow him as their leader.

---

[44] Joshua 3:7 AMP

GOD TOLD JOSHUA:

> Take twelve men from the tribes of Israel, one from each
> tribe. When the soles of the feet of the priests who bear
> the ark of the Lord of all the earth shall rest in the Jordan,
> the waters of the Jordan coming down from above shall
> be cut off and they shall stand in one heap.[45]

So Joshua steps out in faith and obedience according to
God's word, activating the anointing of God in the supernatural.
Joshua puts his trust in God's abilities over his own abilities,
releasing the authority and power to overcome the impossible!

When the feet of the priests that were carrying the ark
touched the Jordan,

> the waters which came down from above stood and rose
> up on a heap far off...and the people passed over opposite
> Jericho. And while all Israel passed over on dry ground,
> the priests who bore the ark of the covenant of the Lord
> stood firm on dry ground in the midst of the Jordan, until
> all the nation finished passing over the Jordan.[46]

God actually parted the waters of the Jordan just like He
parted the waters of the Red Sea for Moses, allowing Joshua
and the Israelites to overcome the impossible in order to finally
possess their promised land.

EVERYTHING IS POSSIBLE

There is a young couple in our church named Jesse and
Lyndsey Rehm who recently discovered how to overcome an

[45] Joshua 3:12-13 AMP
[46] Joshua 3:16-17 AMP

impossible situation in their own life so that they could begin to live on the right side of the cross.

Jesse says, "We had decided that we wanted to have a baby, but two and a half years passed by without any success. Finally, Lyndsey decided that she wanted to go to the doctor and have some testing done to make sure that everything was working properly with her body. I decided to get tested as well.

"Our test results came back free from any negative results, but we were told that the help of medication would be necessary for Lyndsey to get pregnant. The doctor told us that if Lyndsey was not pregnant within three months, then we should come back for more extensive testing. Three months came and went, and we still did not have any baby. It was especially hard for Lyndsey since she works in a family practice clinic and sees pregnant women every day.

"We had become discouraged and started speaking the wrong things over our lives by agreeing with what the world and the enemy said about us. We finally turned to the Word of God. Mark 11:23 said that we could have what we speak if only we would not doubt. I showed Lyndsey that Romans 4:16 tells us that we are the seed of Abraham and the heirs of the promise through faith in Jesus. I then took her to Deuteronomy 7:14-15, showing her that none of the seed of Abraham shall be barren, and God will remove all our afflictions.

"She took possession of that word, receiving it as a rhema word. She decided not to go back to the doctors anymore for testing; she quit taking the medication and established God's promise in her heart and words. Our friends and family had been praying for us for months. Many at our church had prayed for us and had faith when we had none, but it was not until we accepted God's Word for ourselves and started speaking in agreement with it that we actually began to experience His Word come to pass in our lives.

"Once Lyndsey accepted that word for herself, God turned her anxiety into peace and our discouragement into trust. Instead of wondering if she would get pregnant, Lyndsey started talking about when she 'got pregnant.' The doubt was gone, and the words from her mouth agreed with God's Word! According to Matthew 18:16 which says, 'in the mouth of two or three witnesses every word is established.' Our words are containers of God's power!

"I want to encourage people that God wants His power to manifest in your life, but we need to be speaking the right words in our life for it to be established. God's promise is that if we will agree with Him in our heart and with the words we speak, everything is possible for us. Two months after Lyndsey quit her medication, standing on the Word of God, Lyndsey was pregnant. This testimony is not that Lyndsey is pregnant, but that there is real power in our relationship with God and the words that we speak! Start speaking words that agree with God and you will experience God's power in your own life."[47]

MIXING THE MESSAGE

What impossible thing in your life is keeping you from experiencing the abundant life? Is there something in your life that you cannot accomplish in your own strength and abilities? Is there an area of sin in your life that you have tried to overcome many times, but now have given up on altogether? Is fear of

---

[47] Jesse Rhem, Revival Cry Newsletter, Volume 1, Issue 8 (Bozeman, MT: Revival Cry Ministries, 2006)

failing again keeping you paralyzed from moving forward in your life? Then it is time for you to cross the Jordan and start mixing the message of the Gospel with faith so that you can start living on the right side of the cross!

> For indeed we have had the glad tidings (*Gospel of God*) proclaimed to us just as truly as they (*the Israelites of old did when the good news of deliverance from bondage came to them*); but the message they heard did not benefit them, because it was not mixed with faith (*with the leaning of the entire personality of God in absolute trust and confidence in His power, wisdom, and goodness*) by those who heard it.[48]

The Israelites heard the message of the good news but it did not benefit them because it was not mixed with faith. What is faith? Here it speaks of leaning on the entire personality of God in absolute trust and confidence in His power, wisdom, and goodness.

Faith is a result of building a trust relationship with Holy Spirit. It is not enough to hear the information from the message of the gospel alone. We must mix our hearing of the gospel message with a relationship resulting in revelation of the personality of God so that we can have faith to trust Him in order to experience the benefits of living on the right side of the cross! Many Christians are still living on the wrong side of the cross.

We are fighting battles that have already been defeated by Christ. We are still trying to accomplish what Christ has already accomplished on our behalf. We could spend our whole lives fighting and never inheriting the promises of God, if we take

---

[48] Hebrews 4:2 AMP

what Christ did on the cross and make it invalid by trying to accomplish for ourselves all that He has already accomplished for us. When will we stop fighting battles where Jesus has already given us the victory? We are living on the wrong side of the cross!

We could experience the promises of God because Jesus has already given us everything we need to experience the abundant life. Instead, we know deep down inside ourselves that we are still trusting in our own abilities rather than in a relationship based on Christ's accomplishments. As a result, we live in fear of facing the impossible obstacles in our lives that would allow us to live in the promises of God. We look across the Jordan and see those who have trusted Him experiencing the abundant life, as we make excuses to ourselves saying, "One day I will trust God and overcome the impossible things in my life and experience the promises of God for myself."

The problem is that it doesn't get any easier to trust God "one day," when everything in our life is put together just the way we want it. If we cannot trust Him now, we probably will not trust Him later. You have been called to live the abundant life. You do not have to wait until tomorrow. You could start living it today. You have been called to rest in the promises of God because of what Christ has already accomplished on your behalf.

IT IS ALREADY FINISHED

We have all tried to make things happen in our own strength and abilities. Our authority in Christ rests solely on what He has already accomplished at the cross! It is time to start living on the right side of the cross!

CHAPTER 3

RESTING IN HIS ACCOMPLISHMENTS

IT IS IRONIC THAT I AM WRITING THIS CHAPTER of the book on "Resting in His Accomplishments" from my wife's hospital room. God had put it in Tammi's heart to have four children since she was a little girl. She is now nine weeks and four days pregnant with our fourth child, and she has had very difficult pregnancies with all three of our previous children. This time she made a strong decision to trust God for divine health during her pregnancy. Since then, she has been under constant attack from the enemy resulting in the continued deterioration of her health in the natural realm.

Yesterday she went to see a doctor to get relief from a sinus infection that she had been fighting for about two weeks. During the visit she found out that her blood pressure was two hundred and five over one hundred fifteen. The doctors told us that her health situation could possibly cause a stroke or a heart attack. Furthermore, because she was in the early stages of her pregnancy, the doctor was concerned about the survival of the baby. As a result, she was sent to the obstetrician to determine if the pregnancy was in danger and to receive further diagnosis of her condition.

At that point Tammi called me on the phone to tell me about the doctor's report while on her way to see the obstetrician. I heard Holy Spirit say, "Tell your wife that the baby is healthy." I told my wife that I believed that the baby was healthy and that I would meet her at the obstetrician's office immediately. We determined at that moment to believe God's Word together, over the report of the doctor. When I arrived at the doctor's office they performed an ultrasound on my wife, confirming the report of the Lord!

The doctor then sent my wife to the emergency room for intravenous medical treatment for her high blood pressure. While my wife was in the emergency room, one of the nurses told her that she was sent there in case her heart stopped as a result of trying to bring down her blood pressure. Five hours later she was admitted to the hospital for further medical treatment, testing, and monitoring over the next three to four days. Since her admission to the hospital she has been constantly in pain and vomiting.

Several doctors continue to rotate the visitation schedule around the clock. Each one tries to prepare my wife with reports for all the possible negative future scenarios. She only felt congested before her initial visit to the doctor's office. My wife and I joke that she had to come to the hospital to get sick! I am writing this story as it is happening so we do not have any results to report yet in the natural, but in the spirit we know, through revelation by Holy Spirit, that Tammi has already received her healing – soon to be manifested as a victorious testimony in Him!

PUTTING ON THE ARMOR

In times like these the Bible says:

Put on God's whole armor (*the armor of a heavy-armed soldier which God supplies*), that you may be able successfully to stand up against (*all*) the strategies and the deceits of the devil.[49]

The phrase "put on" here isn't about something we do by our natural effort. It is a reminder not to forget that our identity is found in the accomplishments of Christ. This means we aren't limited by our natural abilities to stand up against the deceits of the devil. This phrase is best illustrated by the picture of a soldier standing over a battlefield that has already been conquered.

The word here for *deceits* is the Greek word *methodia*. It means "method, trickery, and to lie in wait."[50] In other words, the devil lies in wait, scheming for any opportunity to trick us into doubting the Word of God. The reality is that the devil does not have any real power over those who have received salvation in Jesus Christ. So, he tricks us into believing that things are not as we have believed. He deceives us through the appearance of our circumstances that seem in the natural to contradict God's Word. His goal is to get us to agree in fear with the appearance of our circumstances instead of agreeing in faith with God's Word.

My wife's circumstances have given us the opportunity to put on the full armor of Christ's accomplishments so that we may be able to successfully stand against all the strategies of the devil in order to receive our promises of salvation. The more we prayed and believed for Tammi's health, the worse she seemed

[49] Ephesians 6:11 AMP
[50] Strong's Exhaustive Concordance, Reference 3180

to get! It was so extreme that we knew that the devil was trying to trick us into believing his report about her health circumstances over the report of the Lord! The devil had overplayed his hand! We were not going to play around with the enemy any longer! We were going to another realm!

> For we are not wrestling with flesh and blood (*contending only with physical opponents*), but...against the powers, against (*the master spirits who are*) the world rulers of this present darkness, against the spirit forces of wickedness in the heavenly (*supernatural*) sphere.[51]

ALWAYS READY TO FIGHT

As I sit helplessly at the end of my wife's bed watching her fight mentally, physically, and spiritually for her health, I have come again to realize that our only hope is in Christ's accomplishments. I would like to try and find a way to fix everything, but it is only an illusion in my head. I am unable to change my wife's health circumstances no matter how hard I choose to fight in my own strength. I am learning again that there are battles we have to fight in the promised land, but striving to work harder will never lead us to victory. Christ's accomplishments cannot be earned ... they can only be received as a gift!

Joshua and the Israelites had to fight natural battles in the promised land in the same way we have to fight spiritual battles while living the abundant life. Joshua had just conquered the impossible by leading the people of Israel across the Jordan River and into the promised land. As he stepped into the promised land, he was already looking at his next battle with Jericho. He

---

[51] Ephesians 6:12 AMP

was standing there in the promised land when he saw a man, "near him with His drawn sword in His hand."[52]

Joshua was in the midst of thinking about his next battle plan when a man he did not know appeared out of nowhere with a drawn sword. He was about to go to war, and this man could be one of the adversaries. Joshua was startled but was prepared to fight his potential enemy, so he approached and asked Him, "Are you for us or for our adversaries?"[53]

The man replied, "No (*neither*)" and then revealed His identity, saying, "But as Prince of the Lord's host have I now come."[54] Joshua was starting to get a revelation from God. He was beginning to realize that his victory over the city of Jericho had nothing to do with his own abilities but with the supernatural abilities of His God. Joshua was beginning to understand that being on God's side is much more important than determining who is on his side.

Joshua fell on his face and worshipped the Lord, asking, "What says my Lord to His servant?"[55] The Lord replied, "Loose your shoes from off your feet, for the place where you stand is holy"[56] Joshua took off his shoes, realizing that he was standing on holy ground, as God taught him the right way to prepare for a fight. Then the Lord began to share His plan with Joshua to take the city of Jericho, saying, "You shall march around the enclosure, all the men of war going around the city once. This you shall do for six days."[57]

---

[52] Joshua 5:13 AMP
[53] Ibid
[54] Joshua 5:14 AMP
[55] Ibid
[56] Joshua 5:15 AMP
[57] Joshua 6:3 AMP

At this point Joshua was probably full of excitement, knowing that on God's side he would be victorious in the battle over Jericho. If he was anything like most of us, he was probably even a little excited that God was going to make him look good as a leader in front of all the other Israelites.

In the midst of his thoughts, Joshua could still hear the Lord telling him his battle plan:

> Seven priests shall bear before the ark seven trumpets of rams' horns; and on the seventh day you shall march around the enclosure seven times, and the priests shall blow the trumpets.[58]

As the Lord continued with His plans, Joshua probably switched his thoughts to the upcoming fight. He was a warrior waiting to hear his fighting instructions. He wanted to know his role in the fight. He desperately wanted to get past all the preliminaries and into the action plan. He wanted to know the bottom line for conquering Jericho.

THE LORD CONTINUED:

> When they make a long blast with the rams' horn and you hear the sound of the trumpet, all the people shall shout with a great shout; and the wall of the enclosure shall fall down in its place and the people shall go up (*over it*), every man straight before him.[59]

In other words, the Lord said that all Joshua and the Israelites had to do was to march around the city for seven days and then shout to be victorious over Jericho in their battle. God would

[58] Joshua 6:4 AMP
[59] Joshua 6:5 AMP

take care of the rest on His own! He did not need Joshua to fight for Him in order to win the battle. He did not want Joshua on his own to try and make something happen for Him! Joshua's earlier revelation with the Prince of the Lord's host was now beginning to become a reality in his heart. Joshua was a warrior ready to fight, but God was telling him to march and shout according to the revelation that he had already received.

WHY ARE WE ALWAYS LOOKING FOR A FIGHT?

Joshua and the Israelites marched around the city of Jericho once each day for six days, not saying one word. Joshua told the Israelites before they started marching just as the Lord had said:

> You shall not shout or let your voice be heard, nor shall any word proceed out of your mouth until the day I tell you to shout. Then you shall shout![60]

By the seventh day the people probably knew something out of the ordinary was going to happen!

> They rose early at daybreak and marched around the city as usual, only on that day they compassed the city seven times.[61]

With a warrior like Joshua being their leader, the people of Israel were probably anticipating a fight. On the seventh day, on the seventh time around the city,

> When the priests had blown the trumpets, Joshua said to the people, Shout! For the Lord has given you the city.[62]

---

[60] Joshua 6:10 AMP
[61] Joshua 6:15 AMP
[62] Joshua 6:16 AMP

The Lord had already given them the city of Jericho! It was a part of the promised land. It was a gift from God. Jericho could not be conquered through the Israelites' own abilities to strive and work hard. So all the people of Israel shouted just as Joshua had said:

> And (Jericho's) wall fell down in its place, so that the (Israelites) went up into the city, every man straight before him, and they took the city.[63]

The walls of Jericho fell down!

They had never been penetrated by anyone in the history of their existence. The people of Israel did not even touch the walls of Jericho. They only marched and shouted according to God's plan. They did not have to do anything to conquer the city of Jericho during the battle. God conquered the whole city on His own!

SPIRITUAL BLESSINGS WITHOUT FORMULAS

East of the Jordan we still have to strive in our own strength to get results. It is a place where we are still striving to work hard in our own abilities to receive the promises of God. It is a place where there is no reward for our efforts. It appears that the promises of God are for everyone but us. No matter how hard we strive to work in our own strength and abilities, we never seem to experience the promises of God for ourselves. We are still trying to make things happen that Christ already accomplished. We are – living on the wrong side of the cross!

In the promised land we actually get things done by resting in the revelation of Christ's accomplishments. It is a place where

[63] Joshua 6:20 AMP

we no longer have to strive to work hard in our own strength and abilities to receive the promises of God. It is a place where we are actually experiencing the promises of God in our lives. We are experiencing the abundant life for ourselves!

We are resting in the things Christ has done on our behalf:

Having (*freely*) forgiven us all our transgressions, having cancelled and blotted out and wiped away the handwriting of the note (*bond*) with its legal decrees and demands which was in force and stood against us (*hostile to us*). This (*note with its regulations, decrees, and demands*) He set aside and cleared completely out of our way by nailing it to (*His*) cross. (*God*) disarmed the principalities and powers that were ranged against us and made a bold display and public example of them, in triumphing over them in Him and in it (*the cross*).[64]

Jesus has already overcome at the cross every obstacle that we will ever face. Anything that could ever oppose us, keeping us from receiving God's promises, was cleared completely out of our way and nailed to the cross. We cannot do anything in our own efforts that will improve upon the things that Christ already accomplished in His death on the cross and His resurrection from the dead. Jesus triumphed over every enemy who could ever oppose us! He does not need us to perform for Him in order for us to see all the promises of God accomplished in our lives. He does not need us to fight in our own strength in order to overcome our circumstances to make something happen for Him. He has already finished executing His plan, prepared at a time in the past, to make us victorious.

---

[64] Colossians 2:13-15 AMP

There are no special formulas or legalistic rituals that will help us to receive those things He has already given to us. Many Christians follow a religious formula trying to get their desired results, rather than building an intimate relationship with Christ. After awhile we get tired of believing for things that we never seem to experience for ourselves. All of the information that we have received about Christ does not seem to work for us, because we have not learned to rest in Him.

God never intended for us to do anything for Him. He intended to do things through us based on our revelation of His accomplishments. The abundant life is not about a religion, it is about a relationship with Christ.

We have already been set free from the bondage of striving and working hard in order to inherit the promises of God.

> For it is by free grace (*God's unmerited favor*) that you are saved (*delivered from judgment and made partakers of Christ's salvation*) through (*your*) faith. And this (*salvation*) is not of yourselves, (*of your own doing, it came not through your own striving*), but it is the gift of God. Not because of works (*not the fulfillment of the Law's demands*), lest any man should boast. (*It is not the result of what anyone can possibly do, so no one can pride himself in it or take glory to himself.*) For we are God's (*own*) handiwork (*His workmanship*), recreated in Christ Jesus, (*born anew*) that we may do those good works which God predestined (*planned beforehand*) for us (*taking paths which He prepared ahead of time*), that we should walk in them (*living the good life which He prearranged and made ready for us to live*).[65]

---

[65] Ephesians 2:8-10 AMP

We have been saved by free grace — it does not cost us anything. It is a gift from God based on God's merits and favor. Notice that grace isn't just about forgiveness of the past based on His merits, but it's also about the power and favor of God to accomplish your future destiny. It's time for believers to quit living in part of His grace and start living in the fullness of His grace.

The Greek word for *saved* here is *sozo*. It means "to make safe, deliver, protect, heal, preserve, save, do well, and be (make) whole."[66] Salvation includes much more than a future destination called heaven, it also includes everything that we need during this life to overcome the curse of sin – setting us free to live the abundant life!

Salvation includes our eternal life as well as our healing and success. It includes our preservation as well as our deliverance and protection. We receive all the attributes of salvation at one time. We receive healing and favor at the same time that we receive eternal life. Our deliverance and prosperity are all received the same way we receive eternal life. Salvation is received through faith, not as a result of a person's striving, works, or ability. It is a relationship with the Holy Spirit that results in the revelation of our salvation in Christ. All the accomplishments of Christ are included in our salvation!

YOUR MEALS ARE PAID FOR

An illustration from the book *Your Best Life Now* by Joel Osteen is the best story that I can think of to capture this important principle of God's full plan of salvation for us. The story goes as follows:

---

[66] Strong's Exhaustive Concordance, Reference 4982

"Years ago, before transatlantic flights became common, a man wanted to travel to the United States from Europe. The man worked hard, saved every extra penny he could, and finally had just enough money to purchase a ticket aboard a cruise ship. The trip at that time required about two or three weeks to cross the ocean. He went out and bought a suitcase and filled it full of cheese and crackers. That's all he could afford.

"Once on board, all the other passengers went to the large, ornate dining room to eat their gourmet meals. Meanwhile, the poor man would go over in the corner and eat his cheese and crackers. This went on day after day. He could smell the delicious food being served in the dining room. He heard the other passengers speak of it in glowing terms as they rubbed their bellies and complained about how full they were and how they would have to go on a diet after this trip.

"The poor traveler wanted to join the other guests in the dining room, but he had no extra money. Sometimes he'd lie awake at night, dreaming of the sumptuous meals the other guests described. Toward the end of the trip, another man came up to him and said, 'Sir, I cannot help but notice that you are always over there eating those cheese and crackers at mealtimes. Why do you not come into the banquet hall and eat with us?'

"The traveler's face flushed with embarrassment. 'Well, to tell you the truth, I had only enough money to buy the ticket. I do not have any extra money to purchase fancy meals.' The other passenger raised his eyebrows in surprise. He shook his head and said, 'Sir, do you not realize the meals are included in the price of the ticket? Your meals have already been paid for.'"[67]

---

[67] Joel Osteen, Your Best Life Now (New York, NY: Warner Faith, Time Warner Book Group, 2004), 83-84

Many of us are just like the traveling man in this story. We do not realize that Christ has already paid for everything we will ever need to be successful in God and this life. We have given our lives to Christ, receiving eternal life, but we do not understand all the benefits of Christ's accomplishments on the cross to live the abundant life this side of heaven. Ephesians 1:3 AMP says:

> May blessing (*praise, laudation, and eulogy*) be to the God and Father of our Lord Jesus Christ (*the Messiah*) who has blessed us with every spiritual (*given by the Holy Spirit*) blessing in the heavenly realm!

The word *blessed* in this passage is the Greek word *eulogeo*.[68] It refers to "the act of blessing, to act on one's life in their behalf, to do good for them." Here the word *eulogeo* is an aorist active participle. Now this is what is important. He has blessed us. What does that phrase mean?

> First of all, it is in the aorist tense which means it is already done. Aorist tense is a completed action...The active voice means that Father is the one who has done the blessing...He blessed us in Christ. If it were not for Christ, none of the blessings would be there. ... Thirdly, it is a participle. A participle is a verbal adjective. In other words, it simply describes what the subject has done... He is the Father of our Lord Jesus, and He has blessed us. He has already blessed us.[69]

As sons and daughters of the living God, Christ has already blessed us at a time in the past with every spiritual blessing

---

[68] Strong's Exhaustive Concordance, Reference 2127
[69] Dr. Wayne Barber, Ephesians 1:3 A Call to Praise, Sermon, http://preceptaustin.org/new_page_4.htm, Friday October 19, 2007 9:23 GMT 195K.

> WE DO NOT HAVE TO WAIT UNTIL A TIME IN THE FUTURE FOR EVERYTHING TO BE JUST RIGHT IN ORDER TO RECEIVE OUR SPIRITUAL BLESSINGS.

in the heavenly realms! We do not have to wait until a time in the future for everything to be just right in order to receive our spiritual blessings. We do not have to beg in order to receive our spiritual blessings in the midst of our present state of affairs. We cannot add anything to what Christ has already accomplished by striving to work harder in our own strength. Everything we need to live the abundant life has already been accomplished by Christ on our behalf at a time in the past.

Notice that our spiritual blessings are in the heavenly realms; they cannot be found in the natural realm. Imagine the heavenly realm as a room in our house. We are in the family room in our basement. The heavenly realms containing our spiritual blessings are upstairs in the living room.

Everything that Christ accomplished on our behalf is upstairs in the living room. To receive our spiritual blessings, we will have to get up and leave the family room in the basement, then go upstairs into the living room so we can see, gain access and receive our spiritual blessings.

OPENING THE EYES

Since there is no way for us to receive our spiritual blessings in the natural realm, we must have a way to gain access to the spiritual realm to appropriate the promises of God for ourselves. The problem is that we do not have a natural vehicle with the capacity to take us to a destination called heavenly places. Even if we did have a vehicle with the capacity to transfer us from the natural realm to the spiritual realm, we still do not have a GPS navigation system within our vehicle to help us get to our destination. How do we get to this place called heavenly places?

In Ephesians 1:17 NKJV, the apostle Paul tells us the way to heavenly places in his prayer, "that the God of our Lord Jesus Christ, the Father of glory, may give you the spirit of wisdom and revelation in the knowledge of Him." In our relationship with Jesus Christ, the Spirit of wisdom is able to navigate us in the vehicle of revelation to a destination called heavenly places. The word *knowledge* here is not a reference to information about Jesus Christ. It is referring to the intimate knowledge of a person that comes as a result of experience through relationship with Jesus Christ.

In this kind of relationship we are able to receive the kind of revelation that will allow us to rest in the accomplishments of Christ:

> Having the eyes of your heart flooded with light, so that you can know and understand the hope to which He has called you, and how rich is His glorious inheritance in the saints (*His set-apart ones*).[70]

The veil that has blinded our eyes concerning our own identity in Him is removed, "(*so that you can know and understand*) what is the immeasurable and unlimited and surpassing greatness of His power in and for us who believe."[71] The light of His understanding begins to illuminate His glorious inheritance already in

---

[70] Ephesians 1:18 AMP
[71] Ephesians 1:19 AMP

us through the many accomplishments of Christ, as we begin to get a revelation that our old self image has already been replaced with our new identity in Christ!

The exact, same immeasurable, unlimited and surpassing greatness of power that the Father put in Christ now exists in and for us. "Which He exerted in Christ when He raised Him from the dead and seated Him at His (*own*) right hand in the heavenly (*places*)."[72] The power of Christ in us reigns:

> Far above all rule and authority and power and dominion and every name that is named (*above every title that can be conferred*), not only in this age and in this world, but also in the age and the world which are to come.[73]

It is a power that exceeds the power of every rule, authority, power, dominion, and title that exists!

> He has put all things under His feet and has appointed Him the universal and supreme Head of the church (*a headship exercised throughout the church*).[74]

The Father put every authority and power under the feet of His Son. Then He appointed Jesus to be the authority of the church. The authority given to Him would be exercised through the church. The word *church* here in the Greek is *ekklesia*. It means "the called-out ones."[75] The church is not a building in which people meet! The church is "His body, the fullness of Him who fills all in all (*for in that body lives the full measure of Him who*

---

[72] Ephesians 1:20 AMP
[73] Ephesians 1:21 AMP
[74] Ephesians 1:22 AMP
[75] Strong's Exhaustive Concordance, Reference 1577

makes everything complete, and who fills everything everywhere with Himself)."[76]

FAITH IN HIS WORD

Recently a young couple named Jimmy and Melinda and their new baby boy, Braden, started attending our church. They introduced themselves and wanted to tell me the story of how they had come to our church. They had become familiar with our church as a result of some individuals in the church going door-to-door in the neighborhood sharing the gospel, praying, and inviting people to attend our Sunday morning services. Jimmy and Melinda explained that they already had a church home, but the people from our church still asked if they could pray for them before they left.

Jimmy began to explain how Melinda had been healed by God, allowing them to start a family. Soon Melinda found out that she was pregnant, but one week later she miscarried. The couple was devastated by the bad news, saying, "This tested our faith." A friend suggested that Melinda read the book *Supernatural Childbirth*. God used the book to teach her how to pray and have faith in His Word.

After sharing about their loss, the group prayed with them. As they were praying, one of the women in the group began to prophecy that they would have a baby boy within nine to ten months. They were able to experience the manifestation of that word of revelation ten months later when Melinda gave birth to a baby boy named Braden Nehemiah. Jimmy and Melinda experienced a miracle that day, one that they were unable to accomplish in their own strength and abilities, by agreeing

[76] Ephesians 1:23 AMP

with a word of revelation from God that allowed them to rest in Christ's accomplishments.

PERFECT PEACE

JESUS SAID,

> I have told you these things, so that in Me you may have (*perfect*) peace and confidence. In the world you have tribulation and trials and distress and frustration; but be of good cheer (*take courage; be confident, certain, undaunted*)! For I have overcome the world. (*I have deprived it of power to harm you and have conquered it for you.*)[77]

Jesus speaks revelation to His disciples resulting in perfect peace and confidence in Him. In other words, Jesus is peace! He did not tell His disciples that they would have peace and confidence because their circumstances appeared to be better. He told them they would have peace and confidence in the midst of stressful times because of the revelation that they had received in regards to resting in Him and His accomplishments.

Jesus was not trying to say that we should be happy because our circumstances look negative! He said that we should have a positive outlook because He had already disarmed every power from its ability to harm us. We have to remember that if our circumstances appear to contradict God's Word, we have already overcome them by Christ's work on the cross. The appearance of our circumstances will be changing for our good as we begin to

---

[77] John 16:33 AMP

get a revelation of God's Word. He already conquered the very source of the distress, trials, and frustration on our behalf!

SPIRIT OF TRUTH AND REVELATION

The abundant life is experienced through revelation that comes as a result of being in a relationship with Holy Spirit. The natural result of any relationship is that those in the relationship begin to reveal themselves more and more to one another.

JESUS SAYS,

> I have still many things to say to you, but you are not able to bear them or to take them upon you or to grasp them now. But when He, the Spirit of Truth (*the Truth-giving Spirit*) comes, He will guide you into all the Truth (*the whole, full Truth*). For He will not speak His own message (*on His own authority*); but He will tell whatever He hears (*from the Father; He will give the message that has been given to Him*), and He will announce and declare to you the things that are to come (*that will happen in the future*). He will honor and glorify Me, because He will take of (*receive, draw upon*) what is Mine and will reveal (*declare, disclose, transmit*) it to you.[78]

The disciples had just learned that Jesus was going away and that He would be sending them Holy Spirit. He essentially tells them that "I have much more to say to you, but you cannot handle hearing it all right now. So your relationship with Me is going to have to continue with Holy Spirit." It is the communication that we receive by Holy Spirit that is known as revelation. His

---

[78] John 16:12-14 AMP

job is to receive and draw upon the things that Jesus wants to communicate by declaring, disclosing, and transmitting them to His people.

As God's people, we are called to live by the revelation of the Spirit rather than the information that we get with our natural senses, allowing us to trust God at His Word over our feelings and circumstances. If we are going to trust God as provider, then we must have a revelation of Him as our provider. Often God speaks a word to us and in our uncertainty we change His Word in our minds according to how we feel at the moment. Holy Spirit says, "I want to heal you!" So we change it to say, "God wants to make me feel better."

God responds to us by saying, "If that's what you really want!" He will not force His will on you. He allows us to experience the consequences of the Word in which we choose to agree. If we agree with our circumstances, then we get to continue to live in those circumstances. If we agree with His Word then we get to move out of our circumstances and into the promises of God.

EXPERIENCE IT FOR YOURSELF

In Ephesians 3:19 AMP, the apostle Paul affirms this by saying,

> (*That you may really come*) to know (*practically, through experience for yourselves*) the love of Christ, which far surpasses mere knowledge (*without experience*); that you may be filled (*through all your being*) unto all the fullness of God (*may have the richest measure of divine Presence, and become a body wholly filled and flooded with God Himself*)!

The word *know* in this passage is the Greek word *ginosko*. It means "allow, be aware (of), feel, (have), perceive, be resolved, can speak, be sure, and understand."[79] Paul is making a huge distinction here between knowing Jesus and having knowledge about Him. Knowing someone is based on a personal relationship. Having knowledge about someone or something is based on secondhand information such as another person, book, or something that we may have heard on the radio or watched on TV.

Knowledge is a reference to the information we have in our head. If you want to live the abundant life, then it is not enough to have information about a relationship with Jesus Christ. Information gives us logic and the ability to have sense and reason. This way of thinking has its roots in Greek culture in which most of our society has been influenced. Information by itself is just religious rhetoric, unable to bear fruit-giving evidence of the life of God in you. The information may be good but it will not lead you to the promised land!

Paul is not speaking of working and striving to have a relationship with an external far-away God. He is praying that we would get a revelation diffused throughout our soul about the relationship that we already have with Holy Spirit, so that we would know for ourselves by experience with Holy Spirit the flooding of our mind, will, and emotions with the fullness of God. He is praying that we would receive revelation in our soul, that we are already filled and flooded with the fullness of the supernatural presence of God Himself.

In John 4, Jesus says the Kingdom of God is within us. He tells the Pharisees that we don't have to search here or there for

---

[79] Strong's Exhaustive Concordance, Reference 1097

the Kingdom of God. We don't have to work and strive harder to find revelation. If we would just learn to enjoy the union that we already have with Holy Spirit, revelation would begin to naturally flow supernaturally, as a result, without any effort.

Many Christians are disillusioned and believe that God has let them down. They do not understand the importance of cultivating sensitivity in their spirit to train their spiritual senses. They don't have continual interaction with Holy Spirit resulting in revelation. It is the essence of faith. Without revelation from Holy Spirit, we find ourselves struggling to overcome again and again.

We cannot live the abundant life by the information we receive through the physical senses of our flesh. In the Western world, many Christians fill their heads with information rather than revelation, leading to a life filled with results based on our own intelligence and abilities rather than on His mind and abilities. As a result, we keep finding ourselves unable to possess the promises of God. Eventually, we become discouraged with our constant failures. We grumble and complain that things have not worked out for us as we had believed, and finally it turns into unbelief.

On the other hand, Hebrew thought reflected a more practical, relational, and revelatory perspective of our relationship with our world and Jesus Christ. This can be seen clearly in the Hebrew term *towbunah*. It is translated *understanding*. It means "discretion, reason, skillfulness, and wisdom."[80] In other words, understanding means that you are experiencing a revelation of the information received so that you are actually putting it into

---

[80] Strong's Exhaustive Concordance, Reference 8394

practice in your daily life. It is this concept of understanding that the Bible refers to as real proof of a genuine relationship with God. It is the fruit in a believer's life!

IMPORTANCE OF REVELATION

In Proverbs 29:18 it says, "Where there is no vision...the people perish."[81] Another version says it more accurately, "Where there is no revelation, the people cast off restraint."[82] The Hebrew word for *vision* here is *chazowth*. It means "a sight mentally, dream, revelation, or oracle."[83] Revelation is the unveiling of something that is hidden so that we can see what we have not previously been able to see or understand in the past. God is all knowing and could give us revelation about any number of possible things, including the future, past, present, people, relationships, circumstances, events, direction, purpose, vision, His Word, Himself, our identity, and our inheritance. Revelation is God communicating directly with His people through Holy Spirit.

When we do not have a relationship with God resulting in revelatory understanding for our lives, we will not be able to restrain ourselves to make good choices allowing us to live in the fulfillment of the promises of God. It is like the Israelites when they were in the wilderness ... they kept trying to accomplish God's plan in their own strength and abilities based on their thoughts, not His thoughts. They were moving in the strength of the flesh based on their mind and not the mind of the Spirit. It was the way of the wilderness to strive and work hard in the flesh to fulfill God's promises.

---

[81] Proverbs 29:18 AMP
[82] Proverbs 29:18 NKJV
[83] Strong's Exhaustive Concordance, Reference 2377

Isaiah 55 says that His ways are higher than our ways, and His thoughts are higher than our thoughts.[84] But this is an old covenant Scripture often quoted out of context as a manifestation of the religious spirit. The new covenant says we have the mind of Christ. If we have the mind of Christ we can receive revelation to think His thoughts, and if we can think His thoughts then we can live in His ways.

The wilderness is a place where we come to recognize our weaknesses and failures so that we can learn to quit relying on our own mind and strength. It is the place where we can begin to rely on His mind and strength, trusting Him at His Word. The wilderness is a place where there are no distractions so we learn to develop intimacy with God by waiting on Him through fellowship. It is a place to receive revelation; we are not trying to reach a destination - Jesus is our destination!

We will never be able to believe God at His Word outside of an intimate relationship with Holy Spirit resulting in revelation. Eventually we are going to get tired of striving through hard work and trying to figure it out on our own. Soon we will begin to believe that the promises of God are not for us, realizing that we have accomplished nothing in our own strength. We will become disillusioned with our belief in God, resulting in negativity, complaining, and finally unbelief! We will live our lives, as God bypasses us and waits for a generation willing to rest in His accomplishments. This is what is at stake for the church and our personal lives when we live out of our own mind and strength rather than His mind and strength.

Our victory is a result of revelation from God allowing us to live our lives with meaning, purpose and fulfillment. It gives us

[84] Isaiah 55:9 AMP

a hope for a future that is greater than our present circumstances, allowing us to make good decisions based on His abilities to live the abundant life. As we build a relationship with the Holy Spirit, the result is revelation that encourages and empowers us to become a part of what He is doing in order to walk in faith and put into practice those things God has revealed by His mind. It cannot be realized through the natural realm, but can only be discerned through spiritual eyes that enable us to see in the spiritual realm!

RESTING IN HIS ACCOMPLISHMENTS

East of the Jordan River we are always striving to work hard in our own mind, strength and abilities to earn the promises of God. It is a place where we do not understand that we have already been given everything we need in salvation. We are always waiting for God to do something for us because we do not have any revelation of the things that He has already accomplished on our behalf. We strive and work hard, trying to make something happen for ourselves. It is the way of the flesh. It is living on the wrong side of the cross!

The promised land is a place where we can look back across the Jordan with eyes of revelation and understanding, seeing that everything we have ever needed has already been given to us in Christ!

For we who have believed (*adhered to and trusted in and relied on God*) do enter that rest, in accordance with His declaration that those (*who did not believe*) should not enter when He said, As I swore in My wrath, They shall not enter my rest; and this He said although (*His*) works

83

had been completed and prepared (*and waiting for all who would believe*) from the foundation of the world.[85]

Those who develop a genuine relationship with Christ can obtain the promise of God's rest. It is a relationship that extends beyond a prayer of salvation to receive eternal life. We do not make a commitment to Christ and sit back and wait until we get to a destination called heaven. It is a continual relationship with the person of Christ Himself. He alone is the fullness of our salvation. We are not still waiting for Him to accomplish something on our behalf. His works have already been accomplished and prepared for us since the foundation of the world. They are waiting for everyone and anyone who would adhere, trust, and rely on Him and His accomplishments over their abilities and natural circumstances.

Those without a genuine relationship with Christ are incapable of believing His Word. They will choose to believe in their circumstances over believing in Him. As an example, of those who did not believe to enter His rest, this passage refers again to the Israelite generation that never made it to the promised land. Moses had sent out the twelve spies to scout out the land of Canaan. Ten of the spies:

> brought the Israelites an evil report of the land which they had scouted out, saying, The land through which we went to spy it out is a land that devours its inhabitants. And all the people that we saw in it are men of great stature."[86]

The people of Israel began to believe the evil report of the ten spies over the Word of the Lord, saying:

[85] Hebrews 4:3 AMP
[86] Numbers 13:32 AMP

Why does the Lord bring us to this land to fall by the sword? Our wives and little ones will be a prey. Is it not better for us to return to Egypt?[87]

The Israelites begin to blame God for their circumstances, grumbling and complaining that they would rather go back and live in the bondage of Egypt over the promises of God.

Look at the Lord's response to Moses:

How long will this people provoke (*spurn, despise*) Me? And how long will it be before they believe Me (*trusting in, relying on, clinging to Me*), for all the signs which I have performed among them?[88]

God was upset that these people never learned to trust and rely on Him over their circumstances. They had seen God part the Red Sea and defeat the Egyptian army, but they still could not trust the Word of the Lord over the evil report of ten men concerning their circumstances.

Then, after a long argument with Moses concerning the future of Israel, God said,

Because all those men who have seen My glory and My (*miraculous*) signs which I performed in Egypt and in the wilderness, yet have tested and proved Me these ten times and have not heeded My voice, Surely they shall not see the land I swore to give to their fathers; nor shall any who provoked (*spurned, despised*) Me see it.[89]

---

[87] Numbers 14:3 AMP
[88] Numbers 14:11 AMP
[89] Numbers 14:22-23 AMP

As a result, they never entered the rest of God. "And (*they forfeited their part in it, for*) in this (*passage*) He said, They shall not enter My rest."[90] A whole generation of Israelites never learned to depend on His mind and works over their own mind and works. They never learned to rest in His accomplishments.

The Bible exhorts us to rest in Christ's accomplishments, rather than trying to live by our own mind, strength and abilities.

> The promise remains over (*from past times*) for some to enter that rest, and that those who formerly were given the good news about it and the opportunity, failed to appropriate it and did not enter because of disobedience.[91]

The Israelites had failed to appropriate the promises of God for their lives because of their failure to rest in the revelation of God's Word to them in regards to the promised land. As a result, Jesus has given us:

> (*A new*) Today, (*and gives another opportunity of securing that rest*)...if you would hear His voice and when you hear it, do not harden your hearts.[92]

Today we have been given the same opportunity to experience the abundant life that the Israelites had to possess the promised land – if we will receive the promise of God by resting in a trust relationship with Christ based on His accomplishments. It says here that the promise of a rest "remains over for some to enter that rest."[93] Who are the "some" in this passage of Scripture? They are those who will stop trusting in their own mind, strength and

---

[90] Hebrews 4:5 AMP
[91] Hebrews 4:6 AMP
[92] Hebrews 4:7 AMP
[93] Hebrews 4:6 AMP

abilities and rest in the revelation of His abilities over their own abilities!

All we have to do is keep our hearts soft through an intimate relationship with God so that we will trust His report before we will trust the report of our circumstances. Then we can stop working so hard in our own mind and strength and begin resting in His accomplishments.

> For if Joshua had given them rest, He (*God*) would not speak afterward about another day. So, then, there is still awaiting a full and complete Sabbath-rest reserved for the (*true*) people of God; For he who has once entered (*God's*) rest also has ceased from (*the weariness and pain*) of human labors, just as God rested from those labors peculiarly His own.[94]

This passage is prophetically referring to a day in which all of those who have a genuine relationship with Christ would be given the opportunity to enter God's rest through Christ's accomplishments on the cross.

We are currently living in that day!

We have been given the opportunity to experience the complete fullness of the abundant life. God is eagerly waiting for us to receive that which He has already given to us through building a relationship with Him resulting in a revelation to rest in His accomplishments. We have been set free from the weariness and pain of human labor. We can rest in Christ's accomplishments, receiving all the promises of God. All we have to do is choose to cease from laboring in our own mind, strength and abilities!

---

[94] Hebrews 4:8-10 AMP

CHAPTER 4

RELATIONSHIP, NOT RELIGION

DURING MY SOPHOMORE YEAR of high school, I was invited to attend a weeklong summer Bible camp. I had not grown up in a Christian home and I had never been to a Christian camp. I did not know the proper way to behave with Christian people. After all, I had made a mess of my life up to this point. I was consistently being kicked out of school for fighting with other students. I had been living a self-destructive lifestyle, abusing drugs and alcohol while living a life of promiscuity, since the beginning of junior high school.

I did not think that I belonged in a church environment. So I made every possible excuse I could to get out of going to Bible camp that summer. Every excuse that I could come up with was matched quickly with a solution. A church even offered to pay my way with a scholarship. Reluctantly, I agreed to go, convincing myself that I might meet some cute girls that week.

Monday, the first day of Bible camp, was a lot better than I had expected. We could go swimming, play basketball and volleyball, or just hang out with some of the other students. At night we went to chapel. Hundreds of students were singing songs to God and raising their hands in the air. I did not understand what was happening. I could feel a presence in the room that was foreign to me.

When we were done singing, a man got up in front of us and began talking about God and the Bible. At the end of his presentation he asked students to come to the front of the chapel if they wanted to repent of their sins and receive Jesus Christ as their Lord and Savior. I was amazed to see students swarm to fill the front altar of the chapel, sobbing and crying out to Jesus for forgiveness and help in living for Him.

After chapel that first night I was freaked out and asked to have someone take me home! I did not understand the things I had seen and felt at chapel, things that had filled me with fear and anxiety. I told some of the leaders I wanted to go home, never intending to set foot in the chapel again. As it turned out, nobody was able to come and pick me up so I had no choice but to stay at the camp for at least another night.

The next morning I felt better after having a good night's sleep. I did not feel any urgency to leave the camp as I began to interact with the other students and participate in the activities of the day. I tried to forget about chapel, knowing I would soon have to face it again with night rapidly approaching. I reluctantly survived one more chapel that evening!

Wednesday night I went back to the chapel for the third time. As we started to sing, I could sense a presence in the room that seemed to be stronger than the two previous evenings. In the midst of worship, students began to spontaneously approach the altar to kneel and pray before God. Some students even brought items that they believed to be hindering their relationship with God and laid them on the altar as a sacrifice. The guy who slept in the bunk below me left the service, sprinted back to our cabin as fast as he could to collect all his rock music cassette tapes, returned and then threw them on the altar before falling on his knees, sobbing and asking God for forgiveness.

I could sense the Spirit of God all around me! I determined not to surrender my life to Jesus unless He proved Himself to be real to me personally! At that moment I looked up and saw the camp speaker, Ray Larson, standing in front of me. He began to talk with me about events that had occurred earlier in my life; through a word of knowledge he spoke of things I had never shared with anyone. I knew that Jesus was revealing Himself to me through this man!

Soon I found myself standing at the altar of the chapel, crying for the first time since I was a little boy. I did not want to make a commitment to Jesus unless it was completely genuine. I began to ask God, "Why would You want to have a relationship with me?" I had messed my life up completely, living it my way. I asked God, "How could You love me?" I then began to reason with God, saying, "You must be able to do something better with my life than what I have done with it."

CRUCIFIED WITH HIM

I was given a new heart that night as I prayed, "Jesus, I give You my life to do with whatever You want! Forgive me of my sins! Help me to live for You! I surrender everything in my life to You!" Hours seemed like minutes as I poured out my heart to God. I found myself kneeling at the altar of the chapel with my face buried in the floor, allowing God to exchange the agendas and priorities of my life for His agendas and priorities. I will be forever thankful for that night of August 28, 1985, when Jesus changed my heart from the inside out at Cedar Springs Bible Camp.

JESUS SAID,

> If any person wills to come after Me, let him deny himself (*disown himself, forget, lose sight of himself and his own interests, refuse and give up himself*) and take up his cross daily and follow Me (*cleave steadfastly to Me, conform wholly to My example in living and, if need be, in dying also.*)[95]

This verse exhorts us from a pre-Christian context to look to Jesus rather than ourselves. In the same way, after our salvation experience we are to continue to allow Holy Spirit to daily keep our attention on Jesus rather than on ourselves in order for us to experience all the benefits of resting in His accomplishments. By continually keeping our eyes focused on the author and finisher of our faith, Holy Spirit now gives us fresh revelation of heaven's agendas and priorities with His laws no longer controlling us externally but written internally on our heart.

In his book, *Mystical Union,* John Crowder says, "When Jesus talks about denying yourself and taking up your cross, this is really a passage about ceasing from your own self efforts and self-driven attempts at spiritual advancement."[96] Ben Dunn writes in *The Happy Gospel,* "In the eternal sense, this verse means that we are to follow after Christ's sacrifice, not mimic it,

---

[95] Luke 9:23 AMP
[96] John Crowder, *Mystical Union* (Santa Cruz, CA: Sons of Thunder Ministries & Publications, 2010), 71

but trust in it alone for our salvation and sustainment. The sense here in this Scripture is not self-sacrifice in the way most would see it. It actually is a call to deny any heavenly advancement through self achievement."[97]

When we give our lives to Jesus we are no longer our own. We have given our lives completely to Him to do and to will according to God's purposes. Following Him means that we have already exchanged our life for His life. "I have been crucified with Christ (*in Him I have shared His crucifixion*); it is no longer I who live, but Christ (*the Messiah*) lives in me; and the life I now live in the body I live by faith in (*by adherence to and reliance on and complete trust in*) the Son of God, who loved me and gave Himself up for me."[98]

At the cross, "We know that our old (*unrenewed*) self was nailed to the cross with Him in order that (*our*) body (*which is the instrument*) of sin might be made ineffective and inactive for evil, that we might no longer be the slaves of sin. For when a man dies, he is freed (*loosed, delivered*) from (*the power of*) sin (*among men*)."[99]

Our old nature was put to death with Christ on the cross. Now it is no longer our old self that lives on the resurrection side of the cross, but Christ who lives in us. We were resurrected to a new life in order that we might receive revelation to rest in Him. So the agendas and priorities of our heart have become the agendas and priorities of His heart, not by our own efforts but by daily cleaving to the enjoyment of our relationship with Him.

---

[97] Benjamin Dunn, The Happy Gospel (Santa Cruz, CA: Joy Revolution, 2010), 102-103
[98] Galatians 2:20 AMP
[99] Romans 6:6-7 AMP

In the same way, Joshua and the children of Israel had to put to death their agendas and priorities through the outward work of circumcision in exchange for God's agendas and priorities, in order to experience the fullness of His promises while living in the promised land. Now they had just overcome the impossible obstacle of crossing the Jordan River, while...

> The kings of the Amorites who were beyond the Jordan to the west and all the kings of the Canaanites who were by the sea heard that the Lord had dried up the waters of the Jordan before the Israelites until they had crossed over, their hearts melted and there was no spirit in them any more because of the Israelites.[100]

The entire nation of Israel had just finished walking across the Jordan River on dry land. They witnessed the parting of the Jordan River in the same way that their parents had witnessed the parting of the Red Sea. Now the Israelites are actually experiencing the promises of God for themselves. They are living in the promised land!

The Israelites had just received a new understanding about the power of their God! They had witnessed the miraculous. They had experienced a new revelation about their inheritance in God. Life was good for Joshua and the Israelites. They were living in the promises of God, ready to move forward, to conquer and possess the city of Jericho. The enemies that they were expecting to fight in front of them were now melting in fear, waiting to be defeated by the Israelites!

---

[100] Joshua 5:1 AMP

CIRCUMCISION OF THE HEART

When out of nowhere the Lord said to Joshua, "Make knives of flint and circumcise the (new generation of) Israelites as before."[101] The generation of Israelites before that were circumcised with Moses had already died in the wilderness. Now this new generation of Israelites had never been circumcised according to God's covenant. "So Joshua made knives of flint and circumcised the sons of Israel at Gibeath-haaraloth."[102]

The last thing Joshua was probably expecting to hear from the Lord at this time was instruction on how to circumcise the Israelites. Most likely he was expecting to receive battle strategies to conquer and possess the already promised city of Jericho. Circumcising the men of Israel seemed like bad timing, considering the momentum and confidence of the Israelites and the vulnerability of their enemy. It would not be an easy task to circumcise a nation. It would take time, effort, and organization to make the flint knives. Every male Israelite over eight years of age would need to be circumcised. The men would then need to take time to heal, leaving the entire nation of Israel vulnerable if their enemies were to attack. Why was circumcising the nation of Israel a priority now?

Circumcision was important because it represented a type of purity in the Israelites' lives. God wanted to circumcise the nation of Israel at this point to keep the agendas and priorities of their hearts pure so they would not start relying on their own efforts but would continue to rest in His accomplishments. The Israelites had actually experienced the revelation of the power of God personally working on their behalf. Their enemies had

---

[101] Joshua 5:2 AMP
[102] Joshua 5:3 AMP

become fearful when they heard about God's power display when Israel crossed the Jordan River.

If God had waited to circumcise the nation of Israel, the agendas and priorities of their hearts could have become perverted, betraying themselves by taking credit for their own success. It could have caused them to begin striving again through their own mind, strength and abilities, robbing them of the opportunity to live in the fullness of His promises. As a result, God wanted to circumcise His people in order to keep them devoted to His efforts rather than seeing them return to their own efforts.

What does circumcision have to do with my life as a New Testament believer in Christ? The apostle Paul said, "(*True*) circumcision is of the heart, a spiritual and not a literal (*matter*)."[103] The word *circumcision* here means "something is cut off."[104]

"The gospel cuts away the sinful nature from the believer."[105] "Joshua (*lit. Yeshua, a type of Christ*) circumcised the entire army of Israel by his own hand when they first entered the promised land. In the same way, Christ circumcised the entire corporate entity of sinfulness, bringing us into a land of new existence."[106]

Philippians 3:3 AMP says,

We (*Christians*) are the true circumcision, who worship God in spirit and by the Spirit of God and exult and glory and pride ourselves in Jesus Christ, and put no confidence or dependence (*on what we are*) in the flesh

---

[103] Romans 2:29 AMP
[104] John Crowder, Mystical Union (Santa Cruz, CA: Sons of Thunder Ministries & Publications, 2010), 63
[105] Ibid, 64
[106] Ibid

and on outward privileges and physical advantages and external appearances.

In other words, the above passages of Scripture are saying that our new heart and identity found in Christ did not come as a result of our ability to perform based on our natural efforts. The purity we received with our new heart and identity was based solely on resting in the accomplishments of Jesus Christ through revelation as given by the Spirit. It's a whole new way of living!

DADDY HAS ALL OF ME

There is a story about a father and his little girls that helps to illustrate the kind of purity God is looking to find in the hearts of His sons and daughters. The father tells the story, saying:

In returning from Bible conferences, I usually bring little gifts to my girls. One night I came home after they were asleep. The next morning as I sat in my study, I could hear overhead the patter of little feet. In a moment the oldest girl bounced into the study and entwined her little arms around my legs. Just then I heard the pitter-patter of little feet on the stairs. In a moment the youngest little girl came and stood in the doorway. Tears pearled in her eyes and trickled down her face. She was sad because she had failed to greet me first. The older sister said to her, "See, I have all there is of Daddy!" I reached down, took the tearful one in my arms, and folded her to my heart. Looking down at her sister, she said, "You have all there is of Daddy, but Daddy has all there is of me!"[107]

---

[107] Walter B Knight, Knights Treasury Of 2000 Illustrations: Daddy Has All There Is of Me (Grand Rapids, MI: William B. Eerdmans Publishing Company, 1963), 76

Just like the youngest little girl in this story, circumcision of the heart is about resting in the revelation that the Father has all of us, knowing that there is nothing that we can do in our own efforts to have more of Him. It is about loving and enjoying "God with all your heart and with all your soul and with all your mind (*intellect*)."[108]

He has already consecrated us in His presence, the agendas and priorities of our hearts have already been made pure through relationship resulting in revelation to trust in His agendas and priorities, as we securely rest in His accomplishments to experience the abundant life.

REMEMBERING GILGAL

As we get a revelation about our new identity in Jesus Christ, we can see that we have already been given a new heart downloaded with His agendas and priorities. Ezekiel prophesied about this thousands of years ago: "And I will give them one heart (*a new heart*) and I will put a new spirit within them; and I will take the stony (*unnaturally hardened*) heart out of their flesh, and will give them a heart of flesh (*sensitive and responsive to the touch of their God*)."[109]

Paul testifies to this new covenant reality, saying, "You show and make obvious that you are a letter from Christ delivered by us, not written with ink but with (*the*) Spirit of (*the*) living God, not on tablets of stone but on tablets of human hearts. Such is the reliance and confidence that we have through Christ toward and with reference to God."[110]

---

[108] Matthew 22:37 AMP
[109] Ezekiel 11:19 AMP
[110] 2 Corinthians 3:3-4 AMP

As a believer it's important to understand that the resurrection power of the cross already resides in us. Every force that would oppose us has already been defeated at a time in the past. All authority and power has already been given to us as believers, and His heart was already given to us when we were born again!

> Martin Luther once said that the gospel is nothing less than laughter and joy. You are not the slavish people of Ishmael. Ishmael was fully grown when he was circumcised. He had to feel the pain, because he represented the old, do-it-yourself covenant on Sinai. But the little baby Isaac was different! He was only eight days old when he was circumcised. Isaac doesn't remember what happened to him. He has no memory of the pain. Your death found its substitution in Christ.[111]

> In Him also you were circumcised with a circumcision not made with hands, but in a (*spiritual*) circumcision (*performed by*) Christ by stripping off the body of the flesh (*the whole corrupt, carnal nature with its passion and lusts*).[112]

The spirit of religion wants to try and convince us that we must work and perform for what we have already been given in Christ. He wants to us to believe that we still need to try and accomplish His works, which have already been completed. He wants to blind us through a veil of legalism based on our own efforts so that we will unconsciously reject grace based on the efforts of His finished work.

---

[111] John Crowder, Mystical Union (Santa Cruz, CA: Sons of Thunder Ministries & Publications, 2010), 65
[112] Colossians 2:11 AMP

Many of us have received wrong instruction about our identity in Christ. We have been told that we need to strive and work harder to get everything in order on our own. But the more we strive and work harder, the more things fall apart and go wrong. We have been deceived into trying to perform for an inheritance that we have already been given.

We only betray ourselves when we forget who we are in Christ and try to take back the control that we have already given to Him, making excuses for all the reasons that we are not living the abundant life. Unmet expectations turn to frustration as we begin to tell God that we're not going to do things His way anymore, but we are going to start doing things our way again. Frustration turns to anger as we try to manipulate people and circumstances externally in order to try to re-establish more control in our lives.

The angrier we become, the more we seem to lose control. The inability to change our circumstances causes feelings of helplessness leading to resentment and bitterness internally. Finally, resentment and bitterness begin to manifest outwardly through our negativity and complaining, keeping us from ever experiencing the promises of God. This isn't who we are in Christ!

We were buried therefore with Him by the baptism into death, so that just as Christ was raised from the dead by the glorious (*power*) of the Father, so we too might (*habitually*) live and behave in newness of life. For if we have become one with Him by sharing a death like His, we shall also be (*one with Him in sharing*) His resurrection (*by a new life lived for God*).[113]

---

[113] Romans 6:4-5 AMP

This passage says we were buried at a time in the past with Him! How many times do we have to die before we are considered dead? How dead is considered dead enough? When will we quit preaching the wrong message to the wrong audience?

We often hear messages taught to those in the church who have already been buried with Him, that "whoever would preserve his life and save it will lose and destroy it, but whoever loses his life for My sake, he will preserve and save it."[114] This verse was never meant to be taught as a way of life for those who are already in Christ. How can I preserve my life if I am already dead? It's no longer I that live, but Christ that lives in me. Jesus was speaking to a pre-Christian audience!

Jeremiah says our "heart is deceitful above all things, and it is exceedingly perverse and corrupt and severely, mortally sick! Who can know it (*perceive, understand, be acquainted with his own heart and mind*)?"[115] But this is an old covenant Scripture! The new covenant says we have already been given a new heart and a new spirit. It is His heart and His Spirit!

It's time for the church to get a revelation of the time and season in which we are currently living, instead of sometimes living out of the old covenant and other times living out of the new covenant. The veil has already been torn! This allows us to live and behave in newness of life. We don't have to live in deception on the wrong side of the cross, striving and working hard in our own strength.

In remembering Gilgal, we receive revelation of our new heart and all that has already been given to us in Christ! This is the place where the Lord your God circumcised "your hearts

---

[114] Luke 9:24 AMP
[115] Jeremiah 17:9 AMP

and the hearts of your descendants, to love the Lord your God with all your (*mind and*) heart and with all your being, that you may live.[116]

Then, with a revelation of pure heart we can experience the true power of God by resting solely in His accomplishments as He puts "curses upon your enemies and on those who hate you, who persecute you."[117] We can begin to experience the abundant life as "the Lord your God will make you abundantly prosperous."[118]

PURITY IS POWER

Many Christians have been traditionally taught that purity is about trying to live a holy and righteous life. What that means is that if they try hard in their own strength and abilities to behave holy and righteous, they will eventually obtain a heart of purity in order to become holy and righteous. Nothing could be further from the truth!

Our behaviors don't determine who we are. Who we are determines our behaviors! Holiness and righteousness are not just behaviors to be manifested, they are promises already fulfilled in the finished work of Jesus Christ. The truth is that we have already been made holy and righteous!

Many times 1 Peter 1:16 is quoted legalistically, saying, "You shall be holy, for I am holy."[119] This is often done with the best of intentions in order to put pressure on believers to work in their own strength and abilities to behave holy. The problem is that it

---

[116] Deuteronomy 30:6 AMP
[117] Deuteronomy 30:7 AMP
[118] Deuteronomy 30:9 AMP
[119] 1 Peter 1:16 AMP

causes us to walk in the deception of trying to work and perform for what we have already been given.

The above verse is actually best translated, "you be holy because I am holy." In other words, this Scripture is a prophetic proclamation about your being, rather than a command about your doing. And your doing should always be a result of your being. It's His decree about who you are!

In the same way, our behavior doesn't determine our righteousness. The finished work of Christ already made us righteous. We don't have to work to become righteous! The Bible says that we are the righteousness of God in Christ Jesus! The amplified translation says it this way, "For our sake He made Christ (*virtually*) to be sin who knew no sin, so that in and through Him we might become (*endued with, viewed as being in, and examples of*) the righteousness of God (*what we ought to be, approved and acceptable and in right relationship with Him, by His goodness*)."[120]

The true power of God only flows through the purity of a heart that has been birthed in relationship resulting in revelation to rest in the finished work of Jesus Christ.

> For the eyes of the Lord run to and fro throughout the whole earth, to show Himself strong on behalf of those whose heart is loyal to Him.[121]

The word *perfect* here is the Greek word *shalem*. It means "complete, friendly, full, just, made ready, peaceable, quiet, or whole."[122]

---

[120] 2 Corinthians 5:21 AMP
[121] 2 Chronicles 16:9 NKJV
[122] Strong's Exhaustive Concordance, Reference 8003

It is not referring to the actions of someone who is perfect outwardly by their own efforts. It is referring to a heart that is perfect in devotion, faithfulness, dedication, consecration in thought, affection toward His strength and ability to be strong on our behalf. It is the purity of our faith in His efforts that creates a perfect heart. This verse says that God is looking for those with a perfect heart in order to display His power to be strong on behalf of them. It is the purity of a perfect heart that manifests His power!

> The Bible speaks of man's perfection in covenant with God. This is the perfection which the Old Testament demands of God's people ... and ascribes to individual saints ... loyal, sincere, wholehearted obedience to the known will of their gracious God. It is faith at work, maintaining a right relationship with God by reverent worship and service. This perfection is essentially a matter of the heart ... outward conformity to God's command is not enough if the heart is not perfect.[123]

For example, this can be seen in the reign of Amaziah where he "did right in the Lord's sight, but not with a perfect or blameless heart."[124]

If we are going to experience the abundant life, then we will have to have revelation that the agenda and priorities of His heart have already become the agenda and priorities of our heart. Genuinely crucified with Him on the cross, I have chosen to become a part of what He is doing. I did not simply choose to add Him to my life for my own success. As a result, I have been

---

[123] New Bible Dictionary (Wheaton, IL: Tyndale House Publishers, 1962), 911

[124] 2 Chronicles 25:2 AMP

given a brand new heart with His agendas and priorities written on it.

We must renew our minds with revelation of our new identity in Christ so we are no longer tossed to and fro, deceived by reminders of our old identity. We no longer have to perform for the character and nature that we have already received in Him. Making excuses is based on the lie that we cannot receive the promises of God as we continue to live on the wrong side of the cross. We know there is no power to overcome and possess the promises of God in our own strength and abilities.

The power of God to rest in the accomplishments of Christ only flows through the purity of trusting, "the Lord your God with all your (*mind and*) heart and with all your being."[125] Clinging in relationship with revelation of your new identity, "you shall live and multiply, and the Lord your God will bless you in the land into which you go to possess."[126] The Bible says that this type of relationship "is not too difficult for you, nor is it far off."[127] You do not have to be a spiritual giant in order to experience the promises of God. "It is not (*a secret laid up*) in heaven."[128] It's Christ in you, the hope of glory!

As believers we do not need someone else to go to God on our behalf to give us more information in order to receive the promises of God. We are able to go directly to Holy Spirit in relationship with Jesus Christ. He is not difficult to find. The power of the Word of God already lives in you. "The word is

---

[125] Deuteronomy 30:10 AMP
[126] Deuteronomy 30:16 AMP
[127] Deuteronomy 30:11 AMP
[128] Deuteronomy 30:12 AMP

very near you, in your mouth and in your mind and in your heart, so that you can do it."[129]

John 1:1 says, "In the beginning (*before all time*) was the Word (*Christ*), and the Word was with God, and the Word was God Himself."[130] Notice what the Bible says about itself. In the beginning before all time there were no Bibles. The written word known as the Bible is not the word of God. It's the testimony of the Word of God. Jesus Christ is the Word of God!

Often times I hear Christians say that we need to take God out of the box. What they mean is that we need to stop allowing our traditional view of church to limit the creativity of God. But the real problem isn't that we don't want to let Him out of the box! It's that we don't want to let Him out of the Bible!

As soon as we accept Jesus Christ as our Lord and Savior His Word comes to live in us. He comes to live in our minds and hearts so that we can experience revelation of the promises of God through relationship with Him. The agendas and priorities of our hearts have become the agendas and priorities of His heart. "But if your (*mind and*) heart turn away"[131] from living in a love relationship resulting in revelation of the finished work of Jesus Christ, then deceived we will return to our own efforts, striving and working hard in our own mind, strength, and abilities just like those east of the Jordan, unable to experience the promises of God for ourselves. Then the Lord says:

> That you shall surely perish, and you shall not live long in the land which you pass over the Jordan to enter and possess.[132]

[129] Deuteronomy 30:14 AMP
[130] John 1:1 AMP
[131] Deuteronomy 30:17 AMP
[132] Deuteronomy 30:18 AMP

CHOOSE LIFE!

The promises of God will begin to perish, manifesting death to all we strive to accomplish by our own efforts. "For He is your life and the length of your days, that you may dwell in the land."[133] In the old covenant the Lord gave Israel two choices, saying, "I have set before you life and death, the blessings and the curses; therefore choose life that you and your descendants may live."[134]

Choosing life meant that they would live in a relationship with God, trusting in His mind, strength and abilities. Choosing life would result in effortless blessings to experience the promises of God. They were gifts of God that could not be received by their own efforts. Choosing death meant that they would trust in their own mind, strength and abilities. Choosing death would result in living absent from the promises of God.

Absent from the promises of God, they would work hard in their own strength and abilities to live an unfulfilling life of mediocrity, just like those who decided to live on the east side of the Jordan instead of living in the promised land west of the Jordan. We can see God does not want to see His children settle for less than blessed, by instructing them to "choose life."[135]

A New Testament understanding of the preceding verse reveals Jesus through relationship with Holy Spirit as our life. This relationship results in revelation to live the abundant life based on the efforts of His finished work. It's in the absence of the revelation of His accomplishments that we begin to experience the restrictions of our flesh!

---

[133] Deuteronomy 30:20 AMP
[134] Deuteronomy 30:19 AMP
[135] Ibid

The promises of God cannot be received in the natural through our own physical efforts. They are spiritual blessings received by Holy Spirit through revelation in our spiritual senses, based on the unrestricted results of Christ's accomplishments. "He who sows to his own flesh (*lower nature, sensuality*) will from the flesh reap decay and ruin and destruction, but he who sows to the Spirit will from the Spirit reap eternal life."[136]

It's time to get a revelation of who you are. You already made a choice! You have already been born of the Spirit, receiving a new nature that is no longer limited to the natural realm. You are no longer limited to reaping what you have sown, but now you can reap by the Spirit what He has sown. It's time to manifest who you are!

HOLY SPIRIT EMPOWERED

Being filled with Holy Spirit is not only a scriptural truth but also an experiential reality. As seen in Scripture, you will know when you have been filled with the Spirit. You will see the effects of this river in your personal life and a new empowerment to...experience the abundant life![137]

When Jesus was with the disciples:

He commanded them not to leave Jerusalem but to wait for what the Father had promised, of which (*He said*) you have heard Me speak. For John baptized with water, but not many days from now you shall be baptized with (*placed in, introduced into*) the Holy Spirit.[138]

---

[136] Galatians 6:8 AMP
[137] Sean Smith, Prophetic Evangelism (Shippensburg, PA: Destiny Image Publishers Inc, 2004), 127
[138] Acts 1:4-5 AMP

In chapter one, I wrote about the word *wait* in this passage. It is the Greek word *perimeno*. It means "to stay around, to wait for, and to fellowship with."[139]

The baptism of the Holy Spirit was to be a direct result of relationship through fellowship with the Holy Spirit. Jesus said:

> If any man is thirsty, let him come to Me and drink! He who believes in Me (*who cleaves to and trusts in and relies on Me*) as the Scripture has said, from his innermost being shall flow (*continuously*) springs and rivers of living water.[140]

HE WAS:

> Speaking here of the Spirit, whom those who believed (*trusted, had faith*) in Him were afterward to receive. For the (*Holy*) Spirit had not yet been given, because Jesus was not yet glorified (*raised to honor*).[141]

Jesus knew that we would need both a special boldness and divine "overflow"[142] in order to walk in the manifestation of His promises. The Scriptures teach us that every believer born of the Word and the Spirit automatically has the Holy Spirit within. The Holy Spirit came and took up residence in you at the moment of your salvation. We also see in Scripture that the Holy Spirit's empowerment was, in many cases, a subsequent, deliberate and repeated experience for all believers.

---

[139] Strong's Exhaustive Concordance, Reference 4037
[140] John 7:37-38 AMP
[141] John 7:39 AMP
[142] Sean Smith, Prophetic Evangelism (Shippensburg, PA: Destiny Image Publishers Inc, 2004), 126

The indwelling ministry of the Holy Spirit is automatic; you did not have to seek His indwelling presence when you first got saved. He came and took up residence in your heart at the moment of your salvation. The empowering of the Spirit is not automatic. It usually comes in response to prayer.[143]

As we learned in chapter one, the Greek word for *baptism* here is *baptizo*. It means "to be overwhelmed."[144] The idea is to continue to repeat the same process until an object is fully saturated. It is often illustrated by the picture of a pickle being saturated in dill brine by dipping it over and over again. If an object is completely saturated, it means that it can no longer contain the substance in which it is saturated. It is overflowing out of the saturated object and getting all over everything that it comes in contact with.

In *Prophetic Evangelism*, Sean Smith writes, "When we are baptized by Christ in the Holy Spirit, we become 'partakers of the divine nature' at the optimal level."[145] He is not trying to say that we have to receive the baptism of the Holy Spirit in order to become partakers of the divine nature. He is emphasizing the point that the divine nature that is already in us is activated to operate at the optimal level in our soul through the baptism of the Holy Spirit.

In essence, the gifts of the Spirit are the manifestation of a believer being diffused throughout their soul with revelation. They are the "distributions of endowments (*gifts, extraordinary*

---

[143] Sean Smith, Prophetic Evangelism (Shippensburg, PA: Destiny Image Publishers Inc, 2004), 126

[144] Strong's Exhaustive Concordance, Reference 907

[145] Sean Smith, Prophetic Evangelism (Shippensburg, PA: Destiny Image Publishers Inc, 2004), 126

powers distinguishing certain Christians, due to the power of divine grace operating in their souls by the Holy Spirit)."[146]

> Each one is given the manifestation of the (*Holy*) Spirit (*the evidence, the spiritual illumination of the Spirit*) for good and profit. To one is given in and through the (*Holy*) Spirit (*the power to speak*) a message of wisdom, and to another (*the power to express*) a word of knowledge and understanding according to the same (*Holy*) Spirit; To another (*wonder-working*) faith by the same (*Holy*) Spirit, to another the extraordinary powers of healing by the one Spirit; To another the working of miracles, to another prophetic insight (*the gift of interpreting the divine will and purpose*); to another the ability to discern and distinguish between (*the utterances of true*) spirits (*and false ones*), to another various kinds of (*unknown*) tongues, to another the ability to interpret (*such*) tongues.[147]

"All these (*gifts, achievements, abilities*) are inspired and brought to pass by one and the same (*Holy*) Spirit."[148] "The Holy Spirit introduces a radically different dimension – a power plant that propels us into another realm of effectiveness."[149] Jesus told the disciples "you shall receive power (*ability, efficiency, and might*) when the Holy Spirit has come upon you"[150]

On the day of Pentecost:

> There came a sound from heaven, as of a rushing mighty wind, and it filled the whole house where they were

[146] 1 Corinthians 12:4 AMP
[147] 1 Corinthians 12:7-10 AMP
[148] 1 Corinthians 12:11 AMP
[149] Sean Smith, Prophetic Evangelism (Shippensburg, PA: Destiny Image Publishers Inc, 2004), 126
[150] Acts 1:8 AMP

sitting. Then there appeared to them divided tongues, as of fire, and one sat upon each of them. And they were all filled with the Holy Spirit.[151]

Later, we find Peter and John praying with their companions after sharing a report about being commanded by the chief priests and elders not speak or teach in the name of Jesus.

And when they had prayed, the place in which they were assembled was shaken; and they were all filled with the Holy Spirit, and they continued to speak the Word of God with freedom and boldness and courage.[152]

They had received power by being filled with the Holy Spirit, diffusing revelation throughout their souls resulting in freedom, boldness, and courage as a result of waiting on the Holy Spirit in fellowship and prayer.

Notice that this passage of Scripture says they were all filled with the Holy Spirit. Many scholars say that they had probably returned to the same Upper Room with many of the same disciples to pray where they had waited for the original promise of the Holy Spirit. At the very least, Peter and James, if not all the other apostles, had already been filled with the Spirit on the day of Pentecost. The disciples were all filled with the Holy Spirit again after they had already been filled with the Holy Spirit, indicating that the baptism of the Holy Spirit was never meant to be a one-time experience!

It was meant to be an experience with Holy Spirit that we would repeat over and over again, in relationship resulting in revelation being continually diffused throughout our soul. As

[151] Acts 2:2-4 NKJV
[152] Acts 4:31 AMP

a result, this would activate the extraordinary gifts of the Holy Spirit in us, in order to distinguish us as Christians operating with a supernatural grace!

THE TREE OF LIFE

The story of Dr. Meyer illustrates this point as he struggled with a crucial transitional time in his life. He sat dejectedly in his study contemplating his choices, saying, "My life and ministry are unfruitful, lacking spiritual power." Suddenly Christ seemed to be standing next to him, asking, "Let Me have the keys to your life." The experience was so realistic that he reached into his pocket and took out a bunch of keys!

Jesus asked the man, "Are all the keys here?" "Yes, Lord, all except the key to one small room in my life," he answered. Then Jesus said to him, "If you cannot trust Me with all the rooms of your life, I cannot accept any of the keys." Dr. Meyer was overwhelmed, feeling that he was pushing Christ out of his life by excluding Him from one interest in his life. He began to cry out to Jesus, "Come back, Lord, and take the keys to all the rooms of my life."[153]

Just like Dr. Meyer, we must receive revelation by Holy Spirit to unlock all the potential that has already been given to us, activating the authority of Holy Spirit to diffuse revelation throughout all the rooms of our soul! We are no longer limited by our own mind, strength, and abilities, but are free from deception of the tree of the knowledge of good and evil that is void of a life-giving relationship with Jesus. We can now

[153] Walter B Knight, Knights Treasury Of 2000 Illustrations: Take All The Keys Lord, (Grand Rapids, MI: William B. Eerdmans Publishing Company, 1963), 73

enjoy our relationship with Him, the Tree of Life, resting in His accomplishments enabling us to live the abundant life.

In the beginning of creation, "the Lord God planted a garden toward the east, in Eden (*delight*)."[154] It contained everything needed for Adam and Eve to enjoy the abundant life, "every tree that is pleasant to the sight or to be desired – good (*suitable, pleasant*) for food."[155] They were living in an unobstructed relationship with God while they were resting in the goodness of His provision.

The Garden included "the tree of life also in the center of the garden, and the tree of the knowledge of (*the difference between*) good and evil and blessing and calamity."[156] The Lord told Adam and Eve that they were free to eat from any tree:

> But of the tree of the knowledge of good and evil and blessing and calamity you shall not eat, for in the day that you eat of it you shall surely die.[157]

Life and death stood in the middle of the Garden with a clear word from the Lord concerning His intentions. Adam and Eve could choose to eat from the Tree of Life resulting in continued relationship with God, or they could choose to eat from the tree of calamity resulting in spiritual death. It is the first test of free will! The Lord obviously wanted them to choose Him, the Tree of Life, or He would not have warned them of the consequences of eating from the tree of the knowledge of good and evil.

Then the serpent convinced Eve that she would not die if she was to eat from the tree of the knowledge of good and evil:

[154] Genesis 2:8 AMP
[155] Genesis 2:9 AMP
[156] Ibid
[157] Genesis 2:17 AMP

For God knows that in the day you eat of it your eyes will be opened, and you will be like God, knowing the difference between good and evil.[158]

The serpent deceived Eve, tricking her with her own desire to be like God.[159] In reality she was already like God, created in His image. But when she saw the:

tree was good (*suitable, pleasant*) for food and that it was delightful to look at, and a tree to be desired in order to make one wise, she took of its fruit and ate; and she gave some also to her husband, and he ate.[160]

The serpent twisted the agendas and priorities in her heart by offering her the appearance of the abundant life. It was the abundant without the life. He offered the appearance of godliness without a relationship with God.[161] It was a subtle suggestion that she could become wise like God so that she no longer needed Him. He gave the illusion that she could provide for herself in the same way that God had already provided on her behalf. He tempted her with an opportunity to be her own god.

Everything changed that day for Adam and Eve when they disobeyed the Word of God in order to eat the fruit of the tree of the knowledge of good and evil. They had sinned, separating themselves from a relationship with God. They had chosen religion over relationship. The Lord said to Eve:

---

[158] Genesis 3:5 AMP

[159] Ted Haggard, The Life Giving Church (Ventura, CA: Regal Books, 2001), 53

[160] Genesis 3:6 AMP

[161] Ted Haggard, The Life Giving Church (Ventura, CA: Regal Books, 2001), 53

I will greatly multiply your grief and your suffering in pregnancy and the pangs of childbearing; with spasms of distress you will bring forth children. Yet your desire and craving will be for your husband, and he will rule over you.[162]

The curse of her actions would cause pain instead of pleasure in a moment originally intended for joy and blessing. The Lord dealt with the motives of Eve's heart. He declared that her desire would no longer be for her own cause but for the cause of her husband. Not only would she not have the opportunity to be her own god, she would have to submit to the rule of both her husband and God. The Lord wanted her to desire relationship, not religion!

The consequence was to experience the fruit of calamity on every level, bringing death to every blessing that they had effortlessly enjoyed in their relationship with God. The Lord told Adam that because of their sin, "the ground is under a curse because of you; in sorrow and toil shall you eat (*of the fruits*) of it all the days of your life."[163] The blessings freely received in the past would now have to be pursued through the curse of striving and working hard in their own strength. The ground was under the curse of religion, separating them from the fruit that they had previously enjoyed without effort in the Garden through relationship with God.

RIGHT AND WRONG

We can see a parallel story being told about Adam and Eve in the Garden and the Israelites who had left Egypt with

[162] Genesis 3:16 AMP
[163] Genesis 3:17 AMP

116

Moses. When it came time to take the promised land, they chose to believe in their own strength and abilities over God's Word to discern whether the circumstances were right or wrong to possess their inheritance. So the Lord told them, "in spite of this word you did not believe (*trust, rely on, and remain steadfast to*) the Lord your God."[164]

As a result, the Lord told them that not one of them would see the promised land. Only Joshua and:

> your children who at this time cannot discern between good and evil, they shall enter Canaan, and to them I will give it and they shall possess it.[165]

The promised land would be possessed by Joshua and those who could not discern between good and evil. It would be a generation that would trust, rely on, and remain steadfast to their relationship with God, rather than a religion built on their own strength and abilities.

The tree of the knowledge of good and evil has the appearance of living the abundant life, but it is not the abundant life. It is a form of religion without a relationship with Jesus Christ. It represents the understanding of right and wrong resulting in the curse of independence and selfish ambition. Its appearance tries to deceive us of our true identity, so we will strive and work in our own mind, strength and abilities to try to receive all that has already been given to us in Christ.

The Tree of Life represents a genuine relationship with Jesus Christ, a relationship of dependency upon God. It not only has the appearance of the abundant life, but it actually is the

---

[164] Deuteronomy 1:32 AMP
[165] Deuteronomy 1:39 AMP

abundant life. It never stops bearing fruit for those who have a circumcised heart, having already surrendered their heart for His heart. They are free to enjoy its fruit without any effort of their own. They don't have to strive and work hard to overcome the curse in their own strength, allowing them to rest in His provision.

The original plan of creation never even included us understanding the idea of right and wrong. His plan has never changed for us. We are created to be in relationship with Jesus Christ through Holy Spirit in order to receive revelation of His heart and thoughts as our own. Then, without the effort of our own strength and abilities, His heart and thoughts would flow organically through us, manifesting the promises of God.

LOST AUTHORITY

It's not our destiny to live according to the tree of the knowledge of good and evil, maintaining a form of godliness without power. We are called to live in relationship with the Tree of Life resulting in authority with power to experience our inheritance.[166] The tree of the knowledge of good and evil is limited to a life based on the consequences of right and wrong. It limits us to our own mind, strength and ability to live a righteous life as we try to overcome the wrong of our sin by our own efforts. On the other hand, the Tree of Life offers freedom to overcome those limits based on our relationship with Jesus Christ, as a result of His righteousness, power and authority that has already defeated the curse of sin and death on our behalf.

When God created mankind in the Garden, He gave them:

[166] Ted Haggard, The Life Giving Church (Ventura, CA: Regal Books, 2001), 54

complete authority over the fish of the sea, the birds of the air, the (*tame*) beasts, and over of all the earth, and over everything that creeps upon the earth.[167]

The Lord had given Adam and Eve authority over the entire earth, including everything on it. He did not give them partial authority. He entrusted them with complete God-given authority over the natural realm called earth, saying:

> Be fruitful, multiply, and fill the earth, and subdue it (*using all its vast resources in the service of God and man*); and have dominion over the fish of the sea, the birds of the air, and over every living creature that moves upon the earth.[168]

THE ORIGINAL PLAN OF CREATION NEVER EVEN INCLUDED US UNDERSTANDING THE IDEA OF RIGHT AND WRONG.

The word *authority* and the word *dominion* in the above verses are the same Hebrew word *radah*. It means "to tread down, to have dominion, prevail against, reign, to rule, or to take."[169] God had originally designed mankind "in His own image."[170] In other words, God had designed man with His very own DNA, allowing them to take on the image of God. He had created a family with sons and daughters representing His name. He had distinguished the supremacy of mankind from all the other beasts by making them in His own image and allowing them to inherit His authority and power.

---

[167] Genesis 1:26 AMP
[168] Genesis 1:28 AMP
[169] Strong's Exhaustive Concordance, Reference 7287
[170] Genesis 1:27 AMP

Married into the very identity and purpose of mankind was this idea of living in dominion. God had made them to dominate by His Word. Every natural thing on earth was subject to the rule of mankind. They would tread down anything that would oppose their authority. God had chosen to share His dominion of heaven and earth by giving His authority over earth to mankind. God would continue to rule the spiritual while mankind would rule the natural.

When the serpent came to deceive Adam and Eve in the Garden, tempting them with the desire to be like God, he was trying to take away the authority that God had given to mankind. The serpent had no legal authority of his own to take it away by force. It was a gift that had been freely given to them by God. Only the authority of God in the spiritual was higher than the authority of mankind in the natural.

As long as they were resting in relationship with God, the serpent did not have the right to take the authority that had been given to them by God Himself. On earth the serpent would have to submit to the authority of mankind. Mankind had complete authority over all the earth. The serpent did not have any authority or power over mankind or the earth. He would have to trick them into giving him their authority by their own free will!

Unfortunately, the enemy was able to deceive Adam and Eve from resting in God. He successfully separated them from their identity in relationship with God. As a result, the enemy severed them from the image they were created in; they lost the authority, dominion and power that had been given to them over the earth. Satan literally tricked them through the appearances of circumstance to hand over the natural authority given to them by their own free will.

Adam and Eve were deceived into trying to receive by their own effort all that they had already been given by God. They decided to disobey God, eating of the tree of the knowledge of good and evil. They trusted in their own mind, strength and abilities to accomplish right and wrong. All the while, God's desire was for them to rest in relationship with Him, eating of the Tree of Life. He wanted them to choose the source of life over the appearance of life, depending on His mind, strength and abilities, instead of giving away the authority that God had entrusted to them by betraying themselves and breaking relationship with Him.

The good news for us is that when Jesus Christ died on the cross, He rose again and He defeated the enemy, death, and the curse of sin. He became a substitute for us by paying for our sins with His life. "The first man Adam became a living being (*an individual personality*); the last Adam (*Christ*) became a life-giving Spirit (*restoring the dead to life*.)"[171]

Adam had lived according to his individual personality based on his own mind, strength and abilities. Jesus Christ became a life-giving Spirit resting in the mind, strength, and abilities of the Father, trusting Him in laying down His own life. His death became life to all those who were under the curse of sin and death, trying to rely on their vain efforts to receive His promises. He took back the authority based on His efforts that mankind had given away in the natural. The authority that was given away in the natural was now restored in the spiritual.

In one of our church services a woman attending was suffering from acute pain in both her back and neck. I was leading the church in prayer when I began to feel this sharp pain in my

---

[171] 1 Corinthians 15:45 AMP

neck. The pain had surfaced out of nowhere and for no apparent reason. I knew Holy Spirit was using this pain in my neck to get my attention in order to prompt me to pray for someone's neck in the meeting.

At that moment, I asked anyone in the church who was experiencing acute pain in the right side of their neck to come to the front of the church so I could pray for them to be healed. Three women came forward that morning to receive prayer for healing. Following the meeting a woman who had been experiencing acute pain in her back and neck came to find me and tell me that her neck had been healed. She told me that she had been suffering in this condition for several years. Now for the first time in years all the pain in her neck was gone!

FILLED WITH THE GODHEAD

During the next Sunday morning service, I heard Holy Spirit tell me that there was someone in the service who was experiencing pain in the right side of their lower back. Again, I asked anyone who was experiencing pain in the right side of their lower back to come to the front of the church so that I could pray for them to be healed. Surprisingly, the woman who was healed the week before came forward to receive prayer for chronic lower back pain. Amazingly, she was not only healed again, but made completely whole!

This woman responded to revelation given by Holy Spirit based on the authority of Christ who is seated in the spiritual sphere called heavenly places. It's this authority originating in the spiritual sphere that resulted in the manifestation of this woman's healing, demanding every natural authority and power to submit to Him. In other words it's the supernatural realm, with dominion over the natural realm, that allowed this woman to receive the manifestation of Christ's rule and authority!

The Lord has chosen to use His people to release His authority and dominion in heaven on earth. He has already equipped us with everything we need in the spiritual realm. He has restored in us the authority originally given away by Adam and Eve. Our enemy has already been defeated, having to submit to the authority of "Christ in you!"

"For in Him the whole fullness of Deity (the Godhead) continues to dwell in bodily form (*giving complete expression of the divine nature*)."[172] In other words, this verse says the same supernatural divine substance of the Godhead continues to live in Jesus Christ. Everything about who God is dwells in Christ. This is the complete substance and expression of the fullness of God's supernatural power and authority which also dwells in and through us in bodily form on earth!

It's not "a part" or "a copy" of the substance and expression of the supernatural divinity of God. It's the exact same fullness! It's not a different expression! It's the exact same substance!

Don't believe it! Look at the next verse! "And you are in Him, made full and having come to fullness of life (*in Christ you too are filled with the Godhead – Father, Son and Holy Spirit – and reach full spiritual stature*)."[173] You are in Christ! Again, in Him you have been made full with the fullness of the substance and expression in Him.

In other words, everything that God made to live in Christ now lives in us. The word *full* actually means "full and complete in substance and expression." The same full and complete su-

[172] Colossians 2:9 AMP
[173] Colossians 2:10 AMP

pernatural divine authority and power that lives in Christ also dwells in us. "And He is the Head of all rule and authority (*of every angelic principality and power*)."[174]

What does this mean for us as believers? Jesus is above all authority and power in heaven and earth. He is more powerful than anyone or anything in heaven or earth! The devil, every one of his demons, and any other power must submit to His authority. As soon as we become born again the same power and authority of all the Godhead came to dwell in us through Jesus Christ.

The powers that must submit to Jesus must submit to His authority in us. When we come to a fight we do not come alone in our own strength. We come with the power and authority of God the Father, God the Son, and God the Holy Spirit. The enemy does not even stand a chance! It is not even a fair fight!

Most churches have a doctrine that says Jesus Christ is fully God and fully man. The above verses indicate that in Christ we are, too! Traditional backgrounds are more comfortable in saying, "We are the hands and feet of Jesus!" Why use such extreme language?

I am not advocating we worship ourselves as God! I would be the first in line to object to such an idea! The Bible clearly says Jesus is pre-eminent. This means He was first, indicating that we only have what we have in Christ because of all that He already accomplished first on our behalf. But we still have it, and it was His idea!

A religious spirit has hijacked the identity of the church, convincing many Christians that they do not have anything in them worthwhile to offer anyone. In addition, it appears like the

---

[174] Ibid

church is the only institution in the world where it's okay to tell people that they are nothing, as religious leaders try to keep the people of God humble. They are seduced by a spirit of fear that believers will become arrogant and prideful if we recognize the greatness in them, put there by God Himself.

The problem for most Christians isn't that they think too much of themselves. It's that they don't think enough of who they are in Christ. God doesn't think that you are nothing. It was God Himself who created you to be something. He thought you were important and valuable enough that it was worth giving His life. You are awesome! You were made to rock!

I don't know how many times I have heard believers say, "I am not God!" or "We are not God!" – as an excuse to continue to live from their own natural abilities rather than stepping out in faith to be used in His supernatural abilities! And they often portray this statement as an act of humility deserving a badge of honor! In reality, it's a religious spirit masked in humility but full of insecurity, fear, and pride!

A NEW CREATION

In the midst of exclaiming this powerful revelation above, the Apostle Paul seems to stop and change direction right in the middle of this truth to what appears at first glance to be an unrelated topic, saying:

> In Him also you were circumcised with a circumcision not made with hands, but in a (*spiritual*) circumcision (*performed by*) Christ by stripping off the body of flesh (*the whole corrupt, carnal nature with its passions and lusts*).[175]

---

[175] Colossians 2:11 AMP

Why did the apostle Paul change the topic suddenly to circumcision? It is because he wants us to understand that as soon as we receive Jesus Christ into our lives, entrusted with the complete fullness of His power and authority, He simultaneously circumcised our hearts, stripping off the body of flesh the whole corrupt, carnal nature with its passions and lusts. He wants us to know immediately that we are not the same person that we were. He wants us to understand that we have a new identity!

This is the opposite of many churches today teaching that even with our new nature we are still going to continue to have struggles with our old nature. This is not what it means to have our hearts circumcised. It literally means that we have put to death our old nature by cutting it off. The apostle Paul is revealing a profound mystery unlocking revelation about the fullness of the operational power of God in us.

The fullness of God's authority and power only flows through His purified heart which has already been given to us as a result of our being united with Him. It is the purity of this new heart and spirit in us activated by revelation that allows us to operate in the fullness of His authority. It is not a moral purity based in the tree of the knowledge of good and evil, and right and wrong. It is a purity that we received with no effort of our own by becoming one in relationship with Christ, the Tree of Life resulting in our death and resurrection to a newness of life in Him.

> (*Thus you were circumcised when*) you were buried with Him in (*your*) baptism, in which you were also raised with Him (*to a new life*) through (*your*) faith in the working of God (*as displayed*) when He raised Him up from the dead.[176]

[176] Colossians 2:12 AMP

Kris Valloton teaches that baptism is not a symbolic act. It is a prophetic act. It's not like we died. We actually died! In baptism we are submerged in water publicly, testifying that our old nature and lives have already been buried with Christ. The motives of our heart died with us and our old heart on that day. We received a new heart and spirit with His purity as we were raised with Him to a new life through our faith in His finished work!

> Therefore if any person is (*ingrafted*) in Christ (*the Messiah*) he is a new creation (*a new creation altogether*); the old (*previous moral and spiritual condition*) has passed away.[177]

This is good news! The old you with your old nature was buried with Jesus! The new you with your new nature was raised with Him by your faith in the working of God to new life in the resurrection of Christ. You are a new creation altogether. Your old previous moral condition passed away. It died! It no longer exists!

> You were united with Him in His death. What died? The entire fallen personality...The new self is completely restored to childlike innocence and trust. Ultimately, the new you is righteous, pure and holy. The old you does not exist any longer.[178]

Stop owning the sinful nature as if it's still hanging around for you to kill. Stop owning fearful, anxious thoughts that belonged to the past. Believe that you are in Christ and that Christ is in you. Negative or sinful feelings can come on strong...really strong! And it is impossible at times

---

[177] 2 Corinthians 5:17 AMP
[178] John Crowder, Mystical Union (Santa Cruz, CA: Sons of Thunder Ministries & Publications, 2004), 30-31

to stop them. But that does not mean that you have to agree with them or own them. Instead, agree that the old corrupted emotional life died with Christ. Now, you are a recipient of new, resurrected emotions. You are a joint participant in the emotional life of Christ.[179]

Is there a difference in your life since you have accepted Christ? The testimony being that we have been buried with our old nature and we are no longer living for ourselves. We are no longer victims of our past, just trying to survive. The person that we were before Christ is dead! You now have a new life that isn't just reproducing fruit for yourself, but others!

This is what Jesus said would happen when we died:

I assure you, most solemnly I tell you, unless a grain of wheat falls into the earth and dies, it remains (*just one grain; it never becomes more but lives*) by itself alone. But if it dies, it produces many others and yields a rich harvest.[180]

Of course, in this passage Jesus was speaking to pre-Christians who had not died with Him, because He had not died yet! Although, there have always been those who have chosen to stop at the cross, unwilling to die with Him. Some just want to add Him to their lives, hoping to be blessed, but they don't want to die with Him and they will never get to experience His promises through the resurrection power of the cross!

Salvation requires getting on the cross and dying with Him. There is no other way to enter His kingdom. There is no other way to live the abundant life. You may go to church. You may

---

[179] John Crowder, Mystical Union (Santa Cruz, CA: Sons of Thunder Ministries & Publications, 2004), 35
[180] John 12:24 AMP

be a good person. You might even believe in Jesus! But if you haven't died, you can't live again! Without death there cannot be a resurrection! "As we die to our own agenda and self absorption, we will be reapers of the harvest in great measure."[181]

If we died to our old self with Christ but forget who we are in Him and become deceived, betraying ourselves in resurrecting the old self with all his agendas and priorities, we will never experience the promises of God (sometimes it seems like believers are better at resurrecting their old nature than resurrecting the dead). It doesn't matter how hard we strive and work in our own strength and abilities, the promises of God will never come to fruition because His promises can only be found resting in Him!

YOU BELONG

Circumcision is a sign of belonging. So when God told the Israelites to "circumcise the foreskin of your (minds and) hearts,"[182] He was giving them a revelation of their identity in Him. One of the reasons the Israelites had to be circumcised is that God wanted them to know they were His people. God wanted them to remember in everything they did that they belong to Him!

In the same way, God circumcised our hearts with Christ on the cross in union with Him so that no matter where we are or what we are doing, we will remember that we belong to Him. Our new hearts have already been downloaded with revelation of our new identity as sons and daughters. So we no longer have to pretend to be something that we are not, or to perform for

[181] Sean Smith, Prophetic Evangelism (Shippensburg, PA: Destiny Image Publishers Inc, 2004), 41
[182] Deuteronomy 10:16 AMP

acceptance that we have already received. We have been liberated from religion to just be who we are in relationship with Christ!

We no longer represent our old self – we manifest Christ in us, the hope of glory, with every thought, word, and deed. We manifest Him at work, to strangers, with our friends, and in our families. God is looking for those who know who they are in Him. He is looking for a people who know they belong to Him!

We are no longer living for our old self! We voluntarily died with Christ on the cross, resurrected to new life in Him. We had the option, based on our own free will, to keep our lives for our old self or to give them away to Him. Now it is no longer I that live, but Christ that lives in me!

Why continue to settle for the wrong side of the cross, where we live east of the Jordan, watching everyone else living in the promised land, feeling like we don't belong as they experience the promises of God? Crucified with Christ, we can now enjoy the resurrection side of the cross where we belong, with Him. Knowing "that our old self was put to death on the execution-stake with him, so that the entire body of our sinful propensities might be destroyed."[183]

We will be resting in His authority and power, experiencing the abundant life for ourselves! Where we belong!

---

[183] Romans 6:6 CJB

CHAPTER 5

LIVING IN REVELATION

OUR GOOD FRIENDS, BRIAN AND NICOLE McConville, served as our associate pastors for almost seven years. They joined our ministry about a year and a half after my wife and I had planted our church, Word of Life Christian Center. They had felt called by God to full-time ministry after becoming a part of our local church. It has been our privilege to train and equip them as they have unselfishly sacrificed everything in their lives in order to serve God and His people. They've been our armor bearers and we have learned to trust them with our lives. It has been a joy to serve the Lord with such good friends!

For several years Brian and Nicole tried to have children without any success. Our church continually rallied around them in prayer as they continued to stand in faith, trusting God at His Word for children, regardless of the appearance of their circumstances. Nicole testifies to their experience saying:

"Ever since I can remember it was my dream to be a mommy. I love children and could not wait to have some of my own. The day I was married I felt closer to that dream than ever before in my life. Although my husband did not feel ready to have children right away, we never took any precautions to prevent a pregnancy. After three years without a baby in sight we began to question whether something was wrong with us.

"When seeking the Lord in prayer, I felt a peace from the Lord to go and see a doctor regarding our situation. I went to a specialist who performed several tests, including ultrasounds, which concluded that I was in excellent physical shape to have a baby. Brian was also tested, proving that he was physically healthy and able to biologically produce children. As a result, the doctor began to talk with us about our options in conceiving a baby. As we continued to seek the Lord in prayer I felt God's peace as He spoke to my heart to just trust in Him.

"Over the next few years we received prophetic word after prophetic word about having children. The Lord knew just how to help encourage us to continue to put our trust in Him. These words always served as a confirmation to the things the Lord had already spoken to us in our special private times with Him. In one of those times God told me that we would have a son and to name him Judah, 'Praise to God.'

"The appearance of our circumstances continued to contradict God's Word during this season. I was diagnosed with fibromyalgia resulting in chronic pain and fatigue. Many times I was totally incapacitated, but I did not stop seeking the Lord for healing. One day while I was praying, Jesus told me to stop taking any medication. He was delivering and healing me from any sickness and disease in order to prepare my body for a child.

"On January 1, 2005, the Holy Spirit told me that I was healed and set free! I felt better physically and began to sleep through the night for the first time in months. At my next doctor's appointment it was a joy for me to share my testimony of being healed. I told my doctor about the promise I received from God about conceiving a child. He responded by saying, "I'll see you in a few months when you're pregnant!" In May of 2005, I became pregnant with our miraculous son, Judah Grant McConville! I know that each life is miraculous, but to experience this firsthand has been so amazing. God literally spoke our son into being!"

Brian and Nicole had been experiencing the manifestation of the promises of God through the birth of their new son for eight weeks when they noticed that a skin deformity had developed on top of Judah's head. They brought him to a doctor, who diagnosed a pin sized opening that went from the top of his head down into his skull, possibly containing a cyst or tumor that could cause meningitis. Judah needed to have surgery to fix the defect, but would have to wait another month before it could be scheduled.

During the next thirty days Brian and Nicole continued to put their trust in God on behalf of their son. One day they heard the Lord say, "Judah will have to go through the surgery, but I will take care of Him!" As promised, God protected Judah in surgery. Afterwards the surgeon told them that the opening in Judah's head appeared to penetrate his skull resulting in a seventy five percent chance that he would need to have brain surgery in the near future. Six months later Judah was to return for a follow-up exam, including an MRI.

In the meantime, Brian and Nicole continued to pray that Jesus would heal their son. During this time the Lord told them, "I will make it apparent to everyone, including the doctors, that I have healed Judah!" In the natural this seemed impossible to them. The doctors had already told them that an MRI would only reveal problems of more growth. It would not be able to reveal any progress toward healing.

They knew that they served a creative God, but wondered how He would make Judah's healing apparent to everyone. After completing the MRI at the follow-up exam, the surgeon met with Brian and Nicole to review Judah's medical file with them. The doctor began to awkwardly explain that he had remembered doing the surgery in this case and seeing an opening that penetrated the skull. Now in reviewing the MRI the doctor could not see any indication of an opening that still existing in Judah's skull. Nicole said that it was as if someone was literally giving the doctor the words to speak as he proclaimed, "I would have to say Judah is healed!"

BATTLES IN THE PROMISED LAND

Over the years we've watched Brian and Nicole come to experience the promises of God in their own lives. If they would have tried to fight the above crisis in their own strength they would never have witnessed the miraculous healing power of God on behalf of their son, Judah. They didn't have the ability to overcome this impossible situation in the power of their own strength. In the midst of experiencing the promises of God, they had to learn to overcome new obstacles by resting in Him in order to continue to experience the manifestation of His promises.

There are battles we have to overcome to be in the promised land so we can continue to enjoy the fullness of God's promises. Joshua and the Israelites had already overcome the impossible obstacle of crossing the Jordan River. This allowed them to possess their promised land. Then as soon as they got to the promised land, God stopped them and began to prepare their hearts through circumcision for their next battle in Jericho.

Joshua and the Israelites were living in the promised land. They were experiencing the promises of God for themselves, and they still had battles to fight to receive the manifestation of God's promises. They would have to prevail in several impossible battles, starting with the city of Jericho, in order to possess all that God had already given them in the promised land.

"Jericho (*a fenced town with high walls*) was tightly closed because of the Israelites; no one went out or came in."[184] The walls of Jericho had survived many battles without being penetrated by anyone in its history. Now, if Joshua had gone out in his own strength, he would never have conquered the walled city of Jericho. Joshua had no sooner overcome the impossible obstacle of crossing the Jordan River than he was facing another impossible situation in conquering the city of Jericho.

Why were Joshua and the Israelites still fighting battles once they had possessed the promised land?

Like most of us, Joshua and the Israelites probably thought that possessing the promised land meant they could stop fighting and begin to relax and enjoy the fruits of His promises. After all those years of wandering in the wilderness, dreaming about the opportunity to possess the promised land, Joshua probably never imagined having to continue to overcome battle after battle once in the promised land. God was teaching His people that the fullness of His promises could only be found in Him. He did not want them to see the promised land as an accomplished event without a continued need to be in relationship with

[184] Joshua 6:1 AMP

Him. He wanted them to continue to be dependent upon Him through relationship. Only in relationship could they experience the revelation that they needed in order to continue to rest in the fullness of His promises.

Jesus wants us to recognize that He is our promise! Oftentimes we see the fulfillment of a promise in God as our destination. We can become distracted and stop maintaining a relationship with the source of our promise, the One who is our destination. We forget who we are in Him, revert back to the ways of the flesh and try to accomplish the fullness of His promises in our own strength and abilities, living from the tree of the knowledge of good and evil.

Now, we try to overcome battles based on information we have learned from the Bible, which is not the Word, but is the testimony of the Word! The Bible is not God Himself! This Bible says about itself in John 1:1, "In the beginning was the Word, and the Word was with God, and the Word was God."[185]

This is the first step to betraying ourselves, as we are deceived from enjoying a relationship with God Himself that results in revelation. We become content with information, testifying about Him. This doesn't devalue the importance of the Bible. It brings it to life as we receive revelation from Holy Spirit to experience revelation of the information testifying of Him!

Many Christians are trying to overcome impossible battles based on information from their natural senses concerning their circumstances, forgetting who they are in Him. They chart a course of action according to their interpretation of right and wrong based on that information, instead of knowing that they belong in relationship with Him, which would result in

[185] John 1:1 NIV

revelation from the spiritual realm and be diffused throughout their soul to overcome every obstacle in the natural realm. They become disillusioned in their faith, not being able to experience for themselves the things they believe, as God does not show up as they supposed, and He doesn't do all they thought He was going to do in their circumstances!

Everyday circumstances can beat us up when we try to exercise our authority in Christ through our own strength and abilities. Our words return void as the enemy taunts us with thoughts that the promises of God must not be for us, as we try to speak regurgitated information to a mountain that will not move based upon anything less than revelation (only found in a genuine relationship with Him). Instead of living in the fullness of the promised land, we find ourselves retreating to wander once again in disillusionment, filled with doubt, unbelief, and fear, since only revelation can activate the manifestation of His finished work!

INFORMATION VERSUS REVELATION

It is important for us to understand that there is a biblical distinction between information and revelation. We will continue to talk about this in greater depth in chapter six. In the meantime we need to understand, we receive information through the natural senses of our flesh and in the same way, we receive revelation in the spirit through our spiritual senses.

The abundant life is the manifestation of revelation received through our union with Holy Spirit, so we can activate the faith diffused throughout our soul to experience the things that we believe. This is not faith based on our natural ability to hope for positive things. This is faith based on His supernatural reality!

Many Christians misunderstand the term *faith*. They apply it to positive confession based on hope from information received by our body's natural senses. They say things like, "I'm trusting in faith that God is going to give me this new job I applied for yesterday." If God did not say He was giving them a new job, then it is not based in revelation; it is not biblical faith! It is hope!

There is nothing wrong with hope. The Bible lists it as one of three things that will remain for all eternity. But hope can only take us so far before we need faith to take over. The problem occurs when hope is disguised as faith. If the above person doesn't get the job described, they can become disillusioned about their faith in God, as they believe He has let them down once again, when all along it wasn't Him speaking!

Even the Bible can be reduced to information without a relationship with Holy Spirit resulting in revelation. It doesn't work to just quote information from chapter and verse of the Bible without revelation. It is not enough to know about the things of God. You must personally have revelation from God Himself in order to have authority to experience the manifestation of those promises.

The Holy Spirit gives us revelation so we can live in the purpose and victory of that revelation. When we do not live in the activation of that revelation, we set ourselves up for defeat. The abundant life is about getting a revelation and then living according to that blueprint in our thoughts and actions. The enemy cannot prevail against you when you are resting in Holy Spirit's revelation, but the enemy can prevail against you as you rely on information through your own strength and abilities.

Often as believers we can get a little information coupled with hope, go in our own strength and ability, and be deceived as we try to make something happen for ourselves. Then we call it faith, although we are doing our own thing; we expect God to show up and make us look good, instead of waiting to hear from Holy Spirit before launching out to do anything in the first place! As a result, God will say, "Let Me get out of your way so you can try it on your own!" We are reminded that we are not acting like ourselves, and the words of Jesus echo in our thoughts, "Apart from me you can do nothing."[186] God does not bless all things! He only blesses those things of which He is a part!

RECEIVING GREATER REVELATION

We have to understand, there is a divine order to living in the promises of God. The apostle Paul prays for the "eyes of your heart to be flooded with light,"[187] so we might get a revelation of the things we have already read and heard. Paul prays that God would break us out of our current religious paradigms in the natural realm by flooding our hearts with revelation in the spiritual realm to release the creative move of His Spirit in us.

We need revelation diffused throughout our soul to know and understand with our heart "the hope to which He has called you, and how rich is His glorious inheritance in the saints (*His set-apart ones*). And (*so that you can know and understand*) what is the immeasurable and unlimited and surpassing greatness of His power in and for us who believe,"[188] so we can be activated

---

[186] John 15:5 NIV
[187] Ephesians 1:18 AMP
[188] Ephesians 1:19 AMP

with supernatural faith to experience the manifestation of His promises!

Many Christians unconsciously feel that we do not need to learn anything new from the Bible, let alone receive revelation from His Spirit. I recently read a book that said that by the age of eight most Christians believe that they have learned all they need to know from the Bible to live the Christian life. They believe they have read or heard it all before. But it is important to keep a teachable spirit, because the true promises of God cannot be received through our natural understanding. They only come through revelation by the Spirit!

There is always something more the Lord wants to reveal to us. Jesus once asked the disciple Philip, "Have I been with all of you for so long a time, and do you not recognize and know Me yet?"[189] The disciples had spent over three years with Jesus, day and night, and still did not have a full revelation of Him. In another place, Jesus says, "I have still many things to say to you, but you are not able to bear them or to take them upon you or to grasp them now."[190] Jesus was telling Philip that He had a lot more things to reveal to Him, but that he was not able to perceive them with the current level of understanding in his soul. There is always a greater revelation for us to receive from God!

Today we receive revelation directly from Holy Spirit who resides in us.

He will guide you into all the Truth (*the whole, full Truth*). For He will not speak His own message (*on His own authority*); but He will tell whatever He hears (*from the Father; He will give the message that has been given to Him*),

[189] John 14:9 AMP
[190] John 16:12 AMP

and He will announce and declare to you the things that are to come (*that will happen in the future*).[191]

Living the abundant life requires sensitivity to the communication of the Holy Spirit. The more we enjoy our relationship with Him, the more our soul becomes sensitive and able to discern between information that comes from our flesh versus revelation that comes from the Spirit of God. He leads us into all the promises of His Word by equipping us to overcome with the knowledge of future events to come.

Jesus told His disciples that many of those who listened to His parables, "having the power of seeing, they do not see; and having the power of hearing, they do not hear, nor do they grasp and understand."[192] The information attained by their natural senses paralyzed them from being able to receive the revelation imparted through their spiritual senses. The information they were seeing with their natural eyes and ears was not enough to live in the promises of God. The natural realm had become a box that limited them from experiencing the true Kingdom of God.

Information we obtain in the natural realm is not enough to experience what we believe about God and His Word. We get in trouble when we try to overcome natural battles with natural resources. On the other hand, we have been equipped to overcome our natural battles with supernatural resources. The manifestation of His promises can only be released by the limitless authority of the spiritual ream that rules over the limits of the natural realm.

Most of the answers to our problems are in a place that is different from what we can see with our natural eyes and hear

[191] John 16:13 AMP
[192] Matthew 13:15 AMP

with our natural ears. Many Christians believe that if we work harder with the information received from our flesh to change things in the natural, then God will bless us. Jesus told His disciples the opposite in regards to the spiritual realm, "Blessed (*happy, fortunate and to be envied*) are your eyes because they do see, and your ears because they do hear."[193] A life of being blessed, happy, and fortunate enough to be envied sounds a lot like the abundant life.

Jesus said, "(*Things are hidden temporarily only as a means to revelation.*) For there is nothing hidden except to be revealed, nor is anything (*temporarily*) kept secret except in order that it may be made known."[194] In other words, there are spiritual realities hidden from us in the natural, but only as a means to activate our spiritual senses by reason of use to obtain revelation. Everything that we cannot see or hear with our natural eyes and ears can be seen and heard with our spiritual eyes and ears. The veil has already been removed!

During the first full day of our short-term mission trip to Jamaica, we went to Burger King for lunch. We had that day to get settled from traveling before we would begin our ministry time the next day. While waiting in a long line to order my food, a couple of young Jamaican men in their late teens began to engage me in small talk. Our conversation ended as they came to the front of the line to order.

As I was standing next in line to order, I heard the Holy Spirit say, "I was doing something in your conversation with those boys in order to change their hearts for Me, and you missed it." I began to think about how easily those young men had begun

---

[193] Matthew 13:16 AMP
[194] Mark 4:22 AMP

to converse with me. I knew that I had missed an opportunity that had been hidden in the spiritual realm from my physical senses. Now, regretfully, when these young men were finished ordering and were on their way out the door to leave, I still had to wait to order my food.

FAITH BY HEARING

A couple of minutes later I received my food order and noticed that these young Jamaican men were still standing outside at the corner of the restaurant talking with another guy on a bike. I hurried outside to redeem the opportunity that I had lost. Once outside, I was able to re-engage them in conversation. I began to share the gospel with them right there in the parking lot. Within a few minutes I was praying with all three of them as they received Jesus Christ as their Lord and Savior!

After inviting them to the ministry meetings that we were going to be doing that week in Jamaica, I began to return to the restaurant. Then I heard the Holy Spirit say to me, "All you need to do is learn to recognize what I am doing and become a part of it." I would not have led those three young Jamaican men to the Lord that day if the Holy Spirit had not diffused revelation into my soul concerning His purposes for that moment. It was in the midst of receiving revelation that my faith was activated to trust Him with the manifestation of His spoken word!

Romans 10:17 AMP says, "Faith comes by hearing (*what is told*), and what is heard comes by the preaching (*of the message that came from the lips*) of Christ (*the Messiah Himself*)."

Another translation says it this way, "Faith comes by hearing, and hearing by the word of God."[195] The Greek word here

---
[195] Romans 10:17 NKJV

for *Word* is *Rhema*. It means "preaching from the lips of the Messiah Himself or an utterance (individual, collective, or specific), by implication of a circumstance or topic."[196]

In essence, faith could be defined as the fruit of a relationship with the Holy Spirit resulting in revelation to trust Him. The word *hearing* implies there must be an exchange of communication between at least two people in a relationship. One person has to be speaking for another person to be listening to that which is being spoken. In this passage, the person hearing comes as a result of the Word being communicated directly from the Messiah Himself, Jesus Christ! Specifically, faith is the result of a specific word that comes from Jesus Christ through Holy Spirit as a direct result of being in union with Him!

Notice that faith is not a blind leap into the unknown.

Faith is the assurance (*the confirmation, the title deed*) of the things (*we*) hope for, being the proof of things (*we*) do not see and the conviction of their reality (*faith perceiving as real fact what is not revealed to the senses*).[197]

Our assurance comes in trusting God's specific Word to us regarding our own specific circumstances, so we can perceive the reality of the spiritual realm as real fact even though it has not been revealed to our natural senses. It is the proof of the things we cannot see in the natural realm and confirmation of the things we previously had only hoped God would do for us.

God has given us a title deed in the spiritual realm as proof of our divine inheritance in Him. A title deed is proof of our ownership in the natural realm. If I own a house and someone

---

[196] Strong's Exhaustive Concordance, Reference 4487
[197] Hebrews 11:1 AMP

tries to say that it is not my house, all I have to do to prove that I am the rightful owner of the house is to produce my title deed.

In the same way, when the enemy or someone else tries to get us to question our faith, all we have to do is produce the title deed of His specific Word to us. True faith is about trusting the things God has revealed to us with our spiritual senses over those things which were revealed by our physical senses. It is about trusting God's specific Word to us as fact, rather than continuing to believe in the appearance of our natural circumstances.

> IN ESSENCE, FAITH COULD BE DEFINED AS THE FRUIT OF A RELATIONSHIP WITH THE HOLY SPIRIT RESULTING IN REVELATION TO TRUST HIM.

WITHOUT FAITH

In Genesis 13 we find Abraham trying to keep peace with his brother Lot. As a result, Abraham stood on a hill, giving his brother first choice of the land before them, saying:

> If you take the left hand, then I will go to the right; or if you choose the right hand, then I will go to the left.[198] Lot looked and saw that everywhere the Jordan Valley was well watered.[199] Then Lot chose for himself all the Jordan Valley and (he) traveled east...[200]

Abraham literally allowed Lot to take his promised land away from him. It appears that Abraham must have been discouraged, with his eyes to the ground, because after Lot had left him, God said,

[198] Genesis 13:9 AMP
[199] Genesis 13:10 AMP
[200] Genesis 13:11 AMP

Lift up now your eyes and look from the place where you are, northward and southward and eastward and westward; For all the land which you see I will give to you and to your posterity forever. And I will make your descendants like the dust of the earth, so that if a man could count the dust of the earth, then could your descendants also be counted. Arise, walk through the land, the length of it and the breadth of it, for I will give it to you.[201]

Abraham had just lost the promised land when God arrived on the scene. It was the land God had promised him! No wonder he was hanging his head. Imagine having to tell God that you lost the land that He had given to you as a promise! It was Abraham's most discouraging and humiliating moment. It is the worst circumstance of his life, but God came to him in this moment and reaffirmed His commitment to give Abraham the promised land.

Every natural appearance and circumstance contradicted the Word that God was now speaking to Abraham. God wanted him to believe His Word over the circumstances, so He made him look up over the land so he could get a vision for the promised land once again. Then God had him walk through the land so he could experience the revelation of His Word for himself. God wanted Abraham to get his eyes off his circumstances and onto His promise.

Just like Abraham, we can all see the problems in our circumstances, but God has already provided solution for each one of us. His solution is to give us preordained revelation concerning our circumstances so we can watch Him accomplish

[201] Genesis 13:14-17 AMP

it. If we are looking for natural solutions for natural problems then we are probably falling short of the promises of God for our lives. It is only through relationship by our union with Holy Spirit that we are able to go into spiritual places to find spiritual solutions that will reverse our natural circumstances.

We cannot allow our physical senses to betray us into living in doubt and unbelief, and still experience the manifestation of promises of God. We must speak life and victory by agreeing with the reality of God's words to us, rather than death and defeat by agreeing with those things that are against us.

Without faith it is impossible to please and be satisfactory to Him. For whoever would come near to God must (*necessarily*) believe that God exists and that He is the re-warder of those who earnestly and diligently seek Him (*out*).[202]

SANCTIFYING YOUR IMAGINATION

We develop relationship with Holy Spirit:

By having the eyes of your heart flooded with light, so that you can know and understand the hope to which He has called you, and how rich is His glorious inheritance in the saints (*His set-apart ones*).[203]

We mention this verse above, but it's important for us to take another moment to look at the word *heart* in this passage. It is also widely translated as the word *understanding* in several Bible

---

[202] Hebrews 11:6 AMP
[203] Ephesians 1:18 AMP

translations. It is actually the Greek word *dianeuo* which is most accurately translated as the word *imagination*.[204]

The Holy Spirit opens up the spiritual eyes of our heart and understanding through our imagination, so we can personally experience revelation from the spiritual realm that we could never see before. "He has released within us the hardware necessary to receive spiritual pictures, impressions, visions, dreams and stirrings,"[205] of our spiritual blessings so we can see and know for ourselves the hope of His calling and the inheritance He has given us to fulfill it.

The more we sanctify our imaginations with the things of the Spirit, the more we will be able to "defeat the hindrances to a greater revelatory release in our life!"[206] Matthew 5:8 says, "Blessed (*happy, enviably fortunate, and spiritually prosperous — possessing the happiness produced by the experience of God's favor and especially conditioned by the revelation of His grace, regardless of their outward conditions*) are the pure in heart, for they shall see God!"[207] Another translation says, "Blessed are the pure in heart, for they shall see God!"[208] In other words we could translate this verse, "Blessed are the pure in imagination, for they shall see God."

Who are the pure in imagination? Those who have not allowed their imaginations to be corrupted by the influence of darkness, by the information received through their physical senses. They have dedicated their imaginations to the things of the light by the revelation received through the spiritual senses of their spirit.

---

[204] Strong's Exhaustive Concordance, Reference 1271
[205] Sean Smith, Sanctifying Your Imagination , 3 CD Set, Disc #1
[206] Ibid
[207] Matthew 5:8 AMP
[208] Matthew 5:8 NKJV

The pure in imagination are blessed because they can see God in the spiritual realm. They are happy, fulfilled, and fortunate as a result of their relationship with Him. The pure in imagination are spiritually prospering and possessing His promises. They are actually experiencing God's favor through the revelation of His operational power, regardless of their outward circumstances. As a result, others around them begin to be motivated with intense desire to have a similar relationship with God.

Sanctifying the imagination of our soul "awakens our spiritual eyes"[209] to receive revelation in our spirit, "yielding awareness to the activities of God."[210] We can "activate our imagination to receive revelation more freely"[211] by not allowing the imaginations of our souls to be defiled by darkness contained within the information that we may receive through our physical senses about the natural world. What kinds of images, sounds, feelings, tastes, and smells dominate your imagination? What kinds of information do we allow to dominate our children's imaginations?

The filling of our lives with entertainment such as pornography, perverse music lyrics, violent video games, and negative movie images degrade the name and values of Holy Spirit. It will only corrupt the hard drive of our imaginations, making it more and more difficult to receive revelation from Him. It is in this context that Paul exhorts the people in Ephesians to "no longer live as the heathen (*the Gentiles*) do in their perverseness (*in the folly, vanity, and emptiness of their souls and the futility*) of their minds."[212] These people who considered themselves Christians were being exhorted to no longer live their lives in the same manner as unbelievers,

---

[209] Sean Smith, Sanctifying Your Imagination, 3 CD Set, Disc #2
[210] Ibid
[211] Ibid
[212] Ephesians 4:17 AMP

because participating in forms of perverse entertainment would create an emptiness of revelation being diffused throughout the imagination of their souls. As a result, their imaginations were "being darkened in their understanding, excluded from the life of God."[213] In other words, the perverse entertainment of a generation was darkening their imaginations to the point that it was excluding them from the life of God.

What happens when the atmosphere of a room becomes darkened? It is no longer exposed by the light, making it more difficult to see things within the room. The atmosphere of the room called our soul containing our imagination can become darkened by perverse, unsanctified images received through our physical senses. As a result, our spiritual senses become desensitized in the room of our soul, making it more difficult to see and receive the sanctified images containing revelation from our spirit.

The people that Paul was addressing in Ephesians were being excluded from the life of God:

> because of the ignorance (*the want of knowledge and perception, the willful blindness*) that is deep-seated in them, due to their hardness of heart (*to the insensitiveness of their moral nature*).[214]

The phrase "moral nature" here is a reference to our spirit. Only the spirit within us is perfect and moral. Here we see a whole generation who were deceived into forgetting who they were in Christ. They had become excluded from the revelatory life of God because of their want to pursue knowledge and perception by information received through their physical senses. As a result, they had become insensitive to the Spirit by ignorantly allowing

[213] Ephesians 4:18 NASB
[214] Ephesians 4:18 AMP

the enemy to capture and harden the imagination of their heart and understanding through the perverse idol of entertainment.

In their spiritual apathy they have become callous and past feeling and reckless and have abandoned themselves (*a prey*) to unbridled sensuality, eager and greedy to indulge in every form of impurity (*that their depraved desires may suggest and demand*).[215]

SABOTAGING YOUR IMAGINATION

In Jonah 2:8 it says, "Those who regard worthless idols forsake their own mercy."

This verse also uses the term "lying vanities" for worthless idols, describing the deceptive smoke screens of all the spiritual substitutes. Do you know what will sabotage a sanctified imagination? It is being distracted by entertainment and personal goals that are not necessarily God's plan for us.[216]

Often we have allowed "the hypnotic trance of modern culture"[217] to fill our minds with entertainment and unsanctified images that pollute our imaginations. As we allow our imaginations to be corrupted with the unsanctified images of darkness, our soul becomes more desensitized to the sanctified images of revelation received from our spirit.

We must not get tied up in the intoxication of our age. Heaven is busy releasing spiritual impressions, spiritual pictures and Holy Visions. We were created to surpass

---

[215] Ephesians 4:19 AMP
[216] Sean Smith, Prophetic Evangelism (Shippensburg, PA: Destiny Image Publishers Inc, 2004), 105
[217] Sean Smith, Sanctifying Your Imagination, 3 CD Set, Disc #3

the challenges of our generation and the time in which we are placed. Sanctifying our imagination is about cleansing our hearts and opening our spiritual eyes to receive heavens downloads. Tapping into this reality requires that your imagination must become the dwelling place of God.[218]

THE HEAVENLY REALM

Our spiritual eyes are opened by the revelation of God's light as the imagination of our heart allows us to see the hidden, supernatural reality of His inheritance that already dwells in us. As we leave the natural realm and enter the spiritual realm, a new revelation begins to shift our current paradigm as we redefine our identity in Him. The things we have known and read in the Bible are now becoming a reality to us, so we can understand that God has truly "blessed us in Christ with every spiritual (*given by the Holy Spirit*) blessing in the heavenly realm!"[219]

Every spiritual blessing has already been given to us "(*so that you can know and understand*) what is the immeasurable and unlimited and surpassing greatness of His power in and for us who believe, as demonstrated in the working of His mighty strength."[220] Only in the spiritual realm can we come to know and understand the spiritual blessings that have already been given to us in the heavenly realm. They cannot be understood through our physical senses in the natural realm.

In chapter three, we imagined the heavenly realm as a room in our house. In review, we pretended that we were in the family

---

[218] Sean Smith, Sanctifying Your Imagination, 3 CD Set, Disc #3
[219] Ephesians 1:3 AMP
[220] Ephesians 1:19 AMP

room of our basement. In addition, we said that our spiritual blessings were upstairs in our living room. In that light, we asked the question, "Where do we have to go in order to receive our inheritance?"

To which we answered, "We would have to get up and leave the family room of our basement and go upstairs into our living room to see and possess our spiritual blessings!" This allows us to conclude that oftentimes when we cannot see and possess our spiritual blessings, it is because we are in the wrong room!

God demonstrated His mighty strength to overcome every authority in the natural realm that opposed us with His authority in the spiritual realm, "which He exerted in Christ when He raised Him from the dead and seated Him at His (*own*) right hand in the heavenly (*places*)."[221] A word study shows that the phrase "seated Him at His own right hand" represents fellowship, acceptance, favor, inheritance, authority, power and dominion. Jesus Christ sits at the right hand of the Father. It is the highest place of authority, power and dominion:

> Far above all rule and authority and power and dominion and every name that is named (*above every title that can be conferred*), not only in this age and in this world, but also in the age and the world which are to come.[222]

The substance of the Father was already given to Jesus as a result of their union of fellowship, acceptance, favor, inheritance, authority, power and dominion. Then, based on His finished work, Jesus took possession of everything that was already given to Him, as the Father established His authority above

---

[221] Ephesians 1:20 AMP
[222] Ephesians 1:21 AMP

all other authority, and "put all things under His feet and has appointed Him the universal and supreme Head of the church (*a headship exercised throughout the church*),"[223] when He was seated in heavenly places.

Jesus takes all the authority and power that was been given to Him and releases it to those called the church, "which is His body, the fullness of Him who fills all in all (*for in that body lives the full measure of Him who makes everything complete, and who fills everything everywhere with Himself*)."[224] So the fullness of the substance of Christ's authority, power and dominion is in His body, as a result of all that Jesus has already given to us through our union of fellowship, acceptance, favor, inheritance, authority, power and dominion, in the same way that Jesus received all that was already given to Him by the Father!

HIS INHERITANCE IN US

Many Christians do not have a revelation of all that Christ did for us on the cross and through His resurrection from the dead. Often we do not have a full understanding of Christ, and we do not have a full understanding of who we are in Christ. All authority, power, and dominion have already been given to us. It is not just something we are going to receive at a time in the future.

WHEN WE GAVE OUR LIVES TO JESUS CHRIST,

He made us alive together in fellowship and in union with Christ; (*He gave us the very life of Christ Himself, the same new life with which He quickened Him, for*) it is by grace

---

[223] Ephesians 1:22 AMP
[224] Ephesians 1:23 AMP

(*His favor and mercy which you did not deserve*) that you are saved (*delivered from judgment and made partakes of Christ's salvation*).[225]

Our spirit was quickened to life with the exact same substance and life of Christ Himself. It wasn't a "copy" or a "part" of His substance and life, but it was the very same new life as when Christ Himself was quickened from the dead! The phrase "made us alive" is past tense. It already happened at a time in the past when you received Christ as Savior. It's not something that we are going to receive in the future based on our own efforts and accomplishments. It was by grace!

Grace is not just the mercy, but it's also favor. It's the mercy of forgiveness that we did not deserve, but it's also the favor for a future that we did not deserve. It's time to quit living in part of His grace and to start living in the fullness of His grace! We aren't just forgiven from our past, but we have received power to accomplish our destiny! Instead of getting what we deserve, we get what He deserves!

Sin, sickness, poverty, fear, failure and death no longer have authority over us in Christ. We were delivered from judgment to partake in Christ's salvation at a time in the past. We've already received all the power, authority and dominion we need for our safety, deliverance, protection, healing, preservation, success and anything else we need to walk in the fruition of His promises. It's all because:

He raised us up together with Him and made us sit down together (*giving us joint seating with Him*) in the heavenly

---

[225] Ephesians 2:5 AMP

sphere (*by virtue of our being*) in Christ Jesus (*the Messiah, the Anointed One*).[226]

The phrase "raised us together with" is translated as the Greek word *sunegeiro*. It means "to rouse from death, to revivify spiritually in resemblance to being raised up together, or to rise with."[227]

The meaning is more literally "raised up together," the pronoun "Him" being added to indicate it was with Jesus we were raised up with. In a secular sense it means "waking up together." Believers do not just receive life, but experience resurrection life in Christ! Practically, this truth means that we now can walk in His resurrection power. The aorist tense of this verb indicates that this co-resurrection is a past completed event.

"Believers are in a solemn, binding, indissoluble covenant with Christ and so are eternally in union with Him and identified with Him. When He died, we died. When He was buried, we were buried. When He was raised up, we were raised up. When He was seated at the right hand of our Father, we were seated at the right hand of our Father in heaven."[228]

The phrase "made us sit down together" is translated as the Greek word *sugathizo*. It means "to give or take a seat in company with and to be a partaker of afflictions."[229] Again, "Paul uses the aorist tense, which here speaks of a past completed action. Paul is so certain of this grand truth that he records it as if it has already occurred! So certain of every Word of God, every promise! Why are we so often, so prone to wonder, so little in

[226] Ephesians 2:6 AMP
[227] Strong's Exhaustive Concordance, Reference 4891
[228] Ephesians 2:6-7, Search by Verse or Phrase:, Whole Bible — OT NT — Law History Wisdom Major Prophets Minor Prophets, Wednesday, November 7, 2007, 12:08 GMT
[229] Strong's Exhaustive Concordance, Reference 4776

our faith? So, with the eyes of faith we see that this seating with Christ has occurred, even if we, from our finite human perspective, cannot fully comprehend its practical import."[230]

We have already been "raised up together" with Him. Christ has already "made us sit down together" with Him at a time in the past. No amount of work on our part will help us to accomplish the things that He has already completed on our behalf. We have already been raised up with Him and we have already been seated with Him!

In addition, the phrase "raised up together" is defined as actually partaking in the raising of another, in the same way that the phrase "made us sit together" is defined as actually partaking in the seating of another.

Jesus literally made us to share in His accomplishments. It is not a future event. It already happened at a time in the past. It is a part of the inheritance that we have already received. He made us to sit down together with Him, giving us joint seating with Him in heavenly places. On the throne next to the Father sits Jesus Christ, and we sit in Him!

It is important to understand that we will never be any more raised or seated with Christ than we are right now! Jesus is the head and we are the body of Christ, seated together at the right hand of the Father in a place of fellowship, acceptance, and power operating in the exact same authority!

It is not just the Head of Jesus Christ that is seated on the throne next to the Father. The Head of Jesus is connected to the body of Christ called the church. We are the body of Christ

[230] Ephesians 2:6-7, Search by Verse or Phrase:, Whole Bible — OT NT — Law History Wisdom Major Prophets Minor Prophets, Wednesday, November 7, 2007, 12:08 GMT

seated in the heavenly realms. We cannot see it in the natural realm because it exists in the spiritual realm. The authority, power and dominion to change the natural realm all exist in the spiritual realm!

JACOB'S DREAM

Our authority in Christ originates in the spiritual realm. Many Christians use Jacob's ladder as a reference today to illustrate how we as believers can receive revelation in the spirit from heaven in order to bring it back to manifest in the natural on earth. Jacob had come to a certain place and, while staying the night, he had a prophetic dream "that there was a ladder set up on the earth, and the top of it reached to heaven; and the angels of God were ascending and descending on it."[231] Throughout the Bible angels are ministers and messengers of God. They minister and deliver messages to people from God. In other words, they were often used to deliver the revelation of God to His people.

In his dream, Jacob saw a ladder that was set upon the earth and extended into the heavenly realm, with the messengers of God ascending and descending upon it.

> And behold the Lord stood over and beside him and said, I am the Lord, the God of Abraham your father (*forefather*) and the God of Isaac; I will give to you and to your descendants the land on which you are lying.[232]

Until this moment Jacob was still trying to accomplish his own agenda in his own strength. Now he received a revelation from heaven confirming the promises of God to his forefathers to be

[231] Genesis 28:12 AMP
[232] Genesis 28:13 AMP

accomplished through him. When Jacob woke up from his sleep, he said, "Surely the Lord is in this place and I did not know it."[233]

Jacob's heart and destiny changed in a moment as he began to trust in a newly found relationship resulting in faith to trust that God would manifest in the natural the revelation that he had received from the messengers of the spiritual realm. His revelation of God and His promises brought him to a place of awe and reverence, saying, "This is none other than the house of God, and this is the gateway to heaven."[234]

It's this verse that many Christians quote and use to pray for an open heaven. This is an old covenant verse that serves as a prophetic type. We are living in the new covenant! We are no longer living in the old covenant! The veil was already torn! His spirit lives inside of me. I can receive revelation anytime and anywhere, which means that everywhere I walk is an open heaven!

> Jesus told Nathaniel in John 1 by word of knowledge that he had just seen him sitting under the fig tree. That represented that Nathaniel was under the old Jewish covenant. Amazed at this prophetic word, Nathaniel immediately believed in Jesus. Jesus essentially said you believe just because I had a word of knowledge? He said to Nathaniel, "I tell you the truth, you shall see Heaven open and the angels of God ascending and descending on the Son of Man."[235]

[233] Genesis 28:16 AMP
[234] Genesis 28:17 AMP
[235] John Crowder, Mystical Union (Santa Cruz, CA: Sons of Thunder Ministries & Publications, 2010), 122

Jesus is saying here that He is not simply a prophet. Don't be mesmerized by visions or words of knowledge. Even a psychic can get those. Jesus is saying, I am more than a prophet. He said I am Jacob's Ladder. That the angels move up and down on Him. Jesus was saying I am Open Heavens.[236]

You have Jacob's Ladder living inside of you right now! Your belly is an international airport for angels. Open Heavens is a person.[237]

ROCK OF REVELATION

One of the reasons we need to receive revelation from heavenly places is so we can see the promises of God manifest in our lives, just like Jacob did. The other reason is to protect us from the attacks of the enemy that could keep us from experiencing these promises.

For we are not wrestling with flesh and blood (*contending only with physical opponents*), but against the despotisms, against the powers, against (*the master spirits who are*) the world rulers of this present darkness, against the spirit forces of wickedness in the heavenly (*supernatural*) sphere.[238]

Our struggle is not in the natural realm. We can try to make it about the natural realm, but would never learn to overcome the battles we face on a day-to-day basis. We can live our entire lives getting beat up in the natural because we did not learn to fight in the spiritual. We have to equip ourselves with revelation from the spiritual realm to live effectively in the natural realm. The battles

[236] John Crowder, Mystical Union (Santa Cruz, CA: Sons of Thunder Ministries & Publications, 2010), 122
[237] Ibid
[238] Ephesians 6:12 AMP

we have been fighting are not against people or circumstances. They are against demonic forces called principalities, powers, and master spirits who are the world rulers of this present darkness, and spiritual forces in the heavenly supernatural sphere.

Notice that the above Scripture says that these demonic forces also live in a place called the heavenly realm. Obviously this means that there are going to be struggles in this life that are impossible for us to overcome in the natural, just like Joshua and the Israelites in the promised land preparing for the impossible battle Jericho. If the forces that oppose us live in the spiritual realm and we live in the natural ream, then we are going to have to learn how to operate in the spiritual realm if we are ever going to experience the promises of God for ourselves.

> (*The purpose is*) that through the church the complicated, many-sided wisdom of God in all its infinite variety and innumerable aspects might now be made known to the angelic rulers and authorities (*principalities and powers*) in the heavenly sphere.[239]

Christ already gave us the victory and ability to live the abundant life. He already gave us all dominion and authority, but it does not really work in the natural realm. Our authority in Christ originates in the spiritual realm. We will never know what is opposing us unless we use our spiritual senses in the spiritual realm. We will continue to live east of the Jordan, unable to experience for ourselves the manifestation of His promises!

Matthew 16:13-16 says, "When Jesus went into the region of Caesarea Philippi, He asked His disciples, Who do people say that the Son of Man is? And they answered, Some say John the Baptist;

---

[239] Ephesians 3:10 AMP

others say Elijah; and others Jeremiah or one of the prophets. He said to them, But who do you (*yourselves*) say that I am? Simon Peter replied, You are the Christ, the Son of the living God."[240]

It's here that we begin reviewing our discussion from chapter one, where Jesus told Peter, "Blessed (*happy, fortunate, and to be envied*) are you, Simon Bar-Jonah. For flesh and blood (*men*) have not revealed this to you, but My Father who is in heaven."[241] Peter had not received this understanding of Jesus' identity through the natural realm but by revelation given to him by the Father in the spiritual realm. And Jesus continues, "on this rock (*Greek, petra–a huge rock like Gilbraltar*) I will build My church, and the gates of Hades (*the powers of the infernal region*) shall not overpower it (*or be strong to its detriment or hold against it*)."[242]

Jesus says that He is going to build His church on this rock. He was speaking about building His church on the rock of revelation! Not only is He going to build His church on the rock of revelation, but the gates of hell will not be able to prevail against it! On the other hand, the antithesis is also true that without revelation the gates of hell will prevail against it.

The church that Jesus was talking about was not a building. It was the people who are the called out by His name. So if you and I are the church, then our ability to prevail in the natural realm against the gates of hell will be determined by our ability to obtain revelation in the spiritual realm through our relationship with Him!

As a result of our union with Christ resulting in revelation, He gives us His authority followed by instructions on how to use it, saying:

---

[240] Matthew 16:13-16 AMP
[241] Matthew 16:17 AMP
[242] Matthew 16:18 AMP

I will give you the keys of the kingdom of heaven; and whatever you bind (*declare to be improper and unlawful*) on earth must be what is already bound in heaven; and whatever you loose (*declare lawful*) on earth must be what is already loosed in heaven.[243]

BINDING AND LOOSING ORIGINATE IN HEAVEN

Notice that it says we are only able to bind or loose things on earth that have already been bound or loosed in heaven. The authority, power, and dominion to bind or loose something on earth originate with revelation about the things that have already been bound and loosed in heaven. We are only able to bind and loose things in the natural realm by agreeing with those things that have already been bound and loosed in the spiritual realm.

All authority, power, and dominion over the natural realm originate in the spiritual realm. We exercise our authority by receiving revelation in order to see it manifested in the earth to change the circumstances in our lives. If we can see the spiritual blessings that God has given us in the spiritual realm, we will be able to live in faith to loose and receive His promises for our life. On the other hand, if we cannot see how the enemy is trying to oppose us in heavenly places, we will not be able to pray proactively to bind the enemy from having authority over the natural circumstances of our life. We would be left to praying reactively over our natural circumstances, allowing the enemy to paralyze us from experiencing the fullness of His promises.

Only in the spiritual realm can we receive revelation to uncover the source of our battles before they are able to manifest in the natural. This allows us to exercise our authority, power and

[243] Matthew 16:19 AMP

dominion in Him so we can bind and loose things in the natural realm, so we can experience those things that have already been given to us. This is all while avoiding the wounds and carnage often suffered in the battle of the natural realm.

UNCOVERING REVELATION

In the natural realm we are blinded to the spiritual realm. Our natural physical senses cannot help us to see into the Spirit to understand and receive the reality of His spiritual blessings in heavenly places.

> But even if our Gospel (*the glad tidings*) also be hidden (*obscured and covered up with a veil that hinders the knowledge of God*), it is hidden (*only*) to those who are perishing and obscured (*only*) to those who are spiritually dying and veiled (*only*) to those who are lost. For the god of this world has blinded the unbelievers' minds (*that they should not discern the truth*), preventing them from seeing the illuminating light of the Gospel of the glory of Christ (*the Messiah*), who is the Image and Likeness of God.[244]

The good news of the spiritual realm can only be revealed by the Spirit! It is hidden from the physical senses of our flesh, so that our soul cannot receive the reality of the heavenly realm! Unless a person is spiritually born again, they do not even have a spirit to perceive the things of the Spirit. The word hidden in this passage is the Greek word *kalupto*. It means "to cover up, cover, or hide."[245]

---

[244] 2 Corinthians 4:3-4 AMP
[245] Strong's Exhaustive Concordance, Reference 2572

The Greek for *revelation* is the exact opposite word *apokalupto*. It means "to take off the cover, disclose, or reveal."[246] "The cover up is what Satan does; the uncovering is what God does."[247] Experiencing the promises of God in our life is a result of revelation being received through a spiritual relationship activated in prayer by the Holy Spirit. He takes off the cover that blinds us in order to disclose and reveal heaven's blueprint in us, allowing us to receive the abundant life which the gates of hell cannot prevail against.

BREAD FOR US

When Caleb was getting ready to go into the promised land to face the battle with Jericho, he stood up and said, do not "fear the people of the land, for they are bread for us. Their defense and the shadow (*of protection*) is removed from over them, but the Lord is with us. Fear them not."[248] After eighty-five years Caleb was still walking in faith with the Lord. He had been no stranger to opposition, spending forty years wandering in the wilderness. He had continued to trust God at His Word through relationship, resulting in revelation in the spiritual realm to overcome the appearance of his circumstances in the natural realm. Every battle had caused him to grow stronger through a relationship that allowed him to see heaven's perspective over earth's perspective. Instead of seeing the battle in the natural, Caleb saw provision in the supernatural.

In the midst of facing an impossible battle, we will either allow revelation of our union to draw us closer in relationship

[246] Strong's Exhaustive Concordance, Reference 602
[247] Sean Smith, Prophetic Evangelism (Shippensburg, PA: Destiny Image Publishers Inc, 2004), 123
[248] Numbers 14:9 AMP

to God to possess the promised land, or we will run away from Him, forgetting our identity back at the east side of the Jordan. It is easy to get depressed over the appearance of our natural circumstances, living in disillusionment land. We must allow the opposition in our lives to drive us back into relationship with Holy Spirit resulting in revelation of our identity in Him. Only then can He take us into the spiritual realm of solution land to see His provision for our problems in the natural realm.

Just like Caleb, God wants to help us see our battles as opportunities that provide for our promises in Him. How else will we learn to be people who overcome if we never learn to overcome the battles that oppose us? There are battles that we have to fight in the promised land, but God has already equipped us with everything necessary in the spiritual realm to make us victorious. We have already overcome at a time in the past by the blood of the Lamb. We must quit relying on our strengths and abilities to overcome in the natural realm, and begin to rest in His accomplishments in the spiritual realm to overcome. Then no weapon formed against us will prosper! Instead, every weapon formed against us, will become bread for us!

CHAPTER 6

HIS SUPERNATURAL DNA IN YOU

IN MAY OF 2004, I CALLED MY STEPFATHER just before the fifth anniversary of my mom's death, a result of a long struggle with lung cancer. I was surprised to learn that he was selling the house and was having a garage sale that weekend to sell most of the contents within the home. I asked, "Are there any things of my mom's that are going to be sold?"

He named a few things and told me that I was welcome to come and take anything I wanted in memory of my mom. Although it was short notice, I knew this would be the last opportunity to receive any sentimental items before they were sold to strangers, never to be recovered again. I made plans that day to drive from Bozeman, Montana, to Seattle, Washington, with my daughter, Jordan, over the Memorial Day weekend.

While we were in Seattle, my stepfather asked Jordan and me to go with him to visit my mother's gravesite on the anniversary day of her death to honor her memory with flowers. It was the first time that Jordan had ever been to a cemetery. As a result, she began to ask a lot of questions about cemeteries, graves, and death. Her mom and I had always told her that when we die we go to live with Jesus in heaven as a result of accepting Him into our hearts as Lord and Savior. After pondering the idea of visiting her grandma at a cemetery for a few moments, Jordan asked me a profound question, "How can my grandma be in a grave if she is supposed to be in heaven?"

I tried the best I could to explain in five-year-old terms that "When we die, our bodies are buried in the ground, which is called a grave, while our spirit and our soul go to heaven to live with God. Our bodies are just houses for our spirit and soul. Our soul is the part of us that thinks, feels, and makes decisions. Our spirit is put in us by God when we receive Jesus into our heart."

"Then the Bible says Jesus is going to come back someday and get all of our old bodies out of the graves and transform them into new bodies for us to live in heaven." Her response to my profound theological breakdown was, "Oh!" Then she said, "Dad, do you think that we could talk about something else now?"

SPIRIT, SOUL, AND BODY

The apostle Paul explains it much better:

But I tell you this, brethren, flesh and blood cannot (*become partakers of eternal salvation and*) inherit or share in the kingdom of God; nor does the perishable (*that which is decaying*) inherit or share in the imperishable (*the immortal*). Take notice! I tell you a mystery (*a secret truth, an event decreed by the hidden purpose of the counsel of God*). We shall not fall asleep (*in death*), but we shall all be changed (*transformed*) in a moment, in the twinkling of an eye, at the (*sound of the*) last trumpet call. For a trumpet will sound, and the dead (*in Christ*) will be raised imperishable (*free and immune from decay*), and we shall be changed (*transformed*).[249]

Paul began by telling us we cannot receive eternal life through the means of flesh and blood. But notice the phrase within this same verse as he continued his thought, "nor does the perishable inherit or share in the imperishable."[250] In other words, we cannot receive eternal life or any other attributes of our salvation through the imperishable of natural means. The antithesis is also true. We receive eternal life and all of the other attributes of salvation through the means of an imperishable spirit. Our spiritual inheritance cannot be received in the perishable realm of flesh and blood but only in the imperishable realm of soul and spirit.

If we were only flesh and blood that would be impossible, but the Bible says that we have been designed by God into three distinct categories called spirit, soul, and body. In 1 Thessalonians 5:23 the apostle Paul prays,

> And may the God of peace Himself sanctify you through and through (*separate you from the profane things, make you pure and wholly consecrated to God*); and may your spirit and soul, and body be preserved sound and complete (*and found*) blameless at the coming of our Lord Jesus Christ (*the Messiah*).[251]

The Greek word for *spirit* here is *pneuma*. It means "God, Christ's Spirit, and Holy Spirit."[252] It is the supernatural divine

---

[249] 1 Corinthians 15:50-52 AMP
[250] 1 Corinthians 15:50 AMP
[251] 1 Thessalonians 5:23 AMP
[252] Strong's Exhaustive Concordance, Reference 4151

substance of God assimilated into a person at conversion, giving them a spirit to be acted upon by the Spirit of God.[253] In other words, the Spirit of Christ was made alive in us so we could have direct relationship with Him, resulting in communication by revelation through our union with Holy Spirit.

The Greek word for *soul* here is *psuche*. It comes from a derivative meaning "breath," by implication spirit in relation to the animal sentiment only. It is distinguished from another derivative in being the rational, immortal soul. Another derivative defines it as mere vitality as with plants. The terms correspond respectively to the Hebrew terms heart, life, mind, soul, us, and you.[254]

It is the inferior part of a person's mental nature giving place to the passions and desires of their natural propensities.[255] It is the part of us that includes our mind, will, and emotions. Our "mind" gives us the ability to process the information we receive through our thoughts, reason, and logic to shape the way we think about ideas, people, and the world we live in. Our "will" allows us to make decisions and determine our actions based on information we process with our minds. Our "emotions" allow us to have feelings about our different thoughts and experiences.

The Greek word for *body* here is *soma*. It means "bodily form or slave."[256] It is the corporeal frame.[257] Our body is the house of our souls and spirit containing everything that gives us our identity as individuals. It has five senses known as the gates to

[253] The Pulpit Commentary, Volume 21 (Peabody, MA: Hendrickson Publishers, 1961), 106

[254] Strong's Exhaustive Concordance, Reference 5590

[255] The Pulpit Commentary, Volume 21 (Peabody, MA: Hendrickson Publishers, 1961), 106

[256] Strong's Exhaustive Concordance, Reference 4983

[257] The Pulpit Commentary, Volume 21 (Peabody, MA: Hendrickson Publishers, 1961), 106

our soul, called sight, sound, touch, taste, and smell. It gives us all the information we need in order to function in our daily lives.

The Bible says that before we knew Jesus Christ as our Savior we "were dead in trespasses."[258] Paul is referring to our pre-Christian status, in which our spirit was dead or non-existent! Our body and our soul were alive, but our spirit was dead. We were handicapped in our ability to discern and make spiritual decisions about our lives and the world around us.

Our bodies collected information from the natural world through our five senses in order to process it with our soul. In our mind we processed the information we received through the physical senses of our bodies to determine the way that we thought about ideas, people, and the natural world. In the same way, our emotions would process the information we received through the senses of our bodies to determine the way we felt about the ideas, people, and world around us.

Then we would use our will to make the daily, practical decisions in our life based on the perceptions we had formed from our thoughts and feelings, from information we had already received. So God in His great mercy,

> Because of and in order to satisfy the great and wonderful and intense love with which He loved us, even when we were dead (*slain*) by (*our own*) trespasses, He made us alive together in fellowship and in union with Christ; (*He gave us the very life of Christ Himself, the same new life with which He quickened Him, for*) it is by grace (*His favor and mercy which you did not deserve*) that you are saved (*delivered from judgment and made partakers of Christ's salvation*).[259]

[258] Colossians 2:13 AMP
[259] Ephesians 2:4-5 AMP

When a person receives Jesus Christ, at the very moment of receiving Christ he is immediately made alive in Christ. That spiritual life comes back within him...The Greek word for "made alive" is *suzoopoieo*. It comes from two Greek words, *sun*, which means "together with," and *zoopoieo*, which means "to make alive or to quicken." It is an aorist indicative active which means "at a certain point in time.

In other words, the very moment I bowed down and received Jesus into my life, immediately I was made alive with Christ. What does it mean to be made alive together with Christ? Jesus rose from the dead, completely and wholly arose from the dead. Jesus now has given us as complete resurrection from a life of sin to a life of righteousness as His body had being raised from the dead.[260]

In chapter five we learned Christ put His Spirit in us through salvation and, "He raised us up together with Him and made us sit down together (*giving us joint seating with Him*) in the heavenly sphere (*by virtue of our being*) in Christ Jesus (*the Messiah, the Anointed One*)."[261] These events were already accomplished for us at a time in the past, and nothing else can be added or taken away from their completion. We literally shared together in the actual spiritual events of Christ's resurrection from the dead, seated together with Him in the heavenly sphere.

How is that possible? Christ put the same Spirit that was in Him in us during our conversion experience. The same Spirit

[260] Dr. Wayne Barber, Ephesians 2:4-6: The Marvelous Grace of Our Loving Lord-Part 2, Friday October 19, 2007, 9:22pm GMT 143k, http://preceptaustin.org/new_page_12.htm
[261] Ephesians 2:6 AMP

that was present in Christ to quicken Him to life from the dead now resides in us. The same Spirit present in Christ when He was seated at the right hand of the Father in the heavenly sphere now resides in us. His spirit did not reside in us before we had received salvation. Our spirit that was dead or non-existent was made alive in us by His Spirit when we became born again.

SPIRITUAL DNA

A Pharisee named Nicodemus came to Jesus in John 3:

Rabbi, we know and are certain that You have come from God (as) a Teacher; for no one can do these signs (these wonderworks, these miracles–and produce the proofs) that You do unless God is with him.[262]

Nicodemus knew that the things Jesus had been teaching and doing could not be performed through the flesh and blood of a natural man. He knew that it must be from God, but it was still a mystery he was unable to comprehend. So here we find Nicodemus trying to ask Jesus about the source of His supernatural abilities.

We know that he was trying to ask a deeper question, because in the next verse it says,

Jesus answered him, I assure you, most solemnly I tell you, that unless a person is born again (anew, from above), he cannot ever see (know, be acquainted with, and experience) the kingdom of God.[263]

The Greek word for born in this passage is gennao. It means "to procreate, to regenerate, bear, beget, bring forth, conceive,

---

[262] John 3:2 AMP
[263] John 3:3 AMP

WHEN WE BECOME BORN AGAIN, GOD GIVES US HIS SUPERNATURAL DNA BY IMPARTING HIS GENES AND HIS SEED INTO OUR SPIRITUAL MAKEUP.

be delivered of, gender, make, and offspring."[264] It is the word in which we get the word *genes*. The Greek word for *again* here is *anothen*. It means "from above, from the first, anew, from the beginning, very first, and the top."[265] It is the word in which we derive the words spore, spora, and seed. So when we become born again, God gives us His supernatural DNA by imparting His genes and His seed into our spiritual makeup.

In the natural, our DNA is the blueprint that patterns our looks and behavior after our natural parents. In the same way, when we become born again, our spiritual DNA gives us the blueprint that patterns after our spiritual Father, in order for us to be conformed to His image. Our spirit which was dead is now born anew. The Holy Spirit sealed our nature and destiny through the supernatural DNA of our Father in us.

Consequently, from now on we estimate and regard no one from a (*purely*) human point of view (in terms of natural standards of value). (*No*) even though we once did estimate Christ from a human viewpoint and as a man, yet now (*we have such knowledge of Him that*) we know Him no longer (*in terms of the flesh*).[266]

When a man and a woman produce a baby, the seed of a man is planted in a woman, producing new life. What did not

[264] Strong's Exhaustive Concordance, Reference 1080
[265] Strong's Exhaustive Concordance, Reference 509
[266] 2 Corinthians 5:16 AMP

exist before now exists! Out of nothing something is created! The natural here is a parallel of what happened by the Spirit. When we gave our lives to Jesus Christ He placed His seed from above in us, making what was dead or nonexistent, alive in us.

Therefore if any person is (*ingrafted*) in Christ (*the Messiah*) he is a new creation (*a new creature altogether*); the old (*previous moral and spiritual condition*) has passed away. Behold, the fresh and new has come![267]

We became a new creation, born anew from above. We serve a God who is able to do more than turn the impossible to possible. We serve a creative God who turns nothing into something!

For neither is circumcision (*now*) of any importance, nor uncircumcision, but (*only*) a new creation (*the result of a new birth and a new nature in Christ Jesus the Messiah*).[268]

Nicodemus still could not grasp what Jesus was talking about, so he said, "How can a man be born when he is old? Can he enter his mother's womb again and be born?"[269] In the natural this would seem to be a logical question, but Jesus was talking about the spiritual realm in this passage and not the natural realm. Obviously, Nicodemus had no grid whatsoever for understanding the spiritual realm.

So Jesus clarified His point further, saying,

Unless a man is born of water and (*even*) the Spirit, he cannot (*ever*) enter the kingdom of God. What is born of (*from*) the flesh is flesh (*of the physical is physical*); and what is born of the Spirit is spirit.[270]

---

[267] 2 Corinthians 5:17
[268] Galatians 6:15 AMP
[269] John 3:4 AMP
[270] John 3:5-6 AMP

In simple terms, Jesus was telling Nicodemus that for us to enter the Kingdom of God it will take more than our substance in the natural realm. It will take more than our natural understanding concerning our information about God. It takes a supernatural birth of the Spirit in our lives that transcends our natural understanding to receive our spiritual blessings in heavenly places. It requires a spiritual birth based on revelation to give us His heart in order to make us supernatural children of a supernatural Father.

I'M NOT GOOD ENOUGH

Two weeks ago our family took a vacation back to the greater Seattle area where I grew up. We had hoped to get together with my stepfather while we were in the area, to ask him once again to receive Jesus Christ into his life as Savior. We were feeling an urgency concerning his salvation since he had been diagnosed with congestive heart failure in addition to having five heart attacks, including three that had occurred within the last nine months.

It was the day before our vacation was going to end and I had still been unable to reach my stepfather by phone. So we decided to stop by his trailer that morning to ask him if we could take him to breakfast. He was not home, so we decided to continue with our own breakfast plans as a family. After breakfast, my wife was not feeling well and we were all a little weary from a week of traveling, so we decided to go back to the place where we were staying to rest for the day.

On the way back we felt led to stop by my stepfather's trailer one last time. This time he happened to be home. We asked him to go have a cup of coffee with us at McDonald's so our children could entertain themselves in PlayPlace while we talked. As we sat and had coffee, I began to share the gospel with my stepfather once again. In response, he began to share with my wife all the reasons he felt he could not accept Jesus Christ as his Savior.

It did not appear that he was any closer to receiving Christ than at any of the other times I had witnessed to him over the last twenty-two years. He explained again that he did not see himself as the church-going type. So I responded to him by saying, "I'm not asking you to go to church! I am asking you what you're going to do with Jesus?"

Then from what appeared to be a place of vulnerability for him, he told us that he already believed in God. So I asked him, "Then what is stopping you from praying to receive Jesus Christ as your Savior?" Still feeling a level of shame that would not allow him to look at me, he basically responded by telling my wife that his behavior was not good enough to be a Christian. He continued to basically say that he would need to get his act together before God could accept him.

At this point I began praying in the spirit as my wife continued to listen to him share his heart. Something in the spiritual atmosphere began to shift as my wife shared about a conversation she had with our five-year-old daughter, Raegan, a couple of months before, when she had prayed to accept Jesus Christ as her Savior. My wife proceeded to tell him that she asked Raegan when she was going to be ready to receive Jesus Christ as her Savior. She continued to tell him about how Raegan's response had broken her heart when she had said, "I'm not good enough."

Finally, I told my stepfather, Jesus is not looking for you to get your act together in order for Him to accept you. He is not looking for you to be perfect. When you give your life to Jesus, then He gives you His heart, empowering you to get your act together. Again, I asked, "So what's keeping you from receiving Jesus Christ as your Savior?" He said, "I do not know how!"

I said, "It's very simple! All you have to do is ask Jesus to forgive you of your sins, to give you His heart, and to help you to live for Him." I told him, "I could lead you in prayer while you repeat after me, believing in your heart." Then, to my surprise, he agreed that he wanted to pray with me to accept Jesus Christ as his Savior, saying, "I'll pray with you when we get back to the trailer."

Back at my stepfather's trailer, I, along with my wife and children, led him in prayer as he gave His life to Jesus Christ! Then I asked my oldest daughter, Jordan, to lay hands on Grandpa Dave and pray that God would heal his body. When we were done praying, my stepfather said, "I never thought I would be converted!" Several minutes later he was saying, "I feel kind of weird." So my wife asked, "Is it a good weird or a bad weird?" He said, "It's a good weird!"

A NEW WAY OF LIFE

That Saturday afternoon my stepfather's spirit was transformed from being dead in his trespasses to being made alive, seated in Christ in heavenly places. Jesus said unless a person is born from the Spirit above, they "cannot ever see (*know, be acquainted with, and experience*) the Kingdom of God."[271] Many religious people think we need to change people's behavior to good before we can lead them to Christ. They spend more time telling them about all the things they should not be doing with their life.

---

[271] John 3:3 AMP

Often well-meaning Christians will tell them that they ought to quit smoking, drinking, or living in adultery and get right with God before they can receive Jesus Christ as their Savior. It is a stumbling block to salvation for the unbeliever!

The Bible says that we are to be preaching the good news, not the bad news. Sinners are supposed to be living in sin. If they were not they would not be sinners in need of grace. We need to see them receive Jesus as Savior before we can expect them to make Him Lord. We cannot change the heart of a person! As a matter of fact, the Bible tells us that no one can confess that Jesus Christ is Lord, except by Holy Spirit.

If we change the behavior of a sinner before allowing Jesus to exchange their heart with His heart, they will not have His identity. They will be pressured to conform from external pressure from others, rather than transformed by the internal government of Holy Spirit. That forces them to act and behave like someone they are not, rather than act and behave out of who they are! It's only a matter of time before they have to act like who they are!

Only Jesus can give them His heart by grace based on His works. So the behavior they manifest will be a reflection of their new identity, rather than performing with their own works to try to be something that they aren't. In the above verse, Jesus makes it clear that unless a person is born of the Spirit, they cannot even see into the reality of the spiritual realm to even know or be acquainted enough with the heart of Jesus to experience the manifestation of His heart and Kingdom for themselves.

The time at which we become born again is the time we begin our new life. As believers we are not just called to be born of the Spirit, we are called to continue to live in and by the Spirit.

It's a new identity with a new way of living! We are no longer called to live solely on the information we receive through our physical senses. We are called to develop, train, and exercise our spiritual senses through a life of relationship in union with Holy Spirit resulting in revelation to see, know, be acquainted with, and experience the manifestation of the things that we believe about the Kingdom of God in our daily lives.

It is through the birth of our relationship with the spirit realm that we receive the substance and source of the DNA of our Father. So we can release our identity, authority, and inheritance as God's children in order to see the Kingdom of God come through us on earth as it is in heaven. Our spirit is different than our soul in that it is already perfect when we receive it. It's the perfection of God living inside of us. That allows us to live in perfect union with Him sanctifying our mind, will, and emotions as we are diffused with revelation by our relationship with Holy Spirit. We wait in expectation to receive our new bodies as our old bodies are transformed at the return of Jesus Christ!

The practical reality is that we were made whole through restoration in Him, allowing our spirit, soul, and body to function together as intended in the original created order. We are reconciled to relationship with Him through our union with Holy Spirit, resulting in a new nature that has the ability to receive revelation from the spiritual realm. We are no longer limited to the information we receive through our physical senses. As born again believers, we continue to make all our decisions about life in the soul with all of the information that we receive through our natural senses, in addition to all of the revelation that we receive through our spiritual senses.

TRAINING SPIRITUAL SENSES

In his book, *Prophetic Evangelism*, my friend Sean Smith puts it this way:

> Divine prescriptions flow when the walls of the outer man and the inner man are broken down and are no longer contrary. When there is unity between the outward man and that inward man...[272]

Our spirit has already been quickened to life, allowing us to discern the bondage breaking will of the Lord for our lives through the sanctification of our mind, will, and emotions. As we develop our spiritual senses we get to reconcile the spiritual with the natural by releasing our spiritual blessings from heavenly places into our natural circumstances on earth!

The apostle Paul addressed this issue of developing and training our spiritual senses in his letter to the Hebrew church:

> We have much to say which is hard to explain, since you have become dull in your (*spiritual*) hearing and sluggish (*even slothful in achieving spiritual insight*).[273]

He is speaking to believers in this passage who have been apathetic in developing their spiritual senses. They are born again, but they have failed to continue to train their spiritual senses through relationship with Holy Spirit resulting in spiritual insight known as revelation. Instead, they have continued to live their Christian life based solely on the information received through their physical senses. As a result, they have become spiritually dull, making it difficult for Paul to explain to

---

[272] Sean Smith, Prophetic Evangelism (Shippensburg, PA: Destiny Image Publishers Inc, 2004), 109
[273] Hebrews 5:11 AMP

them the spiritual realities that they need to grasp to live the abundant life.

Paul continued to point out their failure to grow and mature in the things of the Spirit, saying:

Even though by this time you ought to be teaching others, you actually need someone to teach you over again the very first principles of God's Word. You have come to need milk, not solid food.[274]

These people had been Christians for a long enough period of time that they should have been leading and instructing younger believers in their relationship with Holy Spirit, so they could receive revelation known as spiritual insight to apply with practical understanding. Instead, they needed someone who was mature to come and teach them a second time the very same elementary principles of God's Word which they should have learned in the first place. We know that they were taught once before, because Paul said, "You actually need someone to teach you over again."[275]

In the natural, a baby starts off with a diet consisting of milk alone. As an infant begins to develop and mature through a healthy diet and exercise, they move on to more solid foods. In the same way, a new believer's diet begins with the basic, elementary principles of God's Word. As a new believer develops and matures, they begin to exchange their dietary needs from the elementary principles of God's Word to the revelation of it through relationship with Holy Spirit, while learning to exercise their spiritual senses.

---

[274] Hebrews 5:12 AMP
[275] Hebrews 5:12 AMP

On the other hand:

Everyone who continues to feed on milk is obviously in-experienced and unskilled in the doctrine of righteousness (*of conformity to the divine will in purpose, thought, and action*), for he is a mere infant (*not able to talk yet*)![276]

The implication is that just because you are a Christian does not mean that you are a mature believer in Christ. There is a big difference between growing older in Christ and growing up into maturity in Christ. We all know Christians who are older and yet still immature.

The Bible says:

Solid food is for full-grown men, for those whose senses and mental faculties are trained by practice to discriminate and distinguish between what is morally good and noble and what is evil and contrary either to divine or human law.[277]

Another translation of the Bible says that "solid food is for the mature."[278] The term solid food here represents the revelation received through the Spirit concerning His Word. The mature are those "whose senses and mental faculties are trained by practice."[279] The New King James Version says, "those who by reason of use have their senses exercised."[280] The word used here is also correctly translated as the word *habit*.

Our spiritual senses are developed in the same way that we develop our natural senses. They produce a seasoned maturity

---

[276] Hebrews 5:13 AMP
[277] Hebrews 5:14 AMP
[278] Hebrews 5:14 NIV
[279] Hebrews 5:14 AMP
[280] Hebrews 5:14 NKJV

in our lives as we continue to use and develop them on a regular, consistent basis in our lives. It is by keeping our spiritual senses tuned up that our spirit develops a sensitivity to perceive the things of the spiritual realm to influence our soul with a higher level of persuasion than the information we receive with our physical senses. If we do not exercise our spiritual senses, then they will remain spiritually undeveloped, leaving us in a state of spiritual infancy.

When my youngest daughter, Naomi, was learning to crawl and walk, she had to exercise the muscles in her body to get stronger. If she did not try to use her muscles to move, they would not develop so she'd continue to grow stronger. If she did not continue to grow stronger, she would not learn to crawl. If she did not learn to exercise her muscles through crawling, she would not continue to grow and mature to learn to walk.

The same thing is true for us in regard to the development of our spiritual senses. If we do not use and train our spiritual senses, then we will never grow up into a place of maturity in Christ so we can successfully "discriminate and distinguish between what is morally good and noble and what is evil and contrary either to divine or human law."[281] The NKJV reads, "to discern both good and evil."[282]

We learn to train and exercise our spiritual senses in relationship with Holy Spirit through our union in Him, so we can have wisdom and revelation diffused through our mind, will and emotions, allowing us to gain practical understanding to discern between good and evil in our soul! We apply the revelation received through our spiritual senses to the information received through our physical senses.

[281] Hebrews 5:14 AMP
[282] Hebrews 5:14 NKJV

It is to our advantage to keep our spiritual senses tuned up so they will influence our soul with a higher level of persuasion than our physical senses, noting that the previous Scripture makes reference to those things being good which support His new nature in us, and those things being evil which oppose our new nature in Him. This is so we don't forget who we are in Him, allowing the information received through our physical senses to betray us without the filter of revelation working within our soul to activate His thoughts, purposes and actions.

THE ANOINTING IN YOU

John says:

The anointing (*the sacred appointment, the unction*) which you received from Him abides (*permanently*) in you; (*so*) then you have no need that anyone should instruct you. But just as His anointing teaches you concerning everything and is true and is no falsehood, so you must abide in (*live in, never depart from*) Him (*being rooted in Him, knit to Him*), just as (*His anointing*) has taught you (*to do*).[283]

Why would John say this anointing that is in you is true? Why should you believe what you are sensing is really God speaking through you? What if it is not God? In the process of stepping out, you are going to find out what is and what is not God. You will never know by playing it safe.[284]

Christian maturity is not a result of our developed intellect based on all the information we have received from our physical

[283] 1 John 2:27 AMP
[284] Sean Smith, Prophetic Evangelism (Shippensburg, PA: Destiny Image Publishers Inc, 2004), 215

senses. Maturity is measured by the degree in which the mind, will, and emotions of our soul are controlled, possessed, and sanctified by the Spirit! Our spirit is always in contact with God, in addition to His anointing permanently abiding in us to help us develop our spiritual senses in relationship with Him. So we can learn to correctly discern within our soul those things that the spirit of God is incorporating into His plan for our life from those things that God is trying to separate from our lives in order to protect us in Him.

Knowing that "anointing is going to be on you. The Bible says that the anointing teaches you, it instructs you, it leads you, and it is true and not a lie.[285]

TAUGHT BY THE HOLY SPIRIT

In his first letter to the Corinthians, the apostle Paul said:

When we are among the full-grown (*spiritually mature Christians who are ripe in understanding*), we do impart a (*higher*) wisdom (*the knowledge of the divine plan previously hidden*).[286]

Spiritually mature Christians here were receiving a different level of impartation and revelation from the Spirit than those who were immature. They were receiving an impartation of revelation by the Spirit that could not be understood by information received through the physical senses. It was by the exercising of their spirit that they had learned how to receive:

Wisdom of God once hidden (*from the human understanding*) and now revealed to us by God — (*that wisdom*) which

---
[285] Sean Smith, Prophetic Evangelism (Shippensburg, PA: Destiny Image Publishers Inc, 2004), 215
[286] 1 Corinthians 2:6 AMP

God devised and decreed before the ages for our glorifi-
cation (*to lift us into the glory of His presence*).[287]

Without the spiritual senses that come as a result of being
born again of the Spirit, "none of the rulers of this age or world
perceived and recognized and understood this, for if they had,
they would never have crucified the Lord of glory."[288] They were
unable to understand that there was a realm of the spirit that
contained hidden revelation with authority and dominion over
all the information they had concerning the natural realm. More
importantly, they could not comprehend mankind being created
anew as a spiritual being that could be lifted into the glory of His
presence in order to receive this revelation to walk in the same
authority and dominion as Christ, so we would receive the keys
to the kingdom of heaven to bind on earth through revelation of
all that is bound in heaven and to loose on earth through revelation of all that is loosed in heaven. If they could have perceived
God's plan to take back and multiply His spiritual authority
through spiritual sons and daughters, then they would not have
crucified Jesus Christ.

In the natural realm:

Eye has not seen and ear has not heard and has not
entered into the heart of man, (*all that*) God has prepared
(*made and keeps ready*) for those who love Him (*who hold
Him in affectionate reverence, promptly obeying Him and
gratefully recognizing the benefits he has bestowed*).[289]

No natural eye has ever seen the spiritual realm containing
all of the promises that God has for those who love Him. No

---

[287] 1 Corinthians 2:7 AMP
[288] 1 Corinthians 2:8 AMP
[289] 1 Corinthians 2:9 AMP

natural ear has ever heard the voice of the spiritual realm declaring all of the benefits that He has bestowed upon His children. No natural uncircumcised heart has ever perceived the revelation of all that Christ accomplished on our behalf in the spiritual realm.

Only, "God has unveiled and revealed them by and through His Spirit, for the (*Holy*) Spirit searches diligently, exploring and examining everything, even sounding the profound and bottomless things of God (*the divine counsels and things hidden and beyond man's scrutiny*)."[290] The promises of God that have been prepared for those who love Him are only revealed by and received through the Holy Spirit. He is the only One who is able to search the spiritual realm to give revelation concerning the mysteries of God that are concealed from the physical senses of the natural realm.

> For what person perceives (*knows and understands*) what passes through a man's thoughts except the man's own spirit within him? Just so no one discerns (*comes to know and comprehend*) the thoughts of God, except the Spirit of God.[291]

In other words, no man without the Holy Spirit is able to comprehend in their soul the riches of His inheritance by the information received through the physical senses of our flesh. In addition, they do not even have a spirit to receive revelation from the spiritual realm.

Jesus told the religious teachers of His day that they were forever seeing, but never perceiving. They could see and comprehend the things that they saw in the natural realm, but they could not see or perceive the reality of the spiritual realm. On the other hand, our spirit quickened to life when we

[290] 1 Corinthians 2:10 AMP
[291] 1 Corinthians 2:11 AMP

became born again of the Spirit so we could receive revelation to comprehend the thoughts of all the things that the Spirit of God has made and keeps ready for us in the spiritual realm.

In this light, Paul exhorts the Corinthians to have spiritual eyes and ears. Then they could live according to revelation received through their spiritual senses rather than by information received through their physical senses, so they could experience the promises of God for their lives. In the same way, we could experience the promises of God for our lives by accessing our spiritual blessings in heavenly places, by activating our spiritual senses through reason of use in order to receive revelation in our soul to be manifested in our natural circumstances!

We cannot tangibly experience the promises of God with our natural understanding as a result of information received through our physical senses. We can only experience the promises God has made and keeps ready for us in the spiritual realm by His Spirit, which is already in us. In the natural, our physical senses gather information for us to process in our soul, shaping the way we think about our own success, as we form conclusions about things we must do and people we must be for us to be successful.

All the while, Holy Spirit is trying to get our attention through our spiritual senses to show us who He has already created us to be in Him. So we will not continue to make plans with our lives by the information we have received through our physical senses. The Spirit of God searches the mind of God for His thoughts about us, then brings them back to be diffused throughout our soul so we discern our true identity in Him!

In discovering our identity, we can live a life of agreement with heaven by aligning ourselves with the revelation given to us about the spiritual realm concerning His purposes, plans, and destinies for our lives. This is obviously a very different approach than telling God the things we intend to do with our lives without His input and expecting Him to bless it. When we get revelation from the spiritual realm about our identity in Him, nothing will be able to stand opposed to His blessings already in us!

Many Christians today do not know who they are in Christ! They have been the unfortunate victims of identity theft, knowing the enemy stole their identity and replaced it with a counterfeit image. So, unconsciously they are deceived into forsaking the deposited currency of heaven in them needed to experience their promised inheritance. As they continue to wrestle with who they are, it results in a continual struggle with what they do! As a result, they are not experiencing a revelation of His promises because God does not bless all things. He only blesses those things in which He is already a part!

Only the deep things of our spirit can understand the deep things of the Spirit of God. The reason is that:

> We have not received the spirit (*that belongs to*) the world, but the (*Holy*) Spirit who is from God, (*given to us*) that we might realize and comprehend and appreciate the gifts (*of divine favor and blessing so freely and lavishly*) bestowed on us by God.[292]

As born again believers, we have not received the spirit of this world; we have received the indwelling of the Holy Spirit who is always in contact with God. It gives us our ability to be connected relationally through our union with Holy Spirit as the Spirit searches the mind of God and communicates to our spirit through our spiritual senses, so we can receive revelation to appreciate and experience the gifts of divine favor and blessing

[292] 1 Corinthians 2:12 AMP

freely lavished upon us at a time in the past by God in the spiritual realm!

These spiritual realities are:
Not taught by human wisdom but taught by the (*Holy*) Spirit, combining and interpreting spiritual truths with spiritual language (*to those who possess the Holy Spirit*).[293]

When you became born again and filled with the Holy Spirit, you were given access to operate freely in the spiritual realm, where we are already seated together with Christ with all our spiritual blessings. You cannot learn this through the teaching of a man; you can only learn this through Holy Spirit. This doesn't mean there isn't value in teaching for us as believers. It does mean you need to exercise your spiritual senses in relationship with Holy Spirit so you can receive revelation about the information taught, in order to activate that which He already put in you!

We cannot see it with our natural eyes or hear it with our natural ears. The spiritual realm cannot be navigated by information taught with human wisdom. Only Holy Spirit is able to teach our soul how to combine, interpret and discern the information received through our physical senses and the revelation received through our spiritual senses, in order to see the promises of God manifest in our lives, because it is the spiritual realm that has dominion over the natural realm!

I DON'T HURT ANYMORE!

You have probably heard the saying, "They are so heavenly minded that they are no earthly good!" Many times believers can hear a message like the one in this book and think the same

---

[293] 1 Corinthians 2:13 AMP

thing. What they mean is that the person or message seems to be spiritual, but it's not practical, tangible, or useful to their everyday life, at which point I reply that this is the most practical and useful message you will ever hear in your life, and I proceed to tell them the following story.

On Memorial Day, 2007, my wife and I took our children to the family cabin to get away for the day. We were joined by my father and mother in-law, along with some other relatives. Our four girls love to visit the cabin several times a year to go fishing, camping, and just enjoy being together in the outdoors without the normal distractions of life. As usual, the girls could not wait to start the day off by fishing the brook that runs next to the cabin. They were having a great time when we decided to take a break to eat some lunch.

Most of the adults were still sitting at the table finishing their lunch while the children were playing throughout the cabin. All of a sudden I saw something pink falling through the air out of the corner of my eye, followed by the sound of a thud as it hit the ground. My mind began to comprehend what had happened as several of us jumped up from our seats to find my five-year-old daughter, Raegan, lying on the floor.

It was a parent's worst nightmare as I began to imagine all the horrible possibilities. She had fallen through the ladder entrance of the loft onto the right side of her head, neck and shoulder, from twelve feet up. My father-in-law, Brad, was the first one to arrive by her side, as my wife and I, along with my mother-in-law, Lynn, rushed to gather around her to see how badly she had been hurt. She seemed to be going into shock, and was unable to answer any questions; her eyes were rolling to the back of her head with her pupils extremely dilated.

It became obvious as we tried to assess the damage to her body that she had suffered severe head trauma in addition to several major injuries to the rest of her body. Brad began to pick her up in his arms, moving toward the door and saying, "We need to get her to a hospital right away."

As we were walking across the cabin to leave, Raegan started to show the first signs of emotion as she began crying and saying, "No, I do not want to go to the hospital." We responded by asking if she could tell us where it hurt. She told us that her head, neck, back, shoulders and legs were all hurting.

As we began to examine her complaints, we found that her arms and legs were limp and lifeless. We asked her if she thought she could move her arms or legs. She said, "No." We asked her if she thought she could walk. Again, she said, "No." So we told her that if she could not move her arms or legs, and was unable to walk, we were going to have to take her to the hospital. She began crying again, saying, "I do not want to go to the hospital."

Then I heard the Holy Spirit simply say, "Why don't you pray for her?" Wow! There is an idea! We took her to one of the beds in the cabin and laid her on it. Then we began to pray, "Raegan has already been healed by Your stripes. We thank You for already healing her head, neck, back, arms and legs. We thank You for loving Raegan and making her whole. We love You, and give You all the praise and glory for already healing Raegan."

When we were finished praying, Raegan began to move her arms and legs. She stood up off the bed and began to walk. We asked her if she still had any pain. She said, "No, I do not hurt anymore!" We never did take Raegan to the hospital that day. She spent the rest of the day playing as usual at the cabin. Jesus had already healed her from head to toe!

We got to experience the manifestation of a higher wisdom hidden from the physical senses in the natural realm. We were lifted into the glory of His presence to receive what no natural eye, ear, or heart has perceived, through the unveiling of the spiritual realm through our spiritual senses by Holy Spirit. His DNA in us was able to comprehend the divine favor of His healing and blessing so freely and lavishly bestowed on Raegan by God. The things that we believed about the spiritual realm manifested its dominion over the circumstances of our natural realm!

THE MIND OF CHRIST

It would have been easy for us to allow our physical senses to dominate the influence of our mind, will and emotions that day. All the information received through our physical senses told us that we needed to take our little girl to the hospital. Our will wanted to regain some type of control over the situation. Our emotions were flooded with worry as we felt unable to help our daughter. Our minds searched for a way to make sense of all that was happening in hopes of coming up with a reasonable solution to make it all better.

But that's not who we are! We have already been given the mind of Christ! Healing is already a part of our salvation! A promise already received! His Spiritual DNA has already been quickened to life in us, so our new nature as a spiritual man can dominate the influence of our soul by diffusing revelation into our mind, will and emotions. This is how I could hear Holy Spirit say, "Why don't you pray for her?"

Our spiritual senses were able to receive the revelation needed for us to see our daughter's healing manifested right before our eyes. If we'd been deceived into relying on our physical senses only, Raegan may have died or been paralyzed for life!

The apostle Paul says,

> The natural, nonspiritual man does not accept or welcome or admit into his heart the gifts and teaching and revelations of the Spirit of God, for they are folly (*meaningless nonsense*) to him; and he is incapable of knowing them (*of progressively recognizing, understanding, and becoming better acquainted with them*) because they are spiritually discerned and estimated and appreciated.[294]

The natural, non-spiritual man in this passage is referring to a person who is without Holy Spirit residing in them. He does not exist in them. They are not born of the Spirit, but have only been born of the flesh. As a result, they do not have any spiritual senses, and are incapable of perceiving and discerning the reality of the spiritual realm.

The things of the spirit are meaningless to the natural, non-spiritual man because he has no way to understand and receive the gifts, teaching and revelation from the Spirit of God. Holy Spirit has not been quickened to life in him. His spirit is dead or non-existent. He is still separated from God in his transgressions, cut off from the spiritual realm and his understanding of it.

It is hidden from his physical senses. He cannot see or touch the spiritual realm. He receives information through his physical senses to an unsanctified mind, with unsanctified emotions, using an unsanctified will to decide how to live his life. The spiritual realm does not even exist in the mind of the natural, non-spiritual man.

---

[294] 1 Corinthians 2:14 AMP

In contrast to the natural, non-spiritual man,

The spiritual man tries all things (*he examines, investigates, inquires into, questions, and discerns all things*), yet is himself to be put on trial and judged by no one (*he can read the meaning of everything, but no one can properly discern or appraise or get an insight into him*).[295]

The spiritual man has an advantage over the natural, non-spiritual man because he has been born not only of the flesh, but born again of the Spirit. He has all the same physical senses of the natural, non-spiritual man in addition to all the spiritual senses that come as a result of being born again of the Spirit. He is able to take all the information gathered from his physical senses, and all the revelation gathered from his spiritual senses to examine, investigate, inquire into, question and discern all these things in his soul.

DISCERNING BETWEEN TWO REALMS

God is not asking us to ignore the information we receive with our physical senses about the natural realm. The spiritual man has the ability to discern all the things of the natural realm and the spiritual realm, only the spirit within him, "has known or understood the mind (*the counsels and purposes*) of the Lord so as to guide and instruct Him and give Him knowledge?"[296] The Holy Spirit knows and understands the divine counsels and purposes of God. He is able to guide and instruct us with knowledge for our life, so we can discern how to live our lives in agreement with heaven in order to experience the manifested promises of God.

[295] 1 Corinthians 2:15 AMP
[296] 1 Corinthians 2:16 AMP

As a spiritual people born of the spirit, "we have the mind of Christ (*the Messiah*) and do hold the thoughts (*feelings and purposes*) of His heart."[297] The mind of Christ is the part of our spirit containing the very thoughts, feelings, and purposes of God for our lives, remembering that our soul is able to discern between information received through our physical senses and revelation received through our spiritual senses. We literally are given the mind of Christ, as His thoughts, feelings, and purposes of heart sanctify our imagination.

The preceding verse helps us to understand that when we are born again by the Spirit, not only who we are is different than the natural non-spiritual man, but how we function is also different. Many times people become Christians, yet continue to live their lives in the same way as the natural non-spiritual man. They continue to allow the direction and daily decisions of their lives to be dictated only by the information they receive through their physical senses, instead of training their spiritual senses in relationship with Holy Spirit to allow the direction and daily decisions of their life to be dictated by revelation received from the spiritual realm.

The same thing was happening with some of the people in the Corinthian church when Paul wrote to them about his last visit, saying, "I could not talk to you as to spiritual (*men*), but as to non-spiritual (*men of the flesh, in whom the carnal nature predominates*), as to mere infants (*in the new life*) in Christ (*unable to talk yet!*)"[298] Paul was telling these confessing born again believers that they were a spiritual people who were still functioning and living their lives as nonspiritual people. They didn't know who they were, and

---

[297] 1 Corinthians 2:16 AMP
[298] 1 Corinthians 3:1 AMP

they lived their lives like they didn't know who they were! So, it appeared that their new nature was not causing them to behave differently than the carnal nature of a non-spiritual man.

These were professing believers, continuing to live and make decisions in the same way as an unbeliever. They were still allowing the direction and daily decisions of their life to be dictated only by the information they were receiving through their physical senses, instead of training their spiritual senses in relationship with Holy Spirit to allow the direction and daily decisions of their life to be dictated by revelation received from the spiritual realm.

Paul continued by telling them he had to feed them with milk, "not solid food, for you were not yet strong enough (*to be ready for it*); but even yet you are not strong enough (*to be ready for it*)"[299] In other words, more teaching was not enough for them to become mature. They had already received a lot of information from the teaching of the Word, and yet they were:

> Still (*unspiritual, having the nature*) of the flesh (*under the control of ordinary impulses*). For as long as (*there are*) envying and jealousy and wrangling and factions among you, are you not unspiritual and of the flesh, behaving yourselves after a human standard and like mere (*unchanged*) men?[300]

Paul questioned their salvation in this passage, inferring it's possible that they still have the same nature as an unbeliever, based on their behavior. It was a sensible possibility to think that the old nature had never been crucified with Christ, so

---

[299] 1 Corinthians 3:2 AMP
[300] 1 Corinthians 3:3 AMP

they were never resurrected to new life receiving a new nature. He gave them the benefit of the doubt, implying that if they were spiritual, then they must not know it or they wouldn't be behaving unspiritual. Paul said they were acting like unchanged men, without a new nature!

The phrase here, "still of the flesh," is sometimes translated "for you are still carnal."[301] This is where we get the term "carnal Christian"- someone who is unspiritual. A carnal Christian chooses to live his life by the way of the flesh. They may have received teaching from the Bible, even confessed to being born again of the Spirit, but they do not operate their life out of revelation received in the spiritual realm. They take spiritual principles and process them with their mind, will and emotions based on their physical senses just like the unspiritual man. They consider the information they receive from the world around them and make the best decision they can from their own sense and reason.

In the natural, things appear to be good as can be expected to the carnal Christian. Just like those who chose to settle for less than the promises of God and live east of the Jordan. Without revelation in his spirit, the carnal Christian will have to settle for less than the abundant life. He has no real faith and has never experienced the spiritual realm for himself. He may believe in the information that he has received from reading the Bible or hearing others teach about the spiritual realm, but he does not know from experience for himself the reality of the spiritual realm. Without revelation in his spirit, faith has not been activated to receive his spiritual blessings located in the heavenly realms.

---

[301] 1 Corinthians 3:3 NKJV

The spiritual man chooses to live his life by the way of the Spirit. He takes all the information he receives through his physical senses in the natural realm, he also takes all the revelation that he receives through his spiritual senses in the spiritual realm, and brings it all together in his soul to discern what the Holy Spirit is saying about his life and world. He uses his sanctified mind, emotions and will to discern the voice of God to make life decisions that will enable him to experience the promises of God.

Our spiritual blessings exist in the spiritual realm. The problem is, we live in the natural realm. We need the promises that God has made and keeps ready for us in the spiritual realm to manifest in the natural realm. Only the spiritual man is able to access these promises in the spiritual realm to receive revelation of his spiritual blessings, so he can receive revelation in his soul to experience the manifestation of His accomplishments in order to live on the right side of the cross.

The promises of God are only possessed by the Spirit of God. They cannot be received by living a life based on the physical senses of our natural world. Only the spirit of a believer can inherit the things of the spiritual realm by the Spirit. The Holy Spirit was quickened to life in us so we would know through personal experience the revelation of His promises that have already been freely given to us. We have been born of the Spirit, receiving His DNA to become spiritual sons and daughters, releasing us to operate freely in the spiritual realm of His Kingdom. We do not have to wait until we arrive in heaven someday in the obscure future. We can go into the Spirit realm right now and receive revelation to experience His promises today!

CHAPTER 7

SPIRITUAL

SCHIZOPHRENIA

WHEN I WAS SEVENTEEN YEARS OLD I came home from Cedar Springs Bible Camp to tell my mom that I had committed my life to Jesus Christ. The announcement came as a major shock to her! I had not been raised in a Christian home, and I was the first one in my family to decide to have a relationship with God.

At this time my mom and my sister confessed to be atheists, while my brother was dabbling in the occult. So, for the next several hours, I sat with my mom on the stairwell entry to our house discussing with her my experience at Bible camp. During our conversation she tried to get me to reconsider my decision to become a Christian, expressing concern that I may have joined a cult.

After an awkward pause, my mom asked, "Will you at least think about the commitment you're making for a couple of days before making a final decision?" I had literally just arrived home from Bible camp. It had only been a couple of days since I had given my life to Jesus. And my new commitment to live for Him was already being tested for authenticity.

I could choose to take a stand and continue to have a relationship with Jesus, or I could choose to forsake my relationship with Him to please my mom. But I had already made a decision to be crucified with Christ, allowing Him to live in me. What choice? There was no turning back! I would not be renouncing my new life and commitment to Christ! Soon, I responded to my mom by saying, "I have already decided to give my life to Jesus, and I will not be changing my mind."

I would not have been able take a stand that day for a Jesus I thought existed based on the information received through my physical senses. I was only able to take a stand for Jesus because I had come to know Him through a personal experience as a result of revelation received by Holy Spirit! It's the same for every one of us as believers in our everyday life. We will either live according to His revelatory Word or abandon the revelation of His Word based on the appearance of circumstances.

In stressful times it can be difficult to trust the information we have read in the Bible, especially when are feeling worn out, facing friction and opposition from those closest to us in our lives. But, we are able to trust the information we have read and heard about in the Bible as revelation when His Word is personally diffused throughout our soul from the spiritual realm.

SPIRIT OF RELIGION

Daniel 7:25 says that the antichrist spirit will "persecute the saints of the Most High."[302] For there to be an anti, there has to

---

[302] Daniel 7:25 NKJV

be a pro. Jesus was the Christ! Our relationship with Him is not based on religion through performance, but through our union with Him! The antichrist is a counterfeit, portraying religion as a relationship based on performance and acting like something that he is not and never will be. He wants to us to act like something we are not, so we never will be!

The Hebrew word here for *persecute* is *bela*.[303] It means "to afflict, and to wear out in a mental sense." Here we get a picture of the enemy's end time strategy to wear out the saints through constant conflict by deteriorating their faith and peace through strain and friction, to the point of exhaustion.[304]

The strategy of the devil is to stress us out with our natural circumstances to destroy our lives, families, and ministries. He tries to wear us out by getting us to fight our circumstances like the natural, unspiritual man. The constant stress, strain and friction of fighting our circumstances in our own strength and abilities becomes exhausting. Tired and worn out, we forget about who we are in union with Holy Spirit. No longer training and exercising our spiritual senses to receive revelation through relationship with Holy Spirit, our faith and peace begin to deteriorate, so our physical senses dominate the influence of our soul.

The above verse continues, saying that this antichrist spirit will "intend to change times and law."[305] What does this phrase mean? It means that this spirit of religion intends to exchange our current time and law with other times and law from history. Why would the antichrist want to do that?

---

[303] Strong's Exhaustive Concordance, Reference 1080
[304] Sean Smith, MPR Open Bible Conference, Casper Wyoming, April 24-26, 2007
[305] Daniel 7:25 NKJV

The intention is to deceive God's people so they will return to living under the old covenant based on the law rather than continue to live under the new covenant based on grace. First he wants to persecute us by wearing us out. After wearing us out he intends, in his own deception, to try and change the times and law in order to try and undo the power of the finished work of the cross.

The word *law* here is the same word in which we get the word *instructions*. It's the word in which we get the word *structure*. It means "information to form thoughts, speculations and strongholds." Put it all together and we can see that this spirit of religion wants to set up a government to change the times so we will revert to living under the old covenant of the law. That is based on information to form thoughts, speculations and strongholds to get us to forget our identity in Him, so we will work and strive in our own efforts like the natural, non-spiritual man, rather than resting in Christ's accomplishments as a spiritual man, allowing the antichrist to try and keep the kingdom of heaven from manifesting through believers with revelation on earth!

In contrast, we can see in Isaiah 2:3 that out of God's government will "go forth the law and instruction, and the word of the Lord."[306] This is the same word *law* here that we saw in Daniel 7:25, but it doesn't mean information to form thoughts, speculations and strongholds. It actually means "revelation based on His Word!"

Many churches today are functioning under the deception of the spirit of religion based on the instruction of information to form thoughts, speculations and strongholds. This structure

---

[306] Isaiah 2:3 AMP

often comes through programs made to control and manipulate people and the environment, which is witchcraft. This brings us to the prevalent seeker-sensitive gospel that parallels our culture's system, rooted in a spirit of fear to be politically correct, where pastors feel they have to let everyone know the purpose of every meeting, outlining to the minute exactly what will happen, when it will happen, and why it will happen in the church bulletin, because they are afraid that the spontaneity of the Spirit may cause someone to be uncomfortable or even offended!

As a result, most churches have become purpose-driven, rather than spirit-driven. They teach but no longer activate the people in their spiritual gifts, requiring revelation based on His Word, afraid that activating the supernatural will result in the misuse or misapplication of the gifts being administered to guests and others attending the meetings. This could cause someone to get uncomfortable or offended. As a result, they may decide to leave the church. Then if they leave and take their money with them it could threaten the church's ability to survive.

The problem is that it's not supposed to be about the church! The church is supposed to be about releasing His kingdom. The church should be believers gathering together for worship while being activated in the supernatural for preparation to minister to unbelievers, as they preach the gospel, heal the sick, cast out demons, cleanse the leper and raise the dead in order to demonstrate the Kingdom of God on earth as it is in Heaven. It's the government of antichrist to build a structure based on information to form thoughts, speculations, and strongholds. But the government of God is built from revelation based on His Word!

SHAKING HEAVEN & EARTH

SPIRITUALLY VIOLENT

We will always find the enemy ready to launch a violent assault against those who have learned to spiritually possess the promises of the Kingdom of heaven.

> From the days of John the Baptist until the present time, the kingdom of heaven has endured violent assault, and violent men seize it by force (*as a precious prize — a share in the heavenly kingdom is sought with most ardent zeal and intense exertion.*)[307]

The term violent here is not referring to a natural violence. It is referring to a spiritual violence.

The Kingdom of heaven spiritually imparted into us when we became born again has always endured violent assault from the enemy. It was true in the days of John the Baptist, and it is still true today! As a result, the ability to experience the promises of God set aside for us in the Kingdom will be based on our resting in what has already been given to us through spiritual violence. "God also fashions a strategy that if we will fall into line with, we will see others rescued and set free into God's purposes."[308]

"Spiritual violence denotes a radical intensity in the inner man."[309] It's not a violence that can be accomplished with the physical senses of the natural man. It is about using our spiritual senses to rest in the revelation of His accomplishments by putting "on God's whole armor (*the armor of a heavy-armed soldier which God supplies*), that you may be able successfully to stand up

---

[307] Matthew 11:12 AMP
[308] Sean Smith, Prophetic Evangelism (Shippensburg, PA: Destiny Image Publishers Inc, 2004), 125
[309] Ibid

against (*all*) the strategies and deceits of the devil."[310] The Greek word for *deceits* in this passage is *methodeia*. It means "method, traveling over, trickery, wile, and lie in wait."[311]

The devil lies in wait looking for opportunity to attack us. His method is to devise schemes that will trick us into focusing on the appearance of our circumstances, that through observation with our physical senses we will begin to panic in view of the impossible situations we see before us. Then we will forget who we are and try to put on our own armor rather than God's armor, reverting back to working, striving, and performing like the natural, non-spiritual man, who doesn't rely on revelation from the spiritual realm through Holy Spirit, nor rest in His accomplishments!

The spiritually violent rest in the promises of the Kingdom by staying focused on Jesus Christ and their union with Holy Spirit through relationship with Him. They do not get distracted with the appearance of their natural circumstances, as their imaginations are sanctified with revelation that the promises of God are, "a precious prize—a share in the heavenly kingdom."[312] They are able to possess the precious prize of His promises, already given to them, with much zeal and intense exertion (*not the zeal and intense exertion of the natural man*). It is the zeal and intense exertion of the Spirit through their inner man that allows them to experience the manifestation of His inheritance!

The spiritual man in union with Holy Spirit diffuses revelation throughout our soul to produce an overflow of His promises, resulting in a spiritual violence that breaks yokes of

---

[310] Ephesians 6:11 AMP
[311] Strong's Exhaustive Concordance, Reference 3180
[312] Matthew 11:12 AMP

bondage, and will rescue and set others free to experience His plans, purposes, and destinies for their lives. As we rest in the revelation received from the spiritual senses of our inner man, rather than the information received by the physical senses of our natural man, so we become not only possessors, but distributors of the promises of God!

The abundant life is a result of our spiritual blessings in the heavenly realm becoming a reality for us to discern in our soul through revelation in our spirit. We must be able to see the reality of all that has already been given to us in the spiritual realm for us to have faith in our soul to experience the manifestation of it in our natural circumstances. The inability to live the abundant life is a result of not being able to receive revelation in our soul. If we cannot see the reality of our spiritual blessings in heavenly places, then we will live our lives like the natural, unspiritual man based on information alone that we receive through our physical senses about the circumstances around us.

The realm that dominates the reality of our soul will dictate the outcome of our battles. If our reality is dominated by information received through our physical senses in the natural realm, we will, like the natural, unspiritual man, be limited by the limitations of our reality and resources. As a result, we will not overcome an already defeated enemy, because he is not already defeated in the natural realm. He is already defeated in the spiritual realm. But if our reality is empowered by the spiritual violence of revelation from the heavenly realm, we will, like the spiritual man, be unlimited by the limitlessness of our reality and resources. We thus can overcome our opposition and experience the manifestation of our inheritance in Him.

ONE MIND

At this point it's important for you to understand that, though this chapter is titled "Spiritual Schizophrenia," no one who has received true salvation should ever be spiritually schizophrenic. It's an oxymoron to have already been set free and yet still live like you're in bondage, unless you don't know who you are!

Unfortunately, we can observe believers who don't know that their old nature passed away and was crucified with Christ on the cross, and now they have a new nature. They have been wrongly taught that they still have dual natures, so they live like two people with two different minds who are polar opposites, instead of the new creation they have already been made in Him!

In confusion, they waver in the imagination of their mind between living like the natural, unspiritual man and the spiritual man. In relationship through union with Holy Spirit they can receive revelation through the spiritual senses of their spiritual man to walk in faith. At the same time they are receiving information through their physical senses about the natural realm, that without revelation can cause them to begin to waver, doubt and eventually lose faith, creating a dilemma about which realm they will trust to have the most influence over their soul.

I remember leaving the conversation with my mom, feeling discouraged by her reaction to my new decision to live for Christ. I had spent several hours allowing her to download me with all the reasons to reconsider my relationship with Jesus. The enemy was trying to wear me out by replaying the conversation over and over again in my imagination. As a new believer with almost no revelation about my identity in Christ, I felt tempted to waver, doubt and lose faith.

209

The questions were beginning to multiply before I finally found myself in prayer, being encouraged in relationship with Holy Spirit. The questions began to dissipate from my memory and be replaced with the revelation of His Word, "Do not be discouraged." He continued to reaffirm my relationship with Him saying, "I am your Father. Don't trust in the appearance of your circumstances." And He promised, "I will use you to save not only your mom but your whole family!"

I left that time of prayer empowered with revelation by Holy Spirit diffused throughout my mind, will, and emotions, as the spiritual realm dominated the influence of my soul with supernatural faith! I came to my right mind! One mind! The mind of Christ!

Allowing the revelation of who I am to effortlessly remove the root of all doubt, fear and wavering, I could trust His Word over the appearance of circumstances. As a result, the Holy Spirit revealed a strategy to use me to spiritually rescue not only my mom but my entire family. In addition to their salvation, He would set them free from the enemy's current plan for their lives in order to use them for God's purposes.

TWO MINDS

The Bible says wavering back and forth between thinking, like the natural, unspiritual man and the spiritual man, is to have "two minds (*hesitating, dubious, irresolute*), (*he is*) unstable and unreliable and uncertain about everything (*he thinks, feels, decides*)."[313] Instead of functioning only from the mind of Christ that comes as a result of revelation diffused throughout their soul by Holy Spirit, they waver back and forth between two

[313] James 1:8 AMP

minds — the mind that is like the natural, unspiritual man and the mind of Christ!

Without revelation being diffused throughout their mind, will and emotions, the soul becomes weary, acting like they have a nature that has already been crucified! They behave under the control of ordinary carnal impulses, having to work and strive to accomplish things based on their own efforts rather than His efforts, while the mind of the natural, unspiritual man wants to "wage war against the soul."[314]

The mind of Christ begins to chart a course in faith based on revelation received through union with Holy Spirit. The mind that is like the natural, unspiritual man begins to wage war against the soul with the constant bombardment of information that contradicts the revelation of the mind of Christ. The Holy Spirit knows that God does not want them to waver between the natural, unspiritual man and the mind of Christ. But without revelation being diffused throughout their soul in relationship from a union with Holy Spirit, the mind like the natural, unspiritual man begins to dominate the reality of their soul. As a result, they waver and doubt, without revelation from the spiritual realm, acting like they don't know they are living under the control of ordinary carnal impulses.

Many Christian people today have settled for less than the promises of God for their life. They make excuses why they cannot live a supernatural life, citing all the limitations of their humanity and the natural realm. They think like the natural, unspiritual man who doesn't have revelation of his supernatural union with Holy Spirit or see the manifestation of His promises. As they live a life based on sense and reason from the

[314] 1 Peter 2:11 AMP

information received through the physical senses, they justify why they cannot live any other way! Instead, they live a spiritual schizophrenia where sometimes they live one way, and other times they live a different way altogether, never experiencing the manifestation of His inheritance!

They try to live without the revelation that results in the authority to prevail against the gates of hell. As their lives begin to fall apart based on their own philosophies formed from their own experiences, rather than from the Word of God, they betray their own identity and wonder why God does not seem to be blessing them. In a state of disillusionment, they blame God for the consequences of living by information rather than revelation. How long will we make excuses for not knowing who we are while continuing to live by the way of information received from the physical senses of the flesh, instead of living by revelation received through the spiritual senses of the Spirit?

> INSTEAD, THEY LIVE A SPIRITUAL SCHIZOPHRENIA, SOMETIMES ONE WAY AND OTHER TIMES A DIFFERENT WAY, NEVER EXPERIENCING THE MANIFESTATION OF HIS INHERITANCE!

ALL THINGS POSSIBLE

It was only a few weeks after receiving God's promise to save my family that I was asked by the youth pastor at my church to share my testimony the next week. I went home and told my whole family that I had been asked to speak at the following youth group meeting, and invited all of them to come and listen to my testimony! As a result, only one of my sisters decided to come and listen to me speak at youth group. Unfortunately, I naively included a lot of information about our family's physical and alcohol abuse in my testimony that evening.

My sister proceeded to go home and tell my mom that I had disrespected our whole family in front of the church. When I came home that night, my mom was waiting at the front door to confront me about airing all of our family's dirty laundry in front of the church. I tried to explain to her that my intentions had not been to hurt anyone in the family. I was only trying to testify about my life story and the events that had led to my acceptance of Christ. It just so happened that my family life was a part of my life story.

The enemy would try to twist the purpose of my testimony that night from attracting my mom and family to Christ, to repelling them from Christ. The conversation with my mom that evening ended with her saying, "Don't ever ask me to go to that church again! I would be embarrassed to ever attend that church after you shared all our family's personal problems with everyone! I will never step foot in that church!" It was with those few words spoken by my mom that His spoken promises to use me in the salvation of my family seemed to turn from a difficult task to impossible circumstances.

After that night, it became impossible for me to talk to mom about Jesus. Once in a conversation I ignorantly told my mom that "I was trying to set a good example for her in Christ!" She quickly snapped back at me, "You listen to me, I am the mother and you are the son, and I set the examples for you!" As a result, I began to think twice before sharing Christ with my mom, allowing fear to keep me from it, until our relationship became so strained that we discontinued talking for almost two years.

We will always find impossible circumstances standing between us and the manifestation of the promises of God. In chapters two and three, we saw Joshua conquer the impossible circumstance when crossing the Jordan River to possess the promised land. As soon as he stepped into the promised land, another impossible obstacle awaited him in the battle of Jericho! The Bible says, "Jericho (*a fenced town with high walls*) was tightly closed because of the Israelites: no one went out or came in."[315]

God used the impossibility of these circumstances to teach Joshua that all things are possible through the limitless power of the Spirit rather than limitations of the flesh. The city of Jericho was a fenced town with high walls. These walls had never been penetrated by anyone in the history of their existence. No one had ever defeated Jericho in battle. It was an impossible obstacle!

Jericho represents the impossible that stands between us and the promises of God. A Jericho can keep us from experiencing the manifestation of our promises and fulfilling our destiny in God. The Israelites had to conquer Jericho in order to possess their promised land. What is your Jericho?

As Joshua looked at the impossibility of his circumstances, the Spirit of God spoke to him, saying, "See! I have given Jericho, its king and mighty men of valor, into your hands."[316] Notice, the Lord did not say "I will give this city to you," but "I have given this city to you." The Lord was revealing to Joshua that He had already given Jericho, its king, and the mighty men of valor into his hand at a time in the past.

In the natural realm, nothing had actually been given to Joshua. He was still going to have to fight the battle of Jericho to

---

[315] Joshua 6:1 AMP
[316] Joshua 6:2 AMP

actually possess it. The city of Jericho was still closed up, with no one going in and no one going out. The king and the mighty men of valor were still safe behind those thick walls.

It was in the Spirit that Joshua could see another reality. The spirit realm contradicted the appearance of the natural realm. The reality he saw in the spiritual realm did not look impossible like the reality that he saw in the natural realm. The impossible obstacle before him in the natural realm was already accomplished on his behalf in the spiritual realm.

When the Lord said, "See," He was essentially saying, "Look with your spiritual eyes, not with your natural eyes. No one has ever penetrated these walls, but I have already given this city to you!" He was giving Joshua revelation of the spiritual realm. God was showing him that all things are possible in the spiritual realm! The reality of the spiritual realm would empower him with supernatural faith instead of allowing the reality of the natural realm to dominate his thoughts with fear and doubt.

Joshua was getting a revelation of what it meant to live by faith in God's Word to overcome the impossible obstacle of the battle of Jericho. In the same way, we need to have revelation diffused throughout our soul to see who we are and what we have already been given in Him, so we can conquer the impossible in order to experience the abundant life. We all have the opportunity to face impossible obstacles. If you are not currently facing any impossible circumstances, wait awhile and you will get your chance!

We need the supernatural revelation of the Spirit sanctifying our minds so we can see, in the same way that Joshua was able to see! We need a revelation of the spiritual realm concerning our identity to become a reality in our soul so we can actually experience it in our daily lives. We need the "all things possible" blueprint of the Spirit to conquer the impossibility of our natural circumstances.

I almost allowed fear to keep me from talking with my mom about Jesus Christ. It was one of those impossible things that stood between me and experiencing the promises of God. In the natural, the circumstances with my mom looked impossible, but I did not let go of God's promise to use me to save not only my mom but my entire family. Then one evening out of nowhere the Holy Spirit instructed me to start loving my mom unconditionally, without any judgment. He told me to call my mom on the telephone and apologize for any hurt that I had caused her in the past. As a result, the Lord began to heal our relationship!

Many years later my mom was diagnosed with lung cancer. During that time she allowed us to anoint her with oil and lay hands on her to pray for her healing. Finally, in May of 1999, due to her illness she was admitted to the hospital, as the burden I had to see my mom accept Jesus Christ as her Savior increased! With all the family around, it became difficult to find a private moment to talk alone with my mom. So my wife, Tammi, and I began to pray together for the right time to talk with my mom about giving her life to Christ.

I remember telling my wife that I could not live with the idea of my mom dying and spending an eternity in hell. I needed to know that I had done everything possible to make sure that she was right with Jesus Christ before she died. Finally, the opportunity presented itself to be alone with my mom so that I could share with her the plan of salvation. In May of 1999, God fulfilled His promise to use me in the salvation of my mom. Just two weeks before she passed away at the young age of 48, I had the privilege of leading my mom in prayer to accept Jesus Christ as her Lord and Savior.

All things are possible in Him!

HEAVENLY PERSPECTIVE

The natural circumstances concerning my mom's salvation contradicted the promises of God, just as the natural circumstances of the Israelites' possession of the promised land contradicted the Word of the Lord. Satan has always tried to use the appearance of our natural circumstances to limit our vision to see the promises we've already been given by God. The reason Satan uses this method is that our spiritual blessings cannot be seen or attained through our physical senses.

As long as we are only looking in the natural at our immediate circumstances, we become blinded to our spiritual blessing in the heavenly realms. We have to leave the natural realm and go into the spiritual realm to see and know the promises that God already has for us. Often our current circumstances can hinder us as much by what we see as by what we do not see!

In Genesis 15.1. "The word of the Lord came to Abram in a vision saying, Fear not, Abram, I am your Shield, your abundant compensation, and your reward shall be exceedingly great."[317]

This is the first time we see this phrase, "the word of the Lord," used in the Bible. It is revelation from God to give Abram a different perspective than what he sees in his natural circumstances. In the natural, Abram had not seen any of God's promises fulfilled

---

[317] Genesis 15:1 AMP

in his life. He was still waiting to see the promises of God come into fruition. There was no indication that he would ever see the promises of God come to pass in his life time.[318]

With this in mind, Abram asked the Lord: "What can You give me, since I am going on (*from this world*) childless and he who shall be the owner and heir of my house is this (*steward*) Eliezer of Damascus?"[319]

According to the information received through his physical senses, things did not appear to be headed in the right direction. He continued to tell God about his natural circumstances, saying: "Look, You have given me no child; and (*a servant*) born in my house is my heir."[320]

God needed to deliver Abram from paralysis by analysis. He needed to get Abram to quit living by information from the natural realm, and get him to start living by revelation from the spiritual realm. So again, for the second time: "The word of the Lord came to him, saying, This man shall not be your heir, but he who shall come from your own body shall be your heir."[321]

Then the Spirit of the Lord brought Abram, "outside (*his tent into the starlight*) and said, Look now toward the heavens and count the stars—if you are able to number them. Then He said to him, So shall your descendants be."[322]

Abram wanted God to look at his circumstances, saying, "Look, you have given me no child."[323] But God wanted Abraham to get his eyes off his immediate circumstances so he could get

[318] Sean Smith, MPR Open Bible Conference, Casper Wyoming, April 24-26,2007
[319] Genesis 15:2 AMP
[320] Genesis 15:3 AMP
[321] Genesis 15:4 AMP
[322] Genesis 15:5 AMP
[323] Genesis 15:3 AMP

his eyes onto a heavenly perspective, saying, "Look now toward the heavens and count the stars."[324] God had to bring Abram outside the tent to give him a new vision of the heavens, to get him out of living by the same information received from the natural environment of his tent.[325]

Inside the tent, everything Abram saw limited his perspective, as well as everything he did not see! God had to get Abram out of the tent and under an open heaven in order to get him to receive a new revelation to change his destiny.[326] As a result, Abram, "believed in (*trusted in, relied on, remained steadfast to*) the Lord, and He counted it to him as righteousness (*right standing with God*)."[327]

In the same way, our day-to-day natural circumstances can begin to create a stronghold in our thinking without revelation being diffused throughout our mind, will and emotions. We can forget who we are and what we have been given. So we begin to develop a predisposition about the fulfillment of the promises of God in our lives based on the information we receive through our physical senses about the natural realm, then finding it difficult, if not impossible, to break out of the limitations of our relationships and our environment to receive revelation from the spiritual realm. It is not only the things we see that limit our perspective, but the things that we do not see!

As Christians, we are not called to live our lives out of the limitations of our memory based on the information we have received through our physical senses concerning the impossibilities of our natural circumstances. We are called to live our lives out of imagination based on the revelation that we receive

[324] Genesis 15:5 AMP
[325] Sean Smith, MPR Open Bible Conference, April 24-26, 2007
[326] Ibid
[327] Genesis 15:6 AMP

through our spiritual senses of the heavenly perspective that all things are not only possible in the spiritual realm but they have already been given to us!

BATTLE OF THE MIND

A story about a man named Nick helps us to understand the importance of not allowing our immediate circumstances to dominate the reality of our minds.

Nick was a big, strong, tough man who worked in the railroad yards for many years. He was one of his company's best employees, always there on time, a reliable, hard worker who got along well with the other employees. But Nick had one major problem: His attitude was chronically negative.

Nick was known around the railroad yards as the most pessimistic man on the job. He perpetually feared the worst and constantly worried, fretting that something bad might happen. One summer day, the crews were told that they could go home an hour early to celebrate the birthday of one of the foremen. All the workers left, but somehow Nick had accidentally locked himself in a refrigerated boxcar that had been brought into the yard for maintenance.

The boxcar was empty and not connected to any of the trains. When Nick realized that he was locked inside the refrigerated boxcar, he panicked. Nick began beating on the doors so hard that his arms and fists became bloody. He screamed and screamed, but his co-workers had already gone home to get ready for the party. Nobody could hear Nick's desperate calls for help. Again and again he called out, until finally his voice was a raspy whisper.

Aware that he was in a refrigerated boxcar, Nick guessed that the temperature in the unit was well below freezing, maybe as low as five or ten degrees Fahrenheit. Nick feared the worst. He thought, "What am I going to do? If I don't get out of here, I'm going to freeze to death. There's no way I can stay in here all night." The more he thought about the circumstances, the colder he became. With the door shut tightly, and no apparent way of escape, he sat down to wait for his inevitable death by freezing or suffocation, whichever came first.

To pass the time, he decided to chronicle his demise. He found a pen in his shirt pocket and noticed an old piece of cardboard in the corner of the car. Shivering almost uncontrollably, he scribbled a message to his family. In it, Nick noted his dire prospects: "Getting so cold. Body is numb. If I do not get out soon, these will probably be my last words." And they were. The next morning, when the crews came to work, they opened the boxcar and found Nick's body crumpled over in the corner.

When the autopsy was completed, it revealed that Nick had indeed frozen to death. Now, here is a fascinating enigma: The investigators discovered that the refrigeration unit for the car in which Nick had been trapped was not even on! In fact, it had been out of order for some time and was not functioning at the time of the man's death. The temperature in the car the night that Nick froze to death was sixty-one degrees!

Nick froze to death in slightly less than normal room temperature because he believed that he was in a freezing boxcar. He expected to die! He was convinced that he did not have a chance. He expected the worst. He saw himself as doomed with no way out. He lost the battle in his own mind.[328]

---

[328] Joel Osteen, Your Best Life Now (New York, NY: Warner Faith, Time Warner Book Group, 2004), 72-73

SPIRITUAL SENSES

Nick's story illustrates the power of the mind to determine our perception of reality. It helps us understand the importance of not allowing our immediate circumstances to dominate the reality of our minds. Jesus said, the "Truth will set you free."[329] The Greek word for *truth* here is *aletheia*. It means "true, truly, and verity."[330] Here the word *verity* is defined as "the state or quality of being true; accordance with fact or reality."[331] In other words, the above text can be correctly translated the "reality will set you free."

Jesus was trying to say that the truth of another reality is going to set you free from your current perspective of reality. He was talking about a revelation of a heavenly reality that would deliver and set them free from their current limited perception of a natural reality. If we do not get revelation of a supernatural reality, then we'll always be limited by information of our natural reality.

"The mind once suddenly aware of a verity for the first time suddenly invents it again (Agnes Sligh Turnbull)."[332] Jesus knew that our perception of reality would determine our thoughts, beliefs, and ultimately, our destiny. Proverbs 23:7 reminds us that as a man "thinks in his heart, so is he."[333] The realm that has the greatest influence over our soul (*mind, will, emotions*) will dictate our perception of reality.

If our perception of reality is only influenced by the information we receive through our physical senses about our natural

---

[329] John 8:32 AMP

[330] Strong's Exhaustive Concordance, Reference 226

[331] Dictionary.com, Unabridged (v 1.1), retrieved December 19, 2007, (Random House, 2006), http://dictionary.reference.com/browse/verity

[332] Ibid

[333] Proverbs 23:7 AMP

world, then our perspective will be limited by appearance of our immediate circumstances. This will continually result in our inability to spiritually discern God's design for us to overcome life's challenges in order to experience the manifestation of His promises for our lives. On the other hand, when our perception of reality is empowered by revelation in the heavenly realm, then our perspective of reality will be changed to reflect the influence of our spiritual identity and inheritance in Him.

As I have already written in earlier chapters, we have to go into the spiritual realm to train, exercise and use our spiritual senses. With the Holy Spirit teaching us through relationship based on our union with Him, we can receive revelation of the things that already exist in the heavenly realm. That will be diffused throughout our soul to be manifested in the natural realm.

One of the spiritual senses we can learn to exercise is identified by Jesus as spiritual hearing. In conclusion to telling a parable to a great crowd that had gathered around Him, Jesus said, "He who has ears (*to hear*), let him be listening and let him consider and perceive and comprehend by hearing."[334] Jesus was not trying to separate the hearing from the hearing impaired. He didn't want those listening to hear His words as information to be interpreted through their physical senses about the natural world. He was instructing and exhorting them to use their spiritual ears to discern the revelation He was speaking to them, so they would perceive and comprehend the reality of the spiritual realm over the reality of the natural realm.

"Then the disciples came to Him and said, 'Why do you speak to them in parables?'"[335] They wanted to know why Jesus

---

[334] Matthew 13:9 AMP
[335] Matthew 13:10 AMP

did not talk to the crowds in simple, straight-forward terms that they could understand. Jesus answers their question, saying:

> To you it has been given to know the secrets and mysteries of the kingdom of heaven, but to them it has not been given. For whoever has (*spiritual knowledge*), to him will more be given and he will be furnished richly so that he will have abundance; but from him who has not, even what he has will be taken away.[336]

The secrets and mysteries of the Kingdom of heaven known as revelation have not been given to everyone. They can only be understood by the Spirit. And the things of the Spirit can only be discerned by those who relate to the Spirit. The phrase "spiritual knowledge" in this passage is not a reference to the spiritual information being communicated but the spiritual revelation that comes as a result of relationship with Holy Spirit. Whoever has a relationship with Holy Spirit will be given an abundance of revelation to richly experience. On the other hand, those who do not have relationship with Holy Spirit cannot receive revelation. Even the spiritual information they are currently able to grasp will eventually evaporate!

JESUS SAID:

> This is the reason that I speak to them in parables: because having the power of seeing, they do not see; and having the power of hearing, they do not hear, nor do they grasp and understand.[337]

Those without relationship with Holy Spirit are spiritually paralyzed, unable to receive revelation from the spiritual realm.

---

[336] Matthew 13:11-12 AMP
[337] Matthew 13:13 AMP

They are spiritually blind to seeing anything outside the natural realm. They are spiritually deaf to hearing anything in the spiritual realm. They are rendered spiritually deaf, dumb, and blind with severed spiritual senses, fulfilling the prophecy of Isaiah that says:

> You shall indeed hear and hear but never grasp and understand; and you shall indeed look and look but never see and perceive.[338]

STILL SMALL VOICE

Recently, my wife, Tammi, told me about a conversation that she had with my oldest daughter, Jordan, just last week. Jordan had a spelling test that day at school. We had helped her study for it the night before. When Jordan came home from school that day, Tammi asked her, "How did your spelling test go today?" Jordan said, "It went good. All except for the last question. The teacher asked us to write down the spelling rule for the test. I didn't know the rule. I didn't even know that we were supposed to know the spelling rule for the test. Then I heard God whisper the spelling rule in my ear. So I got it right!" Jordan then asked my wife, "Mom, isn't God a good God?" My wife told me that she laughed and said, "Yes, He is a good God!"

"At times, the Lord speaks to us in a still, small voice from within our spirit. This can be heard as a passing thought, sudden impression or internal 'sense' of something that God is saying. This still, small voice is illustrated in the book of 1 Kings,"[339] where the Word of the Lord came to Elijah, saying.

> Go out and stand on the mount before the Lord. And behold, the Lord passed by, and a great strong wind rent

---

[338] Matthew 13:14 AMP
[339] Kris Vallotton, A Call To War (Redding, CA: KAV 2005), 40

the mountains and broke in pieces the rocks before the Lord, but the Lord was not in the wind; and after the wind an earthquake, but the Lord was not in the earthquake; and after the earthquake a fire, but the Lord was not in the fire; and after the fire (*a sound of gentle stillness and*) a still small voice. When Elijah heard the voice, he wrapped his face in his mantle and went out and stood in the entrance of the cave. And behold, there came a voice to him and said, "What are you doing here Elijah?"[340]

"In this account, God was not in the strong wind or the earthquake, but rather He was in the gentle blowing of the still small voice of God."[341]

VISIONS AND DREAMS

In Matthew 13:16, Jesus identified spiritual *sight* as another of the spiritual senses, when He told His disciples, "blessed (*happy, fortunate, and to be envied*) are your eyes because they do see."[342] The disciples were blessed with spiritual eyes that had been opened to see revelation in the spiritual ream as a result of relationship with Him. Jesus told them "many prophets and righteous men (*men who were upright and in right standing with God*) yearned to see what you see, and did not see it, and to hear what you hear, and did not hear it."[343]

Visions and dreams are two ways the Holy Spirit uses our spiritual eyes to see revelation from the heavenly realm.

Quoting the prophet Joel, the apostle Paul says:

---

[340] 1 Kings 19:11-13 AMP
[341] Kris Valloton, A Call To War (Redding, CA: KAV 2005), 40
[342] Matthew 13:16 AMP
[343] Matthew 13:17 AMP

It shall come to pass in the last days, God declares, that I will pour out of My Spirit upon all mankind, and your sons and your daughters shall prophecy (*telling forth the divine counsels*) and your young men shall see visions (*divinely granted appearances*), and your old men shall dream (*divinely suggested*) dreams. Yes, and on My menservants also and on My maidservants in those days I will pour out My Spirit, and they shall prophecy (*telling forth the divine counsels and predicting future events pertaining especially to God's kingdom*).[344]

There are two types of visions. The first one is a Vision of the Mind, in which the Lord "projects" images and pictures onto the "screen" of our minds. This can be called a "sanctified imagination" or an imagination that is under the influence of the Holy Spirit. Most often, this is how the Holy Spirit speaks to us. For example, if we were asked to picture a pink elephant, we would be able to see it in our mind's eye. The Holy Spirit uses our mind as a blackboard in which He draws pictures or projects images onto our mind's eye. The second type of vision is an Open Vision. This is an image that you are seeing with your natural eyes."[345]

Dreams are also the language of the Holy Spirit. There are two types of dreams. The first could be called a Virtual Reality Dream, occurring while we sleep, remaining in our mind after waking. We can see "an example of a virtual reality dream that Nebuchadnezzar had in the days of Daniel." As you read, be sure to "notice that the dream is symbolic and needs interpretation."[346]

Daniel interpreted the dream for Nebuchadnezzar, saying:

[344] Acts 2:17-18 AMP
[345] Kris Vallotton, A Call To War (Redding, CA: KAV 2005), 35-36
[346] Ibid, 37

"You, O king, saw, and behold, (*there was*) a great image. This image which was mighty and of exceedingly great brightness stood before you, and the appearance of it was frightening and terrible. As for this image, its head was of fine gold, its breast and its arms of silver, its belly and its thighs of bronze, its legs of iron, its feet partly of iron and partly of clay (*the baked clay of the potter*).

"As you looked, a Stone was cut without human hands, which smote the image on its feet of iron and (*baked*) clay (*of the potter*) and broke them to pieces. Then the iron, the (*baked*) clay (*of the potter*), the bronze, the silver, and the gold were broken and crushed together and became like the chaff of the summer threshing floors, and the wind carried them away so that not a trace of them could be found. And the Stone that smote the image became a great mountain or rock and filled the whole earth."[347]

"The second type of dream can be called a Reality Dream. This is a real experience we have while sleeping that we remember after waking. The spirit world never sleeps. Therefore, our spirit can interact with the spirit world while our soul sleeps."[348]

We see an example in this type of dream when, "God came to Abimelech in a dream by night and said, Behold, you are a dead man because of the woman whom you have taken (*as your own*), for she is a man's wife."[349] "Notice in this reality dream it does not say that he dreamt of God, but rather that he had a real encounter with the Lord and that he remembered it when he woke up."[350]

---

[347] Daniel 2:31-35 AMP
[348] Kris Valloton, A Call To War (Redding, CA: KAV 2005), 37
[349] Genesis 20:3 AMP
[350] Ibid, 37

FEELING SENSATIONS

Paul identifies *touch* as being a third spiritual sense to be exercised through our union with Holy Spirit, saying, "in the hope that they might feel after Him and find Him, although He is not far from each of us."[351] Knowing that the Bible says that God is Spirit, then we are unable to feel after Him with the physical senses of our natural bodies. Only in the Spirit are we able to pursue Him as we feel after Him to, "live and move and have our being...For we are also His offspring."[352]

"Sometimes the Lord will communicate His desire to heal someone else's body by causing pain or a sensation in a certain part of the person's body; it typically correlates to the sickness in the person whom God wants to heal. If we receive this kind of revelation from Holy Spirit, it is important that we are aware of what pain or discomfort is common to us. Without clarification, we could mistakenly confuse our pain with a word of knowledge for healing."[353]

SPIRITUAL SCENT

In Song of Solomon we can identify *smell* as a fourth spiritual sense as the psalmist describes a love relationship with God through the picture of a human relationship. During an intimate monologue of flattery he tells his lover that, "the scent of your breath is like apples."[354] It is not about reading the Bible and believing the information about the spiritual sense of hearing, seeing, touch, and smell. It is about knowing, developing, and

[351] Acts 17:27 AMP
[352] Acts 17:28 AMP
[353] Kris Vallotton, A Call To War (Redding, CA: KAV 2005), 46
[354] Song of Solomon 7:8 AMP

experiencing the reality of the spiritual realm personally through our spiritual senses in relationship with the Holy Spirit.

We may be with someone or out somewhere and begin to sense a particular scent with our spiritual senses that may not exist in the natural at that time. This may be the Holy Spirit's way of communicating to us about something that He is doing in a place, or something that He is trying to speak to us about a person. It may come in the way of a familiar smell to remind us of a particular person, place, or event. The Holy Spirit may also lead us to a past memory to remind us of a person, place, or event in order to communicate a particular message to a present or future person, place, or event. The spiritual sense of smell may also be a way for the Holy Spirit to warn us of danger or spiritual warfare.

PROPHETIC TASTING

Finally, we see the psalmist identifying *taste* as a fifth spiritual sense when he says, "taste and see that the Lord (*our God*) is good."[355] We can taste with our spirit senses and see that the Lord is good. We have to go into the spiritual realm and get a revelation of the goodness of God for ourselves. Otherwise, we will believe in the information given to us through our physical senses regarding our present set of circumstances. If our circumstances seem bad, then we may conclude that God is bad. If our circumstances seem good then we may agree that God is good.

"This is similar in nature and application to receiving revelation through spiritual smell. Several times while praying

---

[355] Psalm 34:8 AMP

for individuals, I have suddenly had a very distinct taste in my mouth that was not there previously. When I inquired of the Lord, I realized these tastes were actually prophetic revelation concerning those to whom I was ministering. I was then able to prophesy to them. Others experience this phenomenon when praying for those who are sick."[356]

Spiritual senses are about experiencing the revelation of spiritual realm for ourselves and others. In faith we can bring back His promises to the natural realm to manifest in our daily lives. Instead, many well-meaning Christians try to read the Bible as information on the pages of any good self-help book. They agree with it in their minds, feel good about it with their emotions, and try to do the best they can to live according to it. In a matter of time they begin to recognize that they are not experiencing the same things that they are reading about in His Word. As a result, they become disillusioned with God, taking back control over their lives and thinking that His promises are not for them.

Our spiritual senses help us realize that His promises are for us! Only a revelation of the spiritual realm can change the way we perceive, live, and make decisions in order to experience His promises. It takes more than getting the right intellectual information to our minds to live the abundant life. Information only produces fallible ideas, opinions, and beliefs about our lives, people, and the world around us. It requires a revelation of His Word in our spirit – revelation received as a result of our union with the Holy Spirit. Personal experience through our spiritual senses in the heavenly realm produces faith.

---

[356] Steve Thompson, You May All Prophesy (Charlotte, NC: Morningstar Fellowship Church, 2000), 42

LIFE AND GODLINESS

We need personal knowledge in our spirit that our heart was exchanged with His heart. Only Holy Spirit can diffuse revelation throughout our soul (*mind, will, and emotions*) to free us from belief based on information so we can be illuminated by a spiritual reality.

> For His divine power has bestowed upon us all things that (*are requisite and suited*) to life and godliness, through the (*full, personal*) knowledge of Him who called us by and to His own glory and excellence (*virtue*).[357]

Notice again the past tense usage of the word bestowed in the above text. It is important to understand that God has already given us everything we need for our natural as well as our spiritual lives. It is not going to happen in the future; it has already been completed at a time in the past. It isn't from the natural realm. It is from the spiritual realm.

We already received all that we need for life and godliness through our personal knowledge of Him in union with Holy Spirit. The phrase "personal knowledge" does not mean information received in our soul by our physical senses. It actually implies revelation received through spiritual senses through relationship with Holy Spirit, so we can personally experience the reality of Christ and the heavenly realm, knowing…

> He has bestowed on us His precious and exceedingly great promises, so that through them you may escape (*by flight*) from the moral decay (*rottenness and corruption*) that

---

[357] 2 Peter 1:3 AMP

is in the world because of covetousness (*lust and greed*), and become sharers (*partakers*) of the divine nature.[358]

Enjoying our relationship with Holy Spirit gives opportunity for revelation to come into our life. As we rest in our personal knowledge of our union with Holy Spirit, we are invited by revelation to share in the divine nature of God, revealed in the sensitivity of our spirit and brought back through our spiritual senses to discern in our soul. We can experience the manifestation of His promises in our lives, as we have become partakers in the abundant life.

AGREEING IN FAITH

Many believers have been incorrectly taught that after receiving Jesus Christ as their Savior they will have to wait until they get to heaven to experience the promises of God. Fortunately, that is not biblically sound teaching. The promises of God are not something we hope to receive some day after we die and go to heaven. He has already given us everything that we need right now to live in the fullness of God's promises.

Still other religious people say that we will just have to wait for the revealing of God's sovereign will in regards to His promises. According to Scripture we do not have to wait for God to reveal His will concerning issues He has already spoken to us about in His Word. We may need to get a revelation of His Word in order to experience the manifestation of God's promises for ourselves. But with all certainty the promises of God are the will of God for our lives!

---

[358] 2 Peter 1:4 AMP

All we have to do to live the abundant life is agree with the reality of His promises in the spiritual realm. Joshua and the Israelites had to cross the Jordan River to receive the fullness of God's promises. They could have all stayed on the east side of the Jordan River and never experience life in their promised land, as a result of the impossibility of their natural circumstances based on the information received through their physical senses. Instead, they overcame the impossible obstacle of crossing the Jordan River, entering their promised land by agreeing in faith with the reality of the spiritual realm over the reality of the natural realm.

God is not asking us to pretend that our natural circumstances are not impossible. Holy Spirit is asking us to hope in faith even when there is no hope, by trusting Him to use our spiritual realities to change our natural realities. The God, "who gives life to the dead and speaks of the nonexistent things that (*He has foretold and promised*) as if they (*already*) existed."[359] Remember, Abraham was told by God that he was going to father a child in his old age knowing that "(*human reason for*) hope being gone, hoped in faith that he should become the father of many nations, as he had been promised, so (*numberless*) shall your descendants be."[360]

In the reality of the natural realm, Abraham had no hope. His only hope to see the promise of God fulfilled in his life was to agree in faith with the reality of the spiritual realm over the reality of the natural realm. Abraham, "did not weaken in faith when he considered the (*utter*) impotence of his own body, which was as good as dead because he was about a hundred years old, or (*when he considered*) the barrenness of Sarah's (*dead-*

---

[359] Romans 4:17 AMP
[360] Romans 4:18 AMP

ened) womb."[361] Abraham acknowledged the impossible reality of his natural circumstances and chose to agree in faith with the reality of the spiritual realm over the reality of the natural realm.

> No unbelief or distrust made him waver (*doubtingly question*) concerning the promise of God, but he grew strong and was empowered by faith as he gave praise and glory to God, fully satisfied and assured that God was able and mighty to keep His word and to do what He had promised. That is why his faith was credited to him as righteousness (*right standing with God*). But (*the words*), It was credited to him, were written not for his sake alone, but (*they were written*) for our sakes too. (*Righteousness, standing acceptable to God*) will be granted and credited to us also who believe in, (*trust in, adhere to, and rely on*) God.[362]

Every one of us will face impossible circumstances in our lives. We will all face our own personal Jerichos! It is important to recognize that God has made a way to turn our impossible circumstances to our good, knowing He has already given us everything that we need to be victorious in life and godliness!

Every obstacle is an opportunity for God to release His promises to us. In order to learn to be an overcomer, we must have something to overcome. If we continue to look at the reality of our impossible circumstances in the natural realm, without getting a new perspective from the reality of the spiritual realm, there will always be a Jericho standing between us and the promised land!

---

[361] Romans 4:19 AMP
[362] Romans 4:20-24 AMP

The Israelites would never have received the fullness of the promised land if they had not conquered Jericho. All along, God knew that His people were going to have to face the battle of Jericho. Without the natural reality of the impossible circumstance of Jericho, the Israelites would never have learned to trust the reality of His promises in the spiritual realm. So God said, Joshua look up with your eyes to, "See! I have given Jericho, its king and mighty men of valor, into your hands."[363]

We have to see in order to believe that we have already received!

---

[363] Joshua 6:2 AMP

CHAPTER 8

SHAKING HEAVEN

AND EARTH

"A SEVENTEEN-YEAR-OLD BOY WALKED into a restaurant and heard the Lord tell him to go and sit down next to a certain man. He did so and struck up a conversation. While he was talking to the man, the Holy Spirit began to give him a word of knowledge that the man had a daughter who was dying of cancer. To be sure, he asked the man a few questions. 'Are you married?' he inquired. 'Yes,' came the reply. 'Do you have a daughter?' 'Yes,' the man said. 'Does she have cancer?' he asked compassionately.

"The moment the boy raised that question, the man broke down and started to weep. 'How did you know?' he asked. The young man shared the gospel with the man and told him that God cares so much for him that he would tell a stranger about his daughter. He then asked permission to pray for her. The father was sobbing and said, 'Of course, please pray.'

"As soon as he released the boy to pray, the mother and daughter coincidentally walked into the restaurant! You could see a cancerous growth protruding from the daughter's neck. In boldness, that seventeen-year-old boy, who had already received permission from the father, introduced himself to the mother and daughter and quickly explained that the dad had just given him permission to pray. Before he even got a response, he placed his hands on the daughter's neck and rebuked the cancer in the name of Jesus.

"The cancer fell off right there in the restaurant, and a mini-revival broke out on the spot! The father and mother got down on their knees and began weeping and confessing their sins as fast as they could. People in the restaurant found out what was happening and began turning to God. It was such a commotion that the owner of the restaurant had to call the police to settle down the crowd. Who was that seventeen-year-old boy? He was a believer who used the authority of the name of Jesus!"[364]

NAME OF JESUS

JESUS SAID:

These attesting signs will accompany those who believe: in My name they will drive out demons; they will speak new languages; they will pick up serpents; and (*even*) if they drink anything deadly, it will not hurt them; they will lay their hands on the sick, and they will get well.[365]

In the preceding verse to this passage, the Amplified version defined the person who believes as one "(who adheres to

[364] Che Ahn, The Authority of the Believer and Healing (Colorado Springs, CO: Wagner Publications, 1999), 38-39
[365] Mark 16:17-18 AMP

and trusts in and relies on the Gospel and Him whom it sets forth).″[366] Jesus did not say that these signs will manifest and then we will believe in Him. Instead, these signs accompany those who believe by attesting to the union that they already have with Him. Miracles, signs and wonders are a result of our belief in His name through our relationship resulting in revelation with the Holy Spirit.

Miracles, signs and wonders follow saints!

If our attitude is, "I will believe it when I see it in the natural," then we are operating out of unbelief in the supernatural, based on our belief in the natural, without knowing who we are in union with Holy Spirit. We betray our new nature by trusting in an inferior reality, as we allow it to dominate the influence of our soul (mind, will, and emotions) and cut ourselves off from receiving revelation, the true substance of faith!

"Without faith it is impossible to please and be satisfactory to Him."[367] This is because God is not happy about having a relationship with us if we don't trust Him. Imagine being in an important relationship with someone who didn't trust you. It would be difficult to be pleased, let alone satisfied, with the person and the relationship.

Trust is the foundation for any healthy relationship. As a result, it is important to build relationship with someone to know that they are trustworthy before you can trust them. In the same way, in relationship with Christ through our union with Holy Spirit we receive revelation to know that He is trustworthy, so we can trust in His name!

---

[366] Mark 16:16 AMP
[367] Hebrews 11:6 AMP

There is power released in us by the Holy Spirit when we have faith in the name of Jesus Christ.

God has highly exalted Him and has freely bestowed on Him the name that is above every name, that in (*at*) the name of Jesus every knee should (*must*) bow, in heaven and earth and under the earth, and every tongue (*frankly and openly*) confess and acknowledge that Jesus Christ is Lord, to the glory of God the Father.[368]

Jesus' name is above every principality, every power, any earthly king or government, and over anything in the spirit realm. He is exalted above every other name! The name above all names!

When you are born again, you are seated immediately in heavenly places, regardless of your earthly position. We are in Christ, so if Jesus is in heavenly places, above all principalities, that is where we are also. When operating as an obedient believer, you are not operating from ground level; you are operating from a heavenly level.[369]

"When we exercise our authority, we do so in the name of Jesus and on His behalf. You might liken this to the power of attorney. The power of attorney means you have been given full permission to act with the full power and authority of another individual."[370] "It gives us the right to use somebody else's name for whatever purpose that they said we can use it. If someone has been given the power of attorney over another person's

---

[368] Philippians 2:9-11 AMP
[369] Sean Smith, Prophetic Evangelism (Shippensburg, PA: Destiny Image Publishers Inc, 2004), 198
[370] Che Ahn, The Authority of the Believer and Healing (Colorado Springs, CO: Wagner Publications, 1999), 31-32

estate, they have the power to make all the legal and financial transactions for the estate with their authority. This is the same thing that Jesus has done for us in regards to His name!

"The only difference is that He asks you to exercise faith in using His name. It is like a double signature check that Jesus has already signed. All you must do is sign your name under His and use the authority He has already given. Thus, when you cast out demons in His name, it is as if Jesus Himself is casting out the demons. It is the same with raising the dead. When you pray His name, it is Jesus who is doing the raising. It is His authority and His power that have been delegated to us, and we are co-laboring with Him. That is why it is called the Great Commission. We are laborers with Him, in conjunction with Him."[371]

UNWAVERING FAITH

We need to know that we have already received our requests in the spiritual realm in order to receive them in the natural realm. "For the one who wavers (*hesitates, doubts*) is like the billowing surge out at sea that is blown hither and thither and tossed by the wind."[372] Then if we cannot trust the revelation received as a result of our relationship with God, over the appearance of our circumstances, we will not "receive anything from the Lord."[373] In other words, God is saying that if we cannot trust in what He has said to us, then we should not even bother to think that we will receive anything we have asked from Him. "It must be in faith that he asks with no wavering (*no hesitating, no doubting*)."[374]

---

[371] Che Ahn, The Authority of the Believer and Healing (Colorado Springs, CO: Wagner Publications, 1999), 31-32
[372] James 1:6 AMP
[373] James 1:7 NKJV
[374] James 1:6 AMP

It is an issue of trust in our relationship with God. In the preceding verses to this passage, James says:

> Be assured and understand that the trial and proving of your faith bring out endurance and steadfastness and patience.[375]

This verse is saying that our faith will be put on trial. The revelation we received through the Spirit is going to be tested. At the end of that trial we will return a verdict with our words and actions as to whether we know who we are standing and trusting, the revelation of the Word of God or the information received through our physical senses.

If we will "let endurance and steadfastness and patience have full play and do a thorough work," we will become "perfectly and fully developed (*with no defects*), lacking in nothing."[376] James says, "Consider it wholly joyful"[377] during this trial of our faith. It is an opportunity to trust the revelation of His Word received by Holy Spirit, allowing us to become perfectly and fully developed in our faith through relationship with Him.

We no longer waver as a result of inferior information received through our physical senses about who we are, who He is, and the resources we have already been given in Him. We have learned to trust the revelation of the spiritual realm so we will be found lacking in nothing as it manifests in our natural realm. We have already received everything needed to overcome every trial to experience the promises of God for our lives.

---

[375] James 1:3 AMP
[376] James 1:4 AMP
[377] James 1:2 AMP

POWER AND AUTHORITY

In Luke 9:1-2, AMP, we read:

Jesus called together the twelve (*apostles*) and gave them power and authority over all demons, and to cure diseases. And He sent them out to announce and preach the Kingdom of God and to bring healing.

The word for *power* here is the Greek word *dunamis*. It means "force, and miraculous power through ability, abundance, might, miracle(s), strength, violence, and mighty (wonderful) work."[378] It is the same Greek word in which we get the English word *dynamite*. The word *authority* here in the Greek is the word *exousia*. It means "delegated privilege, force, capacity, competency, freedom, or mastery (concr. magistrate, superhuman, potentate, token of control) through delegated influence; liberty, jurisdiction, power, right, and strength."[379]

Jesus gave the disciples the exact same power and authority contained within the jurisdiction of His name. They were given superhuman authority and power to overcome opposition in the spiritual realm in order to change the circumstances of the natural realm. He delegated His influence to them by sending them out with the explosive power of His supernatural ability in order to share the abundance of the good news of the kingdom of God. They were to demonstrate His might by bringing freedom to those in bondage and releasing the miracle of healing to the sick. It was a right bestowed upon them by His strength as a result of a relationship with Him. In the same way, we have already been given spiritual authority and power to overcome spiritual

---

[378] Strong's Exhaustive Concordance, Reference 1411
[379] Strong's Exhaustive Concordance, Reference 1849

problems in order to see our natural circumstances change by agreeing in faith with His Word.

MAGNIFY THE LORD

Despite the early attacks on my wife's health during the ninth week of her pregnancy, Tammi and I learned to exercise our faith to magnify the power and authority of the name of Jesus over the circumstances of her pregnancy. One of the doctors even implied that she should consider aborting the baby due to her current condition and the history of her health regarding her three previous pregnancies. During this time the Holy Spirit spoke to my wife that she was to continue to believe Jesus' report for divine health in the continuation of her pregnancy over the report of the doctor. In addition, the Holy Spirit promised her that she would be able to go into labor on her own for the first time without having to be induced.

About a month ago, Tammi called me on the phone after one of her regularly scheduled appointments with the obstetrician. She was excited to share the confirmed report of the Lord. During her visit, the doctor told her that she was a "walking miracle." Tammi told her, "Jesus answered my prayers to heal my body during this pregnancy!" The doctor replied, "There is no other explanation for it!" The doctor continued that she never expected Tammi to make it this far in her pregnancy without being transported to a hospital in another city for premature delivery and care. Similar conversations between the doctor and my wife continued for the next several weeks about the miraculous state of her health. At one point the doctor told my wife, "I would like to talk with you more about this prayer thing that you're doing to stay so healthy." She continued to say, "I should consider using you to train all my high risk pregnancy patients in prayer to see if they would receive the same miraculous results as you!"

On the first day of week thirty-eight of my wife's pregnancy, she went into labor naturally on her own as promised by Holy Spirit. Tammi gave birth to Josie Grace Reanier at 1:57 p.m. on September 24, 2007, without any complications. She was our fourth baby girl, weighing 6 pounds and 15 ounces with a length of 20 inches. She weighed more than any of our other girls at birth even though the ultra sound report two weeks prior said that she weighed only about 5 pounds.

The name Josie means, "God adding to His favor!" Grace means, "God's favor through His operational power." Put it altogether and the name Josie Grace means God adding favor to His favor through His operational power. Josie truly is living proof of God adding favor to His already established favor in our lives through the operational power that resides in the magnified name of Jesus!

In Psalm 34:3 David said, "O magnify the Lord with me, and let us exalt His name together."[380] The word *magnify* in this passage is the Hebrew word *gadal*. It means "to twist, to be (cause or make) large (in various senses, as in body, mind, estate or home, also in pride), advance, boast, bring up, exceed, excellent be (come, do, give, make, wax), great, greater, come to…estate plus things), grow (up), increase, be much set by nourish (up), pass, promote, proudly (spoken), tower."[381] It is the same word we use for the name in magnifying glass.

When we view something through a magnifying glass, everything becomes larger. The things outside the view of a

[380] Psalm 34:3 AMP
[381] Strong's Exhaustive Concordance, Reference 1431

magnifying glass stay at the same size so all our focus is on the objects being magnified. When David said, "magnify the Lord with me," it is in the context of magnifying God to be bigger than our problems. As we "exalt His name" we begin to receive revelation to see a God who is larger than all our circumstances.

We can agree with the impossibility of our circumstances, or we can agree with the "(action of His) power that is at work within us, is able to (carry out His purpose and) do superabundantly, far over and above all that we (dare) ask or think (infinitely beyond our highest prayers, desires, thoughts, hopes, or dreams)."[382] In order to overcome the impossible obstacles that stand between us and the abundant life, we need to have a revelation of the power of the name and nature of Jesus that is at work within us. We need to be able to see into the spiritual realm for ourselves that God is able to carry out His purpose for our lives. He is super abundantly far over and above all we ask or think. He is beyond our highest prayers, desires, thoughts, hopes, and dreams. He is certainly larger than the impossibility of our natural circumstances. After all, He is the Name above all names!

Joshua and the Israelites needed revelation to see God as larger than the impossible obstacle they faced to conquer Jericho, before they could experience the fullness of the promised land. What impossible circumstances are keeping you from experiencing the fullness of God's promises in your life? What one impossible area in your life stands between you and the promises of God? Whatever the name of the impossible obstacle, we must have a revelation to see the name of Jesus magnified above that name! We must have a revelation to see that God is bigger than our Jericho!

---

[382] Ephesians 3:20 AMP

If cancer is our impossible obstacle, then we must have a revelation to see the name of Jesus magnified above the name of cancer. If we continue to magnify cancer over the name of Jesus, then we will only continue to magnify and exalt the problem until it gives birth to fear and death in our lives. Without a revelation to see the name of Jesus Christ above all names, fear will limit everything we do! It will keep us spiritually blind and unable to see opportunities to experience His promises for our lives. It will paralyze us as we focus on the appearance of our natural circumstances over His reality in the spiritual realm. We will become a slave to fear until we make it submit to the authority of the magnified name of Jesus Christ!

When we receive a revelation of Jesus, the Name above all names magnified in the heavenly realm, above the name of our impossible circumstance in the natural realm, then our problems will have to submit to His authority. Then we can realize for ourselves that Jesus has already accomplished everything we need to be victorious over every circumstance. He took the keys of death while conquering sickness and disease. Jesus is our deliver and our protector. He has already given us everything we need to preserve, protect, and make us safe. Jesus overcame every obstacle that would keep us from doing well so that we could prosper according to His promises.

GREATER THINGS

Jesus said, "If anyone steadfastly believes in Me, he will himself be able to do the things that I do; and he will do even greater things than these."[383] In other words, He says when we have a genuine relationship of trust established with Him, we

---

[383] John 14:12 AMP

will receive revelation from the spiritual realm to do the same, and even greater miraculous signs and wonders, as He manifested when bringing His ministry from heaven to earth. Jesus tells us that we can be sure of this because, "I will do (*I Myself will grant*) whatever you ask in My Name (*as presenting all that I AM*), so that the Father may be glorified and extolled in (*through*) the Son."[384]

In case we may have thought that we misunderstood Jesus' words, He repeats Himself again, emphasizing, "(*Yes*) I will grant (*I Myself will do for you*) whatever you shall ask in My Name (*as presenting all that I AM*)."[385]

As a believer we have the authority and the power of the name of Jesus Christ living inside of us. God is not a respecter of people. The Bible says "as many as did receive and welcome Him, He gave the authority (*power, privilege, right*) to become the children of God, that is, to those who believe in (*adhere to, trust in, and rely on*) His name."[386]

His authority and power is not just for a few believers with a special call, it is for all who are born again of His Spirit. We need a relationship with Him resulting in revelation of what Christ has done for us and given to us so we can bring back His promises from the spiritual realm to experience them in the natural realm. We need the supernatural to empower our soul so the name of Jesus will be exalted above every other name! We need to see the name of Jesus magnified above the name of our Jericho!

---

[384] John 14:13 AMP
[385] John 14:14 AMP
[386] John 1:12 AMP

MOVING MOUNTAINS

Once Jesus was with His disciples and, "They noticed that the fig tree was withered (*completely*) away to its roots."[387] Peter remembered that Jesus had cursed the fig tree with His words just days earlier, saying, "Master, look! The fig tree which You doomed has withered away!"[388] Interestingly, Jesus replied to Peter by saying, "Have faith in God (*constantly*)."[389]

Then He continued to instruct His disciples by telling them, "Whoever says to this mountain, Be lifted up and thrown into the sea! And does not doubt at all in his heart but believes that what he says will take place, it will be done for him."[390] Jesus said the reason He was saying this was so that whatever we ask for in prayer, we would "believe (*trust and be confident*) that it is granted to you, and you will (*get it*)."[391]

This verse can become a stumbling block to the strongest Christian! Does Jesus actually mean what He is saying in this passage? Is doubt and unbelief keeping us from having the faith to experience the promises of God for our lives? Should we pretend that our circumstances are good when, in fact, we can see for ourselves that they are negative, with no indication of changing?

In the natural we all have reason for doubt and unbelief when left to accomplish results based on our own strength and abilities. Jesus was saying that when we receive revelation as a result of our union with Holy Spirit, we should be able to

---

[387] Mark 11:20 AMP
[388] Mark 11:21 AMP
[389] Mark 11:22 AMP
[390] Mark 11:23 AMP
[391] Mark 11:24 AMP

trust His Word to come to pass. Notice that relationship is a key component to unlocking our ability to have faith in order to trust in God!

We cannot allow doubt and unbelief to dominate our soul based on information from the natural realm. We need revelation received by Holy Spirit to empower our soul, to see with eyes of faith the reality of the spiritual realm magnified over the appearance of our problems. If we receive a Word in our spirit from God and are still controlled by doubt and unbelief, then we obviously have some identity issues that are going to result in difficulty in our lives. Jesus is not saying we should not have doubts and unbelief, if we do not know what God is saying to us. As a matter of fact, we better have some doubts, if we do not know that we have heard from God for ourselves! We can stand in faith when we have revelation to trust Holy Spirit!

The mountain in this passage represents an impossible obstacle in the natural realm standing between us and the promises of God. We have to move this mountain to experience the abundant life for ourselves. All of our natural strength and abilities cannot move the mountain. This mountain can only be moved when we "have faith in God (*constantly*)."[392] As a result of revelation in our spirit, we can trust, agree and be confident in the reality of His authority in the heavenly realm. Then we can speak to the mountain with authority and without doubting so it will move out of our way in the natural realm, because we have already seen it move out of our way in the spiritual realm!

We will not see the mountains in our lives move through positive confessions based on information about the Word of God. These mountains will only move when we speak to them

---

[392] Mark 11:22 AMP

in agreement with revelation from the spiritual realm. It is in agreement with revelation from His Spirit that we can command a mountain to move, and it will move because He said it would move. "What is impossible with men is possible with God."[393] It becomes possible as we are empowered by the spiritual reality of all that we have already been given in Christ.

> The word in the New Testament for confession is homologia, which means say the same thing. Biblical confession is saying what God says—no more, no less. If it is not what God is saying about a situation, it does nothing. But if it is what He says, it accomplishes much.[394] We must understand that it is not an issue of what our words would normally do. It is rather speaking for God, which releases His power to accomplish something. Is not this what happens as we preach or declare the gospel, which is the power of God for salvation?[395]

Our confession as a believer is about agreeing with what Holy Spirit is saying! We don't make positive confessions about the reality of our negative circumstances by pretending that they are positive, when in fact they are negative. We make positive confessions in faith about our negative circumstances in the natural, based on evidence from the superior reality of the supernatural realm, so our positive confessions agree fully with the promises revealed by our spiritual senses through Holy Spirit, allowing our confessions as Christians to be based on the things that Father is saying and doing! Only then will we see the reality of the spiritual realm manifest in the natural realm!

---

[393] Luke 18:27 AMP
[394] Dutch Sheets, Intercessory Prayer (Ventura, CA: Regal Books, 1996), 226
[395] Ibid, 223

Without revelation that Jesus has already conquered the mountain standing between us and the promises of God, we will begin to function out of the wrong identity, allowing ourselves to be limited by information based on the appearance of our circumstances, like the natural, unspiritual man. We rehearse the lies of the enemy in our minds of all the reasons we will never be able to overcome the impossible obstacle before us, all because we cannot see in the spiritual realm that Jesus has already won the battle! We think we still have to win the battle on our own, not knowing that Jesus has already moved every mountain and conquered every Jericho!

We have to quit living on the wrong side of the cross, trying to do the same things that He has already accomplished! Every mountain is an opportunity for us to rest in His accomplishments, as we allow the Holy Spirit to reveal our true identity in union with Him. We can refuse to no longer live a spiritual schizophrenic life based on a wrong identity and begin to sanctify our imagination with revelation from Him, so we can be empowered with eyes to see the reality of the spiritual realm in order to agree fully with His promises for us over the appearance of our natural circumstances.

> If God is for us, who (*can be*) against us? (*Who can be our foe, if God is on our side?*) He who did not withhold or spare (*even*) His own Son but gave Him up for us all, will He not also with Him freely and graciously give us all (*other*) things?[396]

It is important to know that God is on our side! He can't be against us because He can't be against Himself! He is in

---

[396] Romans 8:31-32 AMP

us, therefore He is for us! His nature has already become our nature! Therefore we are victorious, because He is victorious! Our enemies are defeated because His enemies are defeated! His destiny has already become our preordained destiny!

He proved it when giving His own Son for us. We were given His nature and name so no authority and power in the spiritual or natural realm could prevail against us. God is a good God who loves us so much that He wouldn't even spare the life of His own Son for us! As a result, God has already freely and graciously given us every other good thing that we could ever need to experience His promises for our lives!

ALREADY VICTORIOUS

Joshua and the Israelites were getting ready to go into the most difficult battle of their lives against the city and inhabitants of Jericho. In the natural they were facing impossible odds to win the battle! Joshua was looking and contemplating the impossible challenge of defeating Jericho in the battle, when he received a revelation from the Spirit that allowed him to see the Israelites' victory over Jericho before the battle had even begun in the natural realm! No man had ever defeated Jericho, but Joshua knew that he had already won the battle before it even started!

Imagine if you were about to face the biggest battle of your life! Wouldn't it be great to go into that battle like Joshua, knowing that you were already victorious in Him? Would it become easier for you to face the impossible circumstances in your life if you knew you had already overcome them to receive His promises? It could change the whole way we think, act and see our problems in the natural realm!

We would be experiencing the mind of Christ, understanding the new identity we have already been given, with a heavenly perspective that allows us to operate our daily lives out of who we are rather than what we do! We are continually downloaded with revelation from the spiritual realm about our victory in Christ so we can experience the manifestation of those promises!

Jesus wanted us to live by revelation from the spiritual realm to "clearly demonstrate through the ages to come the immeasurable (*limitless, surpassing*) riches of His free grace (*His unmerited favor*) in (*His*) kindness and goodness of heart toward us in Christ Jesus."[397] The phrase here, "His unmerited favor," means the power of God to accomplish our destiny. It's not just favor that reconciles us relationally because He has forgiven our past sins. It's the power to accomplish our future through revelation of the resources that have already been given to us, guaranteeing our success!

HEAVEN ON EARTH

In the Lord's Prayer, Jesus teaches us to pray to the Father, "Your Kingdom come. Your will be done on earth as it is in heaven."[398] He would never ask us to pray for the will of God to manifest on earth as it is in heaven unless it was possible for us to experience the answer to that prayer. "This is the primary focus for all prayer—if it exists in heaven, it is to be loosed on earth. It is the praying Christian who looses heaven's expression here.

When the believer prays according to the revealed will of God, faith is specific and focused. Faith grabs hold of that

[397] Ephesians 2:7 AMP
[398] Matthew 6:10 AMP

254

reality. Enduring faith does not let go. Such an invasion causes the circumstances here to line up with heaven.

> The critics of this view sarcastically say, "So I guess we are supposed to pray for streets of gold." No! But our streets should be known for the same purity and blessing as heaven…Everything that happens here is supposed to be a shadow of heaven. In turn, every revelation that God gives us of heaven is to equip us with a prayer focus.[399]

> The will of God is seen in the ruling presence of God, for "where the Spirit of the Lord is, there is liberty." Wherever the Spirit of the Lord is demonstrating the Lordship of Jesus, liberty is the result. Yet another way to say it is that when the King of kings manifests His dominion, the fruit of that dominion is Liberty. That is the realm called The Kingdom of God. God, in response to our cries, brings His world into ours. Conversely, if it is not free to exist in heaven, it must be bound here. Again through prayer we are to exercise the authority given to us.[400]

> As we read previously in chapters one and five, Jesus says:

> I will give you the keys of the kingdom of heaven; and whatever you bind (*declare to be improper and unlawful*) on earth must be what is already bound in heaven; and whatever you loose (*declare lawful*) on earth must be what is already loosed in heaven.[401]

---

[399] Bill Johnson, When Heaven Invades Earth (Shippensburg, PA: Destiny Image Publishers Inc, 2003), 59
[400] Ibid, 60
[401] Matthew 16:19 AMP

The Greek word *loose* in this verse is *luo*.[402] "The legal meaning of *luo* is (1) to pronounce or determine that something or someone is no longer bound; (2) to dissolve or void a contract or anything that legally binds. Jesus came to dissolve the legal hold Satan had over us and to pronounce that we were no longer bound by his works. He 'voided the contract,' breaking his dominion over us."

"The physical meaning of *luo* is 'to dissolve or melt, break, beat something to pieces or untie something that is bound.' In Acts 27:41 the boat Paul traveled on was broken to pieces (luo) by the force of a storm. In 2 Peter 3:10, 12 we are told that one day the elements of the earth will melt or dissolve (luo) from a great heat. Jesus not only delivered us legally, but He also made certain the literal consequences of that deliverance were manifested: He brought healing, set captives free, lifted oppression and liberated those under demonic control."[403]

"An interesting word is used in 1 John 3:8 (KJV) that adds insight to what happened on the cross. The verse reads, 'For this purpose the Son of God was manifested, that he might destroy the works of the devil.' Destroy is the Greek word, luo, which has both a legal and a physical meaning. Understanding its full definition will greatly enhance our knowledge of what Jesus did to Satan and his works....The question is 'Did Christ luo the works of the devil or do we luo the works of the devil.' The answer is yes. Although Jesus fully accomplished the task of breaking the authority of Satan and voiding his legal hold upon the human race, someone on earth must represent Him in that victory to enforce it."[404]

---

[402] Strong's Exhaustive Concordance, Reference 3089
[403] Ibid, 56
[404] Dutch Sheets, Intercessory Prayer (Ventura, CA: Regal Books, 1996), 56

REPRESENTING JESUS

During my days at Fuller Theological Seminary, I had an opportunity to go on a one-day healing crusade in Mexico. At one of our meetings we were praying for people's needs at the altar. It was not long before several of us were laying hands and praying for one man in particular. He wanted to be healed and set free.

As we were praying, one of the men in the group received a revelation that this man was possessed by a spirit of death, so he began to command the spirit of death to loose this man in the name of Jesus Christ. The man we were praying for began involuntarily convulsing, saliva drooling down the side of his face.

We continued to pray in agreement, commanding the spirit of death to loosen this man in the name of Jesus. Within a short time there was a foul aroma followed by the appearance of a green mist that came out of the man's mouth, leaving our presence to disappear into the air before our very eyes. The countenance of the man's face dramatically changed as he thanked us for our prayers.

He testified that Jesus had set him free and taken away the pain in his body. He was delivered from a spirit of death that had tried to take his life many times, as we were able to represent Jesus that day by enforcing the victory that He had already accomplished in the spiritual realm! It was the authority of Christ in us that destroyed the works of the devil to liberate a demon-possessed man to experience God's promised healing for his life.

MODEL OF JESUS

Many Christian people have never had the joy of destroying the works of the devil by partnering with Jesus. They don't know who they are in union with Holy Spirit. As a result, they are not having a relationship with Holy Spirit resulting in revelation to experience the abundant life. It's the believers actually experiencing the consistent manifestation of the supernatural in their lives who are receiving revelation of His Kingdom directly from the Father through relationship with Holy Spirit! They are seeing their inheritance in the spiritual realm before salvation, healing, freedom and deliverance are manifesting in the natural realm!

This is the way Jesus operated when ministering during His time on earth. We know this because He told His disciples:

> The Son is able to do nothing of Himself (*of His own accord*); but He is able to do only what He sees the Father doing, for whatever the Father does is what the Son does in the same way (*in His turn*). The Father dearly loves the Son and discloses to (*shows*) Him everything that He Himself does. And he will disclose to Him (*let Him see*) greater things yet than these, so that you may marvel and be full of wonder and astonishment.[405]

Jesus revealed His secret here to being able to consistently experience the manifestation of the promised miracles of God in the natural realm. Jesus was limited in the same way we are by the flesh when He made this statement. Nevertheless, He continually manifested the supernatural in the midst of the natural.

[405] John 5:19-20 AMP

Jesus Himself was the ultimate model for us when it came to living in relationship with the Father resulting in revelation. He was unable to perform even one miracle Himself. Every word Jesus spoke and every miracle He performed was a result of revelation received from His Heavenly Father. Jesus demonstrated His way of life to us and explained it to us in His Word so we could live our lives in the same way He lived His life on earth.

Whatever Jesus could see His Father doing in the spiritual realm, He could do it in the natural realm. Whatever Jesus could hear His Father doing in the spiritual realm, He could speak into existence in the natural realm. In the same way, Jesus wants us to train our spiritual senses to see and hear revelation from the spiritual realm so we can experience the manifestation of His promises in the natural. We have to receive it in our spirit before we can release faith in our soul to experience it in our lives.

Jesus said, *"Follow Me."* In other words, "I'm setting the example, so follow My example." Jesus' desire is that His life would be reproduced in us, that we would model our ministry after Him…We can do nothing of ourselves, but that's not the end of the Scripture! What He sees the Father do, the Son can do. Here's the key: If I can see the Father doing it, I can do it. If you can see God do it, you can put your hand to it and partner with Him. The key is the ability to see what He is doing. Let's take it a step further. If you are seeing something that God is doing, it is an invitation for your participation. If you can see it, you can do it.[406]

---

[406] Sean Smith, Prophetic Evangelism (Shippensburg, PA: Destiny Image Publishers Inc, 2004), 209-210

The word used for disclose means to expose to the eyes, to exhibit, to make known...Because the Father loves us, He promises to reveal to us what He is doing so we can partner with Him. The Son did nothing apart from what the Father has shown Him. If you feed on this revelation you will have something released in you that will change everything around you.[407]

Unless I See, I will not Believe!

Every believer can learn to live in revelation when they have a value for the unseen. The problem is that some people want to see it in the natural before they have received it in their spirit. The philosophy is found in a common statement made by people every day, "Unless I see it first, I will not believe it." It does not work that way with God! As a matter of fact, it works just the opposite!

Unless we can believe it first, then we will never see it. "For whoever would come near to God must (*necessarily*) believe that God exists and that He is the rewarder of those who earnestly and diligently seek Him (*out*)."[408] This is the testimony of our salvation experience. First we believed and then we received! We were blind, but now we see!

Although this verse is really intended for the pre-Christian! When we believed, we already received our reward! Isn't Jesus our reward? Now He isn't just near us! He's in us! We have already received our inheritance in Him, including salvation, deliverance, health, provision and success!

---

[407] Sean Smith, Prophetic Evangelism (Shippensburg, PA: Destiny Image Publishers Inc, 2004), 210
[408] Hebrews 11:6 AMP

Jesus said "seek and you will find"...Seeking is not supposed to be a lifelong ordeal. Yes we are daily enjoying Him. Constantly growing in greater and greater revelation of His fullness! But it's a fullness we already have...Isn't your claim to Christianity a very boast that you are no longer looking for answers, but that you have found Him? Christianity is the only religion that can scandalously boast that we are no longer seeking, but have confidently laid hold of God.[409]

It's this greater and greater revelation we are growing in that allows us to see in the Spirit so we can believe in the natural, that we cannot only believe in the natural but see and experience His promises in our lives. We received salvation by revelation, and now we live by revelation! It wasn't meant to be a one-time experience but a new way of life!

Now we have a new nature with Holy Spirit residing in us. It's who we are in Christ, so we can see the reality of His existence and all the rewards He has already given to us in the spiritual realm. The veil was already removed from our eyes to have faith to believe so we may see the manifestation of our heavenly inheritance in our flesh and blood world, where first we believe and then we see!

In his book, *When Heaven Invades Earth*, Bill Johnson says, "Most all the people that I have known who are filled with unbelief have called themselves realists...Those kinds of realists believe more in what is visible than they do in what they cannot see. Put another way, they believe the material world rules over

---

[409] John Crowder, Mystical Union (Santa Cruz, CA: Sons of Thunder Ministries & Publications, 2010), 117-119

the spiritual world."[410] "Unbelief is anchored in what is visible or reasonable apart from God. It honors the natural realm as superior to the invisible. The apostle Paul states that what you can see is temporal, and what you cannot see is eternal. Unbelief is faith in the inferior."[411]

"The invisible realm is superior to the natural. The reality of that invisible world dominates that natural world we live in...both positively and negatively. Because the invisible is superior to the natural, faith is anchored in the unseen. Faith lives in the revealed will of God. When I have misconceptions of who He is and what He is like, my faith is restricted by those misconceptions. For example, if I believe that God allows sickness in order to build character, I'll not have the confidence praying in most situations where healing is needed."[412]

"We are a sensual society with a culture shaped by what is picked up through the senses. We are trained to believe only in what we see. Real faith is not living in denial of the natural realm. If the doctor says you have a tumor, it is silly to pretend that it is not there. That's not faith. However faith is founded on a reality that is superior to that tumor. I can acknowledge the existence of a tumor and still have faith in the provision of His stripes for my healing...I was provisionally healed 2,000 years ago. It is the product of the Kingdom of heaven—a superior reality. There are no tumors in heaven, and faith brings that reality into this one."[413]

Unfortunately, many Christians today have begun to take on the attitude of unbelievers by basing their faith in an inferior

[410] Bill Johnson, When Heaven Invades Earth (Shippensburg, PA: Destiny Image Publishers Inc, 2003), 45-46
[411] Ibid, 45
[412] Ibid, 45
[413] Ibid, 46

reality. They will not believe in the supernatural unless they first see it in the natural. We would expect to hear unbelievers make comments consumed with doubt, but it can be startling to hear a believer make comments that are rooted in such unbelief.

Believers should not be making comments of unbelief based on an inferior reality. They should be making statements of belief based on faith to trust Him. It is not the nature or the character of a believer to operate in unbelief. The character of a believer is built on faith. We believe God according to His spoken Word to us! After all, we are called believers! Isn't that what believers are supposed to do? Believe!

AGREEING WITH HEAVEN

When Joshua was facing the battle of Jericho, God said, "See, I have given you Jericho."[414] Imagine if Joshua would have said, "God, I cannot see what you are seeing, therefore I cannot believe in what I do not see!" Joshua and the Israelites would never have received the fullness of God's promises. Thankfully, Joshua had received a word in his spirit from God!

In the natural, Jericho was still standing! According to all natural appearances, the walls of Jericho would not fall down. Joshua could see in the natural just like every one else in Israel could see that the obstacle before them was impossible! So he "commanded the people, You shall not shout or let your voice be heard, nor shall any word proceed out of your mouth until the day I tell you to shout. Then you shall shout!"[415]

Joshua had already experienced the power of a negative report the first time the Israelites were to take the promised

---

[414] Joshua 6:2 AMP
[415] Joshua 6:10 AMP

land. Only Joshua and Caleb believed the report of the Lord. The negative report of ten spies caused the people of Israel to doubt the spoken word of the Lord. The negative words of a few had kept a whole nation from receiving the promises of God!

The last time they did not believe God's report, they spent forty years wandering in the wilderness. This time Joshua was not going to let anything stand between the people of Israel and the promise of God, including Jericho! As a result, Joshua began to act as if God's Word had already been accomplished in the natural realm. He did not want to take any chances of a possible negative report this time, so he instructed the people not to let "any word proceed out of your mouth until the day I tell you to shout."[416] Joshua had come to know firsthand that faith separates those who do not receive from those who do receive!

Then Joshua began to lead the people of God to march around the walled city of Jericho for seven days, based on the word of the Lord. They marched for seven days without any evidence of anything happening in the natural realm. Imagine the difficulty of trying to keep a nation persevering in the promises of God for seven days without seeing any results.

Joshua did not want the people to be persuaded by unbelief while talking with one another about all the reasons why God's word to them was impossible! It paid off at the end of the seven days when all of Israel shouted a victory shout and the walls of Jericho came down in the natural realm, according to the already fulfilled Word of the Lord in the spiritual realm! Joshua chose to believe in a superior reality over an inferior reality! He had already seen the victory over Jericho in the heavenly realm!

---

[416] Joshua 6:10 AMP

Kenneth Hagin, Jr., said, "I once read a survey that said 95 percent of people live according to what their body and their fleshly desires tell them. Their whole life consists of living from one fleshly desire to another. Only about 5 percent live according to what they believe. And about 8 out of 10 in that group think and believe what others tell them to think and believe! Only a very small percentage of the people in that particular survey truly think and believe in line with God and His Word, and with what He has said about their lives and their futures."[417]

He continued to say, "Our beliefs—what we believe in our heart—should determine our attitude, our mindset or mentality...if we are believing the Word of God, we should have a positive mental attitude. One of the greatest privileges you and I have as believers is that we can take the Word of God and develop the mentality that God wants us to have, that will position us to receive and walk in His abundance...Your thinking will affect your believing and your speaking—what you're saying—about your life. So you absolutely must learn to think right before you'll ever be able to experience the things that God has made available to you."[418]

Jesus said, "If two of you on earth agree (*harmonize together, make a symphony together*) about whatever (*anything and everything*) they may ask, it will come to pass and be done for them by My Father in heaven."[419] This verse says that when we agree with any one thing that is accomplished in the heavenly realm, it will come to pass in the natural realm. We know this because Jesus

---

[417] Kenneth Hagin Jr., Overflow, Living Above Life's Limits (Tulsa, OK: Rhema Bible Church 2006), 28
[418] Ibid, 28
[419] Matthew 18:19 AMP

instructs us in the preceding verse on the way we should agree in order to receive the promises of God in our lives. He says:

> Whatever you forbid and declare to be improper and unlawful on earth must be what is already forbidden in heaven, and whatever you permit and declare proper and lawful on earth must be what is already permitted in heaven.[420]

Our agreement is not just a natural agreement. It's an agreement with heaven. Unity isn't based on our ability to agree with one another. It's based on our agreement with heaven! So when we agree with Him, we agree with one another!

When we agree with the Word that God has spoken to us from heaven, it releases the promises of God to come into fruition in our lives. On the other hand, when we disagree with the Word He has spoken to us it can cause our own future to be found void of the promises of God. Many people never experience the promises of God because they agree with their experiences, circumstances, and other people's negative words, rather than agreeing with the testimony of heaven! When information received through our physical senses dominates over our soul, then we are agreeing with a report that is contrary to the revelation of the spiritual realm. That's not who we are!

As believers, we need the revelation of heaven diffused throughout our soul to empower the way we feel, think and act, so we can stand and agree in faith with heaven, allowing us to experience breakthrough in the natural arena of our lives! Real faith is birthed in relationship through union with Holy Spirit

---

[420] Matthew 18:18 AMP

resulting in revelation in our heart. "For out of the fullness (*the overflow, the superabundance*) of the heart the mouth speaks."[421]

Our faith starts in our hearts but manifests in our actions and words! If our words and actions are filled with doubt and unbelief, then it is a good indicator that we need revelation in our hearts so we can learn to speak in agreement with heaven! The walls of Jericho never fell until the Israelites shouted a victory shout that agreed with the testimony of the spiritual realm! It all began because one man, Joshua, agreed with revelation received from the spiritual realm as a result of relationship with God.

He believed and trusted God according to His spoken word, allowing a whole nation to experience the promises of God. Joshua agreed in his heart with heaven's report and refused to be persuaded to agree with any negative reports about the appearance of the natural realm. Then he put his faith into action by speaking the superior reality of heaven into the inferior reality of earth!

There is power in the actions we perform and the words we speak!

A RIDICULOUS IDEA

If we are ever going to see our faith manifested in the natural realm, then we need to agree with heaven by putting our faith into action. During my junior year at Seattle Pacific University, I attended a church retreat for college students. My friend Scott Campbell and I were driving back home when we felt prompted by Holy Spirit to share our faith with an unbeliever, so we decided to stop at a 7-Eleven convenience store and ask the cashier if we

---

[421] Matthew 12:34 AMP

could talk to them about Jesus Christ in addition to taking their picture as a memory of our conversation.

We went inside the store and began to strike up a conversation with the woman behind the cash register. Scott and I began sharing our testimonies with her about what Jesus had done in our lives. Then we asked the woman if she had a relationship with Jesus Christ. She said, "I have never made a commitment to have a relationship with Him, but I have been to church and heard about Him a couple of times." As we prepared to ask her if she would like to accept Jesus Christ personally as her Savior, we were interrupted by a large number of customers.

It became obvious that we were not going to be able to continue our conversation. We left the store, hanging our heads and thinking we had missed an opportunity for God. It seemed as if all our efforts had failed. We were getting ready to drive out of the parking lot when a woman came running up to the car and began tapping on the window. I rolled down the window just a couple inches to find out what she needed. She said, "My car is broken down! I need a ride! Do you think you guys could give me a ride?"

We agreed to give the woman a ride to where she was going. When she got in the car, she asked, "Are you guys Christians?" Scott and I both said, "Yes!" Without a pause, the woman began to exclaim, "God said He was going to send a couple of Christians to help me!" Then she continued to tell us her life story. She had grown up in a Christian home. Over the last several years she had backslid in her relationship with Christ. As a result, she got involved in an abusive relationship, a relationship her parents had tried to cut off by forbidding her to see him. She had ended up choosing a relationship with her boyfriend over her parents.

The boyfriend had recently left her with no one to turn to for help. As a result, she had felt too shameful to go home and face her parents. Instead she had developed a severe drinking problem, trying to escape the pain of her mistakes. It was not long before we had arrived at the place where she wanted to be dropped off. It was in front of a local bar. She lived in the apartment directly above it.

As she was getting out of the car we told her that we would like to continue our conversation, and asked if we could finish talking with her about Jesus. She said, "I was about to go into the bar and have a drink! We could continue talking in the bar." We agreed, following her into the bar. Once inside the bar we began to talk to this woman about getting right with Jesus once again. We asked her to consider giving up the alcohol and praying with us to recommit her life to Jesus Christ.

Soon she pushed her drink to the side of the table and began to cry, as we began to pray right there in the middle of the bar for her to accept Jesus Christ! We became unaware of all the people around as we continued to stand and pray out loud for all the needs in this woman's life to be met. After we were done, we got some information from her in order to allow some of the women in our church college group to follow up with her new commitment to Christ.

As we were leaving, I stopped to use the restroom while Scott waited outside in the lobby. When I turned to leave the restroom, a man was standing in front of me, sobbing. He said he had heard us praying when we were in the bar. He began to tell me that he was addicted to cocaine and his whole life was falling apart. He said, "I heard you tell that lady about Jesus. I need Jesus to come into my life and help me also!"

Right there in the men's restroom we held hands and began to pray, as that man accepted Jesus Christ to be his Savior! Simultaneously, Scott was out in the lobby praying for another man who had also been touched by the power of the Holy Spirit while we were praying for the woman in the bar. The man, broken, had approached Scott saying his wife was leaving him because of his drinking and gambling problem. So he asked Scott to lead him in prayer to accept Jesus Christ!

Many times we do not step out in faith because we are afraid we will look ridiculous if it does not work. The fear of putting our faith into action stands between us and experiencing the promises of God. If we had been unwilling to act on the prompting of the Holy Spirit that day in the car and stop at the convenience store to tell the cashier about Jesus, we would have missed an opportunity to overcome fear and see three individuals added to the population of heaven. It would have been easy to dismiss the mountain before us as a ridiculous idea! The mountains in our lives will move when they hear our voices speak in agreement with revelation from the heavenly realm in order to shake heaven and earth!

SHAKING HEAVEN & EARTH

In the book of Haggai, chapter two, the prophet received a word from the Lord to propose some questions to the leaders of Israel. "Who is left among you who saw this house in its former glory? And how do you see it now? Is not this in your sight as nothing in comparison to that?"[422]

---

[422] Haggai 2:3 AMP

The word *house* in this passage is a reference to Solomon's temple. It was a dwelling place for the presence of God. It had been destroyed approximately seventy years earlier. The temple had been rebuilt by its current leaders at this point, but not to its original glory. "The words "in comparison to that" ought to be omitted."[423] Instead it should say, "Does it not seem in your eyes as if it had no existence?"[424]

"Zerubbabel the governor of Israel seems to have been unable, with the small resources at his disposal, to execute the original design, even though the proportions were not greatly inferior to those of the earlier temple. But the chief inferiority lay in the absence of the splendor and enrichment with which Solomon adorned his edifice. The gold which he had lavished on the house was no longer available; the precious stones could not be had. Besides these defects, the Talmudists say five things were missing in this second temple including the Ark of the Covenant, with the cherubim and the mercy seat; the holy fire; the Shechinah; the spirit of prophecy; the Urim and the Thummim."[425]

The new house was not only less refined than the old, but it was also missing the manifest presence of God! The temple was meant to be a dwelling place for the Spirit of God, as well as a place where the people of Israel could connect relationally with their God! "It was the first time since the people of Israel had left Egypt that they did not have access to Jehovah relationally by means of the priests and their sacrifices to receive revelations and

---

[423] The Pulpit Commentary, The Book of Haggai, Volume 14 (Peabody, MA: Hendrickson Publishers, 1961), 19
[424] Ibid, 19
[425] Ibid, 19

to be spiritually quickened through the prophets."[426] Without this kind of relationship resulting in revelation they would not prosper in the promises of God. It was understood by all of Israel that "God's spirit was the secret source and ultimate cause of all good in either the church or the nation."[427]

The above passage could be a prophetic picture of the New Testament church today, as many believers seem to have forgotten their identity, trying to live their lives based on their own abilities through a past experience of the presence of God. They become content, living on memories from former glory days of God, passed by in their lives, allowing their souls to become dominated by external images from our physical senses rather than be internally diffused with revelation through our spiritual senses in union with Holy Spirit. So they no longer recognize the need to manifest the mystery of God to our generation.

If we are the church, what do you think history will say about us? Will it have to ask, "Doesn't it seem in your eyes as if the church did not exist?" It is in this context that the prophet exhorts the leaders of Israel with the Word of the Lord:

> Be strong, alert, and courageous, all you people of the land, says the Lord, and work! For I am with you, says the Lord of hosts. According to the promise that I covenanted with you when you came out of Egypt, so My Spirit stands and abides in the midst of you; fear not.[428]

---

[426] The Pulpit Commentary, The Book of Haggai, Volume 14 (Peabody, MA: Hendrickson Publishers, 1961), 19
[427] Ibid, 19
[428] Haggai 2:4-5 AMP

God was calling His people to be strong through living in covenant relationship with Him, resulting in revelation to be alert to the activities of the spiritual realm. Then they would be filled with courage in the knowledge and identity of Him so they could fulfill the work of His call to build a spiritual temple in order to show Himself to a generation, and generations to come!

We can see a parallel between believers being a spiritual temple in the new covenant and the spiritual temple as a building in the old covenant era of Haggai. The Israelites were to make it a national priority to rebuild the spiritual temple to connect relationally with God. In the same way, we can develop relationship with Holy Spirit through our union with Him, so we can receive revelation from heaven to manifest the life-changing presence of God on earth, just like the Israelites would receive revelation to prosper in the fulfillment of the promises of God for their nation.

> For thus says the Lord of hosts: Yet once more, in a little while, I will shake and make tremble, the (*starry*) heavens, the earth, the sea, and the dry land.[429]

The prophet declares in this passage that God will shake heaven and earth! Everything that can be shaken will be shaken! Only those things that are built on relationship resulting in revelation cannot be shaken!

The promises of God cannot be achieved apart from relationship through union with Holy Spirit resulting in revelation. It is time to "consider your ways and set your mind on what has come to you. You have sown much, but you have reaped little; you eat, but you do not have enough; you drink,

---

[429] Haggai 2:6 AMP

but you do not have your fill; you clothe yourselves, but no one is warm; and he who earns wages has earned them to put them in a bag with holes in it."[430]

In contrast, as a spiritual temple resting in union with Holy Spirit through relationship resulting in revelation from Him, God says, "I will take pleasure in it and I will be glorified, says the Lord (*by accepting it as done for My glory and by displaying My glory in it*)."[431] As a result of His pleasure, we get to experience His promise to live the abundant life as we receive revelation that we are already filled with the glory of God! The spiritual realm has already been given to us to experience in the natural realm! We have been set free from living according to the former glory of our own works to live in the latter glory of resting in the peace and the prosperity of His accomplishments.

The glory of spiritual magnificence cannot be compared within a person's heart, as opposed to that of merely material splendor. The temple of Solomon was, after all, but an "earthly house" of polished stone, carved cedar, and burnished gold; but the temple of Jesus Christ is a spiritual house, constructed of lively stones, or believing souls, "a holy temple" erected out of quickened and renewed hearts "for a habitation of God through the Spirit.[432]

When Christ died on the cross, the Bible says there was a seismic earthquake that shook the ground, causing rocks to split open and tearing the veil in the temple in half. "What was behind the curtain? There was a box where God's presence dwelled, but today He lives in you! God ripped the curtain from top to

[430] Haggai 1:5-6 AMP
[431] Haggai 1:8 AMP
[432] The Pulpit Commentary, The Book of Haggai, Volume 14 (Peabody, MA: Hendrickson Publishers, 1961), 29

bottom and what was behind the curtain was heaven on earth. He said, 'I'm going to rip the veil of confusion, not just because I want to let you in, but because I want to get out and let heaven touch your world.'"[433]

We are going to experience a move of God that will be equivalent to a "spiritual earthquake!"...It will seize hearts and affect lives. Right before our eyes, God is going

HE WILL SHAKE HEAVEN AND EARTH BY CO-LABORING WITH US THROUGH RELATIONSHIP RESULTING IN REVELATION IN ORDER TO ACCOMPLISH THE EMERGING AGENDA OF HIS WILL ON EARTH AS IT IS IN HEAVEN.

to break long-standing obstacles! When you think you just cannot get past this person or this situation, God is going to break the rocks right in front of you. He is going to plant His cause in the epicenter of your heart and it will fuel new exploits in your life. When you align yourself with the cause of God, rocks have got to move out of the way![434]

How does God intend to shake heaven and earth? He will shake heaven and earth by co-laboring with us through relationship resulting in revelation in order to accomplish the emerging agenda of His will on earth as it is in heaven. He says:

I will shake all nations and the desire and the precious things of all nations shall come in, and I will fill this house

[433] Sean Smith, Prophetic Evangelism (Shippensburg, PA: Destiny Image Publishers Inc, 2004), 82
[434] Ibid, 82

with splendor…The silver is Mine and the Gold is Mine, says the Lord of hosts. The latter glory of this house (*with its successor, to which Jesus came*) shall be greater than the former, says the Lord of hosts; and in this place will I give peace and prosperity.[435]

[435] Haggai 2:7-9 AMP

CHAPTER 9

SEEDS OF HIS GREATNESS

IN THE NATURAL IT MAY APPEAR that we do not have much to offer in hopes of changing the circumstances of our world, unless we get revelation that we have been born of the Spirit in order to live by revelation through our union with Holy Spirit. We will continue to live east of the Jordan, finding ourselves living short of the promises of God as we continue to struggle with a false identity that is not from Him, knowing that living on the right side of the cross and resting in His accomplishments is a result of agreeing with revelation from the heavenly realm!

As believers we need revelation of the Word of God for ourselves. We must have revelation of the character of our God so we can trust that God is who He says He is in His Word. We need revelation of our identity in Christ so we can believe that we are who He says we are in His Word. And we must have a revelation of all that we have inherited in Christ, so we can have faith that He has equipped us with everything we need to accomplish our future and destiny in Him!

As sons and daughters of the King we have already received the seeds of His greatness within us to live the abundant life. He has already given us everything we need to experience the promises we read about in the Bible. God is calling this generation to relationship with Holy Spirit rather than the empty promises of "religion." By living in revelation through our union with Holy Spirit, His spiritual DNA is activated within us to exercise our spiritual senses as citizens of the heavenly realm.

We have been set free from living as disillusioned, schizophrenic captives dominated by the limitations of an inferior reality. Our imaginations have been sanctified with the unlimited images of a superior reality. We are empowered with revelation diffused throughout our soul resulting in confidence, courage, and faith. The seeds of His greatness within us are coming forth to give birth to His promises in order to shake heaven and earth!

God is doing a new thing! Our past does not dictate our future!

Many Christians today have not experienced the fruit of His promises in the natural realm. It is to these people that God says:

Sing, O barren one, you who did not bear; break forth into singing and cry aloud, you who did not travail with child! For the (spiritual) children of the desolate one will be more than the children of the married wife, says the Lord.[436]

The phrase "barren one" in this passage of Scripture represents those who have yet to experience their spiritual blessings in the heavenly realm manifesting in the natural arena of their lives.

[436] Isaiah 54:1 AMP

Children represent our inheritance! There is a parallel here between producing a natural inheritance by our own means versus producing a spiritual inheritance through our union with the Spirit. God promises that more fruit will manifest in our lives as spiritual children birthed in intimacy with Him, as our identity is established in the spiritual realm, rather than the natural realm!

INHERITANCE MENTALITY

As Christians, it's important to know that God wants us to experience the fullness of our inheritance. His plan is that we would experience the abundant life! It is not that we would experience a little bit more of His promises than we are currently experiencing in our lives. It's that we experience all that He has already given to us!

A revelation of our spiritual blessings in the heavenly realm will change the entire infrastructure of our thinking in order to prepare us to live in the overflow of His promises. The Holy Spirit breaks us out of a captivity mindset by replacing it with an inheritance mindset, saying:

> Enlarge the place of your tent, and let the curtains of your habitations be stretched out; spare not; lengthen your cords and strengthen your stakes, For you will spread abroad to the right hand and to the left; and your off-spring will possess the nations and make the desolate cities to be inhabited.[437]

---

[437] Isaiah 54:2-3 AMP

In the celebration of Passover we can see God delivering His people from a captivity mindset in order to receive an inheritance mentality. Passover represented a new beginning for the Israelites. They were delivered out of captivity from slavery in Egypt in order to receive the promised land as an inheritance. It would be a prophetic reminder of the coming Messiah who would deliver all people from the bondage of sin.

Every year during the celebration of Passover the Hebrew people were to remind their children:

> This is done because of what the Lord did for me when I came out of Egypt. It shall be a sign to you upon your hand and as a memorial between your eyes, that the law of the Lord may be in your mouth; for with a strong hand the Lord has brought you out of Egypt.[438]

In other words, the Hebrew people were to remind their children at Passover of what the Lord had already accomplished on their behalf. God wanted them to remember that they had already been delivered. It had already been accomplished at a time in the past. He did not want His people to continue in the freedom already given to them based on a past slave mentality. He wanted the Hebrew people to see themselves as His children.

They needed to remind themselves that the strong hand of the Lord had already brought them out of bondage. His presence and favor was to be manifested in their day-to-day lives through the present confession of their mouths. In the same way, as Christians we need to remind ourselves that we have already been delivered from the bondage of sin. It is so easy for us to forget who we are and what God has already done for us. We

---

[438] Exodus 13:8-9 AMP

need to remind ourselves daily that we are no longer in captivity to sin, flesh, and the devil.

The word *captivity* refers to being under the control of an enemy. Spiritually it refers to us being restricted to our current surroundings and circumstances. The Holy Spirit is currently exposing the religious mindset of captivity to His people so they can agree with their true identity in heaven. Jesus already took captivity captive! Every stronghold of captivity has already been broken so we can receive the manifestation of all that He has already accomplished on our behalf!

The current surroundings and circumstances of our life might be good, but it is not God's best! The Holy Spirit is releasing His people from a captivity mindset so we can cross over into an inheritance mindset. We have lived like a slave to our natural circumstances for too long! We have learned to live without a revelation of the dominion, authority and power within us! We have been living from a day-to-day survival mindset!

The Holy Spirit is saying, "My people will no longer exist from a survival mindset, but they will live in an inheritance mindset. I will lead you in relationship resulting in revelation to receive your inheritance." In the same way, God directed the Hebrew children:

> In a pillar of cloud to lead them along the way and by night in a pillar of fire to give them light, that they might travel by day and by night.[439]

The Lord says:

I have watched you labor in pain without experiencing the fruit of your inheritance. I am removing the blinding

---

[439] Exodus 13:21 AMP

> WHAT ONCE HELD YOU CAPTIVE IN THE PAST WILL BECOME THE BLESSING OF YOUR INHERITANCE. CAPTIVITY IS TAKEN CAPTIVE!

veil of the captivity mindset through relationship resulting in revelation so that you can see your inheritance for yourself. You will no longer be deceived by the appearance of your natural circumstances. I have already released you with My favor and presence from the spiritual realm to be fruitful and multiply in the natural realm! I have already given you everything you need to experience the fulfillment of My promises for you!

Just as in the day when the Hebrews put blood over their doorways, so the Spirit "passed over the houses of the Israelites in Egypt when He slew the Egyptians, but spared"[440] the Israelites' houses and their children, so it is today that My Spirit has put a mark on your spiritual seed as an inheritance. The Egyptians lost their seed of inheritance when they lost their children. I have already passed over the children of the world and have given their inheritance to you and your children.

It will manifest in the same way as when Pharaoh no longer tried to keep the Hebrew children in captivity. He released them to pursue the promised land by blessing them with the most valued possessions of Egypt. What once held you captive in the past will become the blessing of your inheritance. Captivity is taken captive! As the Israelites left Egypt, Pharaoh told Moses, "take your flocks and your herds, as you have said, and be gone!

---

[440] Exodus 12:27 AMP

And (*ask your God to*) bless me also."[441] The captivity mindset is broken. The one who made you a servant in captivity now serves you as a captive in need of your blessing. "I have already given you the power, resources, riches, and influences that the spirit of this world has controlled as an inheritance. I have already given you the key of favor so that when you ask you will receive."

The Israelites began to clothe themselves with an inheritance mentality and,

> ...did according to the word of Moses; and they (*urgently*) asked of the Egyptians jewels of silver and of gold, and clothing. The Lord gave the people favor in the sight of the Egyptians, so that they gave them what they asked. And they stripped the Egyptians (*of those things*).[442]

In the same way the Holy Spirit says, "Clothe yourself with the revelation of your inheritance in the spiritual realm. You will no longer make excuses associated with a captivity mindset, but you will cross over with faith to ask, in order to experience the manifestation of your inheritance!"

"And when the Lord brings you into the land of the Canaanites, Hittites, Amorites, Hivites, and Jebusites, which He promised and swore to your fathers to give to you, a land flowing with milk and honey (*a land of plenty*), you shall keep this service in this month."[443] In other words, when you experience the natural manifestation of your spiritual promises, continue to make your mouth a memorial to the revelation of His goodness to you! As a result, His favor and presence will continually show

---

[441] Exodus 12:32 AMP
[442] Exodus 12:35-36 AMP
[443] Exodus 13:5 AMP

up again and again in your testimony to be established in your current circumstances, persuading those within your influence to receive Him.

> For the substance (*essence*) of the truth revealed by Jesus is the spirit of all prophecy (*the vital breath, the inspiration of all inspired preaching and interpretation of the divine will and purpose, including both mine and yours*).[444]

The Holy Spirit says, "I will use the fruit of your inheritance to influence every area of culture. I will begin to raise your spiritual sons and daughters with ideas of creativity which the world has never seen. I will use your children to invade the marketplace, business world, investments, arts, sports (professional), music, acting (Hollywood), writing, etc. Where My bride has settled for good in the past, they will now only settle for greatness! I call forth the seeds of greatness that I have already released in and through you to manifest in the natural realm.

"You are the head and not the tail! The world will begin to look to the seeds of my greatness in you as a prototype for living. These seeds will manifest as the standard in which all things are measured. The old cycles that have held you captive have already been broken. You will no longer allow the strongholds of discouragement and disillusionment to paralyze you with a captivity mindset.

"I have called you out of old patterns in order to secure the manifestation of your inheritance. In union with My Spirit resulting in revelation you will overcome every opposition that is contrary to My promise in you! You will stop looking at the appearance of your circumstances. You will stop listening

---

[444] Revelation 19:10 AMP

to your enemies! You will go forward to receive My promises with an inheritance mentality, in order to see your feet firmly established in the future!"

It is a season of new beginnings!

I call the seeds of His greatness in you to manifest now!

Author/Ministry Contact Information

Revival Cry Ministries
Attention: Dennis Reanier
P.O. Box 432
Belgrade, MT 59714

Phone: (406) 522-7107

E-mail: dreanier@revivalcry.com

Website: RevivalCry.com

Additional copies of this book and other book titles from XP Publishing are also available at XPmedia.com

For wholesale prices for stores and ministries, please contact: usaresource@xpmedia.com
In Canada: resource@xpmedia.com

Our books are also available to bookstores through **Anchordistributors.com**

XPPUBLISHING.COM

A department of XP Ministries